STRANGE MEETINGS

Strange Meetings:

The Poets of the Great War

HARRY RICKETTS

Chatto & Windus
LONDON

Published by Chatto & Windus 2010

2 4 6 8 10 9 7 5 3 1

Copyright © 2010 by Harry Ricketts

First published in Great Britain in 2010 by
Chatto & Windus
Random House, 20 Vauxhall Bridge Road,
London SW1V 2SA
www.rbooks.co.uk

Addresses for companies within The Random House Group Limited can be found at:
www.randomhouse.co.uk/offices.htm

The Random House Group Limited Reg. No. 954009

A CIP catalogue record for this book
is available from the British Library

ISBN 9780701172718

The Random House Group Limited supports The Forest Stewardship
Council (FSC), the leading international forest certification organisation. All our titles that are printed
on Greenpeace approved FSC certified paper carry the FSC logo. Our paper procurement policy can be
found at www.rbooks.co.uk/environment

Typeset in Dante MT by Palimpsest Book Production Limited,
Falkirk, Stirlingshire
Printed in Great Britain by
Clays Ltd, St Ives plc

For my father, mother and uncle

There is an extraordinary veracity in war, which strips man of every conventional covering he has, and leaves him to face a fact as naked and as inexorable as himself.

Frederic Manning, *Her Privates We*, 1930

Never such innocence again.

Philip Larkin, 'MCMXIV', 1960

The Somme is like the Holocaust. It revealed things about mankind that we cannot come to terms with and cannot forget. It can never become the past.

Pat Barker on winning the Booker Prize, 1995

Contents

List of Illustrations

4 Siegfried Sassoon, *c*.1916. The Literary Estate of Siegfried Sassoon
   Robert Graves, 1915. The William Graves Collection
5 Edward Thomas, sketched by John Wheatley, 1916 © National Portrait
   Gallery, London
   Wilfred Owen, Hare Hall Camp, November 1915. Reproduced with
   kind permission of the Trustees of the Owen Estate, 2E (a)
6 Ivor Gurney, 1915. Gloucestershire Archives. Copyright 2010, The Ivor
   Gurney Estate. Reproduced with permission
   Rupert Brooke: the frontispiece to *1914 & other Poems*
7 Siegfried Sassoon by Glyn Philpot, 1917. The Fitzwilliam Museum,
   University of Cambridge / Bridgeman Art Library
   Wilfred Owen at Leith, July 1917. Reproduced with kind permission
   of the Trustees of the Owen Estate, 2E (c)
8 Robert Nichols, *c*.1915. Courtesy of Anne and William Carlton, and
   Michael Russell
   Isaac Rosenberg, 1917. Rosenberg Collection, Tower Hamlets Library
   Archives
9 Robert Nichols, 1915. Courtesy of Anne and William Carlton, and
   Michael Russell
   Siegfried Sassoon at Army School, Flixécourt, May 1916. The Literary
   Estate of Siegfried Sassoon
10 Wilfred Owen, Hastings, late August 1918. Reproduced with kind
   permission of the Trustees of the Owen Estate, 1F (L)
   Siegfried Sassoon at Garsington, 1916. The Literary Estate of Siegfried
   Sassoon
11 Edmund Blunden, 1929. The Literary Estate of Edmund Blunden /
   David Higham
   Robert Graves, frontispiece to *Good-bye to All That*, 1929. The William
   Graves Collection
12 Ivor Gurney – the asylum years. Gloucestershire Archives. Copyright
   2010, The Ivor Gurney Estate. Reproduced with permission.
   Edward Thomas at Wick Green, 1913–14. Edward Thomas Archive,
   Cardiff University
13 Vera Brittain, 1934.
   Siegfried Sassoon, early 1940s. The Literary Estate of Siegfried Sassoon
14 Robert Nichols by Catherine Dodgson, 1935–6. Courtesy of Anne
   and William Carlton, and Michael Russell
   Robert Graves at Galmpton, 1943. The William Graves Collection
15 David Jones in his sixties. The David Jones Literary Estate
   Siegfried Sassoon, 'The Great Dictator'. The Literary Estate of
   Siegfried Sassoon

Prologue

The Great War still compels the imagination. It continues to shape how we think about war, and its poets continue to suggest how we might feel about war. American troops training for Afghanistan in 2001 studied not just maps and military procedures but the poems of Wilfred Owen, Siegfried Sassoon and Rupert Brooke. One young sergeant from Portland, Oregon picked out Owen's 'Dulce et Decorum Est': 'Just by what he said you actually can feel it, or you can get a mental picture of the death or the awful sights.' If a single poem now defines the Great War experience for the English-speaking world – and even modern war in general – it is probably that poem of Owen's about the victim of a gas attack: 'If in some smothering dreams you too could pace / Behind the wagon that we flung him in' – for a moment we are in the nightmare, pacing behind that wagon, seeing that face.

Other contemporary markers of the Great War's enduring significance, as event and symbol, come readily to mind. The death in July 2009 of Harry Patch, 'the last Tommy' to serve in the trenches, commanded widespread attention. His funeral was a national event; television and radio documentaries were replayed; Gillian Clarke and the poet laureate Carol Ann Duffy were commissioned to write poems. While the British annual calendar has become increasingly fragmented and eroded, Remembrance Day remains an unassailable landmark, a civic as much as a religious ritual. A few months after Patch's death, the politicians Gordon Brown and David Cameron were both obliged to apologise for seemingly turning the Remembrance Day service at Westminster Abbey into a photo-shoot opportunity – as though they had committed an act of secular impiety, cheated in some test of authenticity. The imaginative power of the Great War and its poets can also be felt in the sheer volume of writing which they continue to generate: history, fiction, biography, poetry, drama, film, art history, the personal essay, literary criticism and theory. Fresh anthologies of the poetry are still regularly published. On a different level of importance, the 2009 England test cricket squad was taken to Flanders Fields as part of its preparation for the Ashes series against the visiting Australians.

Yet the idea of the Great War as a national, cultural, existential benchmark is in some ways quite a recent phenomenon. Forty to fifty years ago, it all looked rather different – certainly as far as the literature was concerned. Sassoon, Robert Graves, Edmund Blunden, David Jones were all still alive when I was doing A Levels in England in the 1960s, but we knew that, except perhaps for Owen, they and the other war poets did not measure up. The modernists were the real twentieth-century literary giants: T S Eliot and Ezra Pound in poetry, James Joyce, D H Lawrence and Virginia Woolf in fiction. Apart from Lawrence, these writers might not actually be on our syllabus but they were the real thing. Since then several seismic reimaginings have so redrawn that literary landscape that it now seems barely recognisable: no longer English literature, but literatures in English. One unexpected consequence has been a renewed interest in a twentieth-century 'English' poetic line with Thomas Hardy as its pre-eminent figure. A number of the poets whose lives and work are explored in this collective biography – Owen, Edward Thomas, Graves, Sassoon, Ivor Gurney, Isaac Rosenberg, Blunden, Brooke – readily take their place in this reconstituted tradition. Their often conflicting and conflicted sense of what it might mean to be 'English' still finds an echo. A new complete poems of Graves in one volume appeared in 2000, previously unpublished letters of Rosenberg in 2007, Thomas's collected poems newly annotated in 2008. Brooke and Gurney have been the subject of recent novels. For Anglophone writers and readers, the Great War and its poets keep renewing themselves.

For many, the connection remains a potent and personal one, if now at some remove. My own father and uncle were both career

British army officers, commissioned in the 1930s and serving in the Second World War. My father survived; my uncle died. One reason why they became soldiers, I remember being told, was because my grandfather was graded medically unfit in the Great War, and always felt ashamed. Growing up in the army, I spent my childhood – like many fag-end-of-empire children – ricocheting from posting to posting: England, Malaysia, England, Hong Kong. School became real life, the holidays what we did in-between. Cricket and poetry – the order eventually reversed – became essential for survival: watching, reading, playing, writing. Cricket I shared with my father, poetry with my mother. *Strange Meetings* – like *The Unforgiving Minute*, my life of Kipling – draws on and grows out of that energy field.

This collective biography presented quite different opportunities and challenges from a single-life biography. Who to include, who to exclude, for instance. Brooke, Owen, Sassoon, Graves, Thomas, Rosenberg were obvious choices, but the more I read, the more their experience, their poetry, gained by being compared and contrasted with that of less celebrated poets like Gurney, Blunden, Jones, Charles Sorley, Robert Nichols and Vera Brittain. Nichols's *Ardours and Endurances* was the poetic hit of 1917. Brittain, though best known for her memoir *Testament of Youth* and her letters and diaries, published a small collection of poems in 1918 called *Verses of a V.A.D.*

A second challenge was structure. Some of the poets had known each other; some had not. Some, like Brooke and Thomas, had literary reputations before the war, while Jones did not publish his Great War epic *In Parenthesis* until 1937. From an early stage, I knew I wanted to include, as a free-standing episode, Rupert Brooke and Siegfried Sassoon having breakfast together in July 1914, just before the start of the war. That was clearly a key moment, and I found myself counting up other encounters: Sassoon and Graves in France in 1915; Sassoon and Owen at Craiglockhart Hospital in 1917; Sassoon and Jones having lunch in 1964.

I came to realise that such meetings might provide my elusive structure – particularly if, together with real meetings, I included vicarious encounters – Thomas twice reviewing Brooke's posthumously published *1914 & other Poems* in June 1915; Blunden and Sassoon angrily annotating Blunden's review copy of Graves's *Good-bye to All That*; Gurney, *circa* 1932, being visited in the Dartford asylum by Thomas's widow Helen. Owen and Thomas were both at Hare Hall training camp between late 1915 and mid-1916, and biographers have speculated that they must have met. Perhaps, I thought, they could have an imaginary conversation à la Walter Savage Landor – in fact, three conversations with differing degrees of probability. In its final version this book includes fifteen meetings: eight actually took place, six are near-encounters of various kinds, and the one between Owen and Thomas is faction, fiction closely based on fact.

The title, *Strange Meetings*, is borrowed of course from Owen, who had himself borrowed it from Harold Monro and from Shelley's *Revolt of Islam* – a meeting within a meeting.

I

Breakfast at Eddie's

Siegfried Sassoon and Rupert Brooke,
Thursday 9 July 1914

Eddie Marsh's literary breakfasts were famous. Promptly at eight o'clock his housekeeper Mrs Elgy served up the kidneys and bacon. Marsh sipped China tea and – a characteristic gesture – stroked his winged eyebrows which seemed on the point of flying off his forehead. Monocled, early forties, he presided over his select gatherings like a university don conducting a tutorial with bright but unpredictable undergraduates. His voice was a distinctive soft squeak, giving his comments, as his biographer put it, the air of a 'witty aside written in faded pencil'. He often began with a 'But, my dear' or 'Now, my dear'.

Marsh's breakfasts were integral to his enthusiastic support of the arts. This support was funded out of what he called his 'murder money': a part-share of a grant originally given to the family after his great-grandfather, the Prime Minister Spencer Perceval, was assassinated in the lobby of the House of Commons in 1812. At first, Marsh used his share to buy the work of promising painters. Then he extended his patronage to promising writers, especially poets. One consequence was the enormously popular anthology *Georgian Poetry 1911–1912*.

Marsh lived in Gray's Inn, in the top flat of 5 Raymond Buildings. His breakfast guests tended to be young, good-looking men. Some,

Left: Siegfried Sassoon, April 1911
Right: Rupert Brooke by Sherrill Schell, 1913

like Marsh himself, came from relatively privileged backgrounds, had been to public school and Oxbridge, and had private means. But Marsh was no snob. Several of his protégés, such as the poet-painter Isaac Rosenberg, were working-class and invited because they possessed, in Marsh's phrase, 'the *feu sacré*'. Having once taken someone up, Marsh became not only a reliable patron but also a loyal friend.

Marsh was a celibate homosexual. Christopher Hassall, a later protégé and his biographer, claimed Marsh was impotent, having contracted mumps together with German measles in his early teens. But since there is no medical reason why those two illnesses, singly or together, should cause impotence, a more likely explanation is that Marsh deliberately chose a life of celibacy. In a world still shadowed by the Wilde trial of 1895, he may even have circulated the story of his supposed incapacity to avoid gossip and scandal. According to the diarist James Lees-Milne, Marsh only allowed himself two acts of worship and transferred desire: 'taking off the hunting boots of his young men friends' and, while holding it against his chest, polishing a favourite's bare foot with his handkerchief.

During Marsh's literary breakfasts, a new poem might be read aloud or a new painting shown and purchased. Hence his acquisition around May 1914 of Rosenberg's *Sacred Love*, which he hung in the spare room along with Stanley Spencer's *The Apple Gatherers*, which he had bought the previous year. At 9.15 sharp, Marsh would set off, impeccably dressed, for his desk at the Admiralty where he was private secretary to Winston Churchill. D H Lawrence, another protégé, thought him 'a bit of a jig-saw puzzle . . . mixing poets and pictures, the Admiralty, and what-not, like somebody shuffling cards'. His boss's opinion was typically brusque. 'You are a good little boy,' Churchill told Marsh, 'and I am very fond of you.'

On this particular morning, Thursday 9 July 1914, there were three breakfast guests: the supertramp poet W H Davies, and two of Marsh's newer young men, the poet Siegfried Sassoon and the painter Paul Nash. The peg-legged Davies had come the furthest, stumping over from his room in Bloomsbury before negotiating the fifty-nine-step spiral stone staircase up to Marsh's apartment. Sassoon had simply popped across from the flat he was renting in 1 Raymond Buildings, while Nash, on a short break from Hampton Court and the restoration of the Mantegna frescoes *The Triumph of Caesar*, had spent the night on Marsh's sofa. The trio were there to meet Marsh's prize protégé Rupert Brooke, just returned from a year travelling in America, Canada and the Pacific.

While they waited for Brooke to emerge from the spare room, Davies did most of the talking. He had eyes like stewed prunes and stiff black hair that stuck up in a natural quiff. He talked with a marked Welsh accent – 'mun' for 'man' – and had a formidable array of stories. He could be a bit of a bore. Nash and Sassoon listened and watched. Sassoon, tall, raw-boned, pleasant-featured with a pronounced cleft chin, was nervous and excited. Although he had never met Brooke before, the latter already aroused in him feelings of 'admiring antagonism'.

This is hardly surprising. Sassoon and Brooke were contemporaries from similar backgrounds: Sassoon, born 1886, Marlborough College, Clare, Cambridge; Brooke, born 1887, Rugby School, King's College, Cambridge. But there the similarity ended. Brooke had recently gained a Fellowship at his old college, was already recognised as the rising poetic star of his generation and seemed to have a glittering career before him. Sassoon had left Cambridge without taking a degree and, for the last seven years, had been stuck in a cul-de-sac of sport and literary isolation. Publicly, he was a fox-hunting man in the winter and a keen cricketer in the summer. Privately, in all seasons, he was a lyric poet. This was made possible by a private income of £600 a year and by living at home with his mother in the Weald of Kent.

So while Brooke had brought out one widely reviewed collection, *Poems* (1911), and had featured prominently in *Georgian Poetry 1911–1912*, Sassoon had plumped for anonymous volumes with titles like *Orpheus in Diloeryum*, privately printed in tiny, expensively produced editions, and circulated only among family and a chosen few. Although he did not lack literary ambition, he deeply feared rejection and the possible reaction of his more sporting friends.

The road to Marsh's breakfast table had taken several twists and turns, but Sassoon held an entry pass to literary circles: Edmund Gosse was a family friend. Gosse, as reviewer and critic, had been a reputation-broker for thirty years, and his Sunday afternoon At Homes were legendary. He was in fact rather more than a family friend of the Sassoons. Happily married, he was also the devoted friend-cum-admirer

of Sassoon's uncle, the sculptor Hamo Thornycroft. At first, the entry
pass failed. Sassoon approached Gosse in 1908 via Uncle Hamo, sending
him *Orpheus in Diloeryum*: Gosse was kind, talked of 'richness of fancy
and command of melodious verse', but otherwise remained non-
committal.

Four years later, Sassoon tried Gosse again. This time he succeeded.
He had been trying to parody the poetic hit of the day, John Masefield's
The Everlasting Mercy, about the moral fall and spiritual rise of a drunken
village blackguard called Saul Kane. Sassoon's take-off, *The Daffodil
Murderer*, was uneven, but much livelier than anything he had written
before.

> At 'Barley Mow' Bill's done with drawing;
> He'll never hear the chaps there jawing
> All evening through, and singing catches,
> And calling out for beer in batches.
> He'll never hear the wind come blowing
> Through door in gusts when some one's going
> Out to the dark where no one fuddles,
> And starlight glints on roadway puddles.

Instead of idealised Greek heroes, he had created a sympathetic Sussex
lad, condemned to hang for a killing he never intended.

The Daffodil Murderer by Saul Kain appeared in February 1913 and
duly bombed. But Gosse, sent a copy by Sassoon, grasped that,
consciously or not, the lines were rather good pastiche – and was at
last impressed. From Gosse, it was a short step to Marsh, who liked
The Daffodil Murderer and asked to see more of Sassoon's work. Sassoon
sent a batch of his usual stuff, full of lines like 'Passion with poisonous
blossoms in her hair', 'Dungeons of dim sighing' and 'Frantic waifs of
plague and sin from direful cities'. Marsh told him it was old-fashioned
and over-literary, but sweetened the pill in his most charmingly
disarming way by telling Sassoon he had 'a lovely instrument to play
upon'. Lunch at the National Club followed, and Sassoon's enlistment
as another of Marsh's promising young men. Which led, during the
summer of 1914, to Sassoon becoming Marsh's neighbour in Raymond
Buildings.

★   ★   ★

It was friendship with Marsh that made Sassoon so acutely aware of Brooke and prompted his feelings of 'admiring antagonism'. Marsh had first encountered Brooke on a visit to Cambridge in November 1906. Brooke, in his first term at Cambridge, had a walk-on part as the Herald in a student production of Aeschylus's *The Eumenides* – performed in the original Greek. Marsh was instantly smitten and never forgot the first impact of that 'radiant, youthful figure in gold and vivid red and blue, like a Page in the Riccardi Chapel'. In 1909 he and Brooke became close, and Brooke started to use the spare room at 5 Raymond Buildings as his London *pied-à-terre*. From that point on, Marsh not only gave Brooke his unconditional affection, but became his warmest critic and unofficial literary patron-cum-agent, helping to ease Brooke's passage through the various London literary turnstiles.

Marsh and Brooke together dreamt up the idea for the first *Georgian Poetry* anthology. One evening in September 1912, they were bemoaning the general lack of interest in contemporary poetry. Brooke, for a lark, proposed a book of avant-garde spoofs – written by himself under various pseudonyms – but passed off as the work of a dozen new poets, six male, six female. Then when the book was hailed as a success, he would blow the gaffe in *The Times*. Marsh had a more practical suggestion. Why not an anthology featuring a dozen or so youngish poets they admired, of whom Brooke naturally would be one?

The idea took off. Marsh secured Harold Monro as publisher and within a fortnight had the nucleus of his collection. He eventually settled on thirty-six poems and extracts by seventeen poets, all male, all British. His initial wish-list had been more inclusive and daring. He had wanted to include Ezra Pound, the young American iconoclast with the red hair and single jade earring. Pound had been rampaging around the London literary scene and was currently masterminding an experimental group of poets he had christened the Imagists. Marsh asked Pound for two poems, 'The Goodly Fere' and (probably) 'Portrait d'une Femme'. Pound vetoed both – the first as too old-fashioned, the second because it was about to appear in his new collection, *Ripostes*. He offered Marsh a free choice from his 1911 collection *Canzoni*, but Marsh thought none of the poems suitable, and the arrangement fell through. At which point Pound dropped out of the reckoning, though he told Marsh that he hoped he might appear in some future *Georgian Poetry* anthology.

Of the final seventeen contributors, a few, like Davies and G K Chesterton, were relative oldies. Other, mostly younger, notables included Walter de la Mare, Lascelles Abercrombie, Wilfrid Gibson, James Elroy Flecker and Gordon Bottomley. Masefield, still riding the popular wave of *The Everlasting Mercy*, was the biggest catch. He even held up publication of a new 300-line poem 'Biography' so that it could make its first appearance in Marsh's anthology. Once Pound dropped out, D H Lawrence was the boldest selection. Lawrence might tick Marsh off, and did, for being 'a bit of a policeman in poetry', but the inclusion of Lawrence's 'The Snapdragon', with its sado-masochistic images of floral throttling, showed Marsh was no prude:

> She laughed, she reached her hand out to the flower
> Closing its crimson throat: my own throat in her power
> Strangled, my heart swelled up so full
> As if it would burst its wineskin in my throat,
> Choke me in my own crimson . . .

This courageous choice made up for tamer selections like Edmund Sargant's 'The Cuckoo Wood', which Brooke failed to warn Marsh off – just as he failed to persuade him to make W B Yeats the anthology's dedicatee rather than Robert Bridges.

Marsh later said that, as editor, the three qualities he particularly looked for were intelligibility, music and raciness – plus, preferably, a discernible form. Brooke, not surprisingly, met all four of Marsh's criteria. He, like Davies, was allowed five entries, including 'The Old Vicarage, Grantchester', 'The Fish' and the more metaphysical 'Dust'. Monro, who was permitted two poems, proved a remarkably reliable and efficient publisher. *Georgian Poetry 1911–1912* was in proof by 5 November, advance copies were ready three weeks later, and, with Marsh sending over a hundred copies to friends, the first edition of 500 (price 3*s*. 6*d*.) had sold out by Christmas.

The anthology appeared under Monro's The Poetry Bookshop imprint. The bookshop itself was devoted exclusively to poetry and situated at 35 Devonshire Street, a poky little side street near the

British Museum. In early 1913 both anthology and shop became fashionable almost overnight. The shop was also used for poetry readings. These took place at around 5.30 p.m. on Tuesdays and Thursdays (price of admission 3*d*.) and lasted for a sensible thirty to forty minutes. Both Brooke and Davies were among the early participants. Davies was apparently nervous but read beautifully, encouraged by the prospect of a 'large whisky afterwards'. Brooke read twice. In late January 1913, six people heard him read selections from Swinburne and Donne. In July 1914, around the time of the breakfast at Marsh's, more than ten times that number heard him read his own poems, wearing a 'broad squash hat'. Actually he had a bad cold, so it was more a case of trying to overhear him. One old lady with an ear-trumpet apparently shouted out: 'Speak up, young man.' Naturally such readings helped to promote *Georgian Poetry*. The anthology was soon in poetry terms a bestseller, and the first volume eventually went on to sell 15,000 copies. By July 1913, six editions had appeared (nine by the end of the year), and Marsh was able to dole out £3 each to contributors. 'I call that manna', wrote Lawrence gratefully.

Marsh naturally tried to convert all his other protégés to Brooke, and Sassoon was no exception. He read *Poems* but later confessed that he found Brooke's 'metaphysical cleverness' confusing and was disturbed by the 'unromantic and provocative character' of the pieces. Also Marsh's obvious adoration of Brooke and his work made Sassoon jealous. Over lunch Marsh would suddenly pull out a recent letter from Brooke in the Pacific, containing yet another masterpiece, and would expect an instantly approving response. On one such occasion Marsh produced and read 'Heaven', which wittily presented existence from a fish's point of view:

> Fish say, they have their Stream and Pond;
> But is there anything Beyond?
> This life cannot be All, they swear,
> For how unpleasant, if it were! . . .

Sassoon, stumped for anything intelligent to say, but reminded of Brooke's 'The Fish' in *Georgian Poetry* blurted out: 'Why does he always write about fishes?' By the time he actually got to meet Brooke that

Thursday morning, Sassoon was both 'agog with excitement' and 'unprepared to find him more than moderately likeable'.

Sassoon was sitting with his back to the spare-room door, so he did not actually see Brooke slip in. Then suddenly there he was at his elbow, being jubilantly greeted by Davies with a 'Welcome home from foreign parts!' Sassoon and Nash were introduced and shook hands. Brooke looked tousled, a little bleary, but this in no way diminished the effect of his famous good looks and general sense of physical ease. He had 'steady, blue eyes' and his 'rosy, clear skin' gave him 'the look of a great girl'. His loose red-gold hair, lightly bleached from the South Pacific sun, was, Sassoon noticed a little primly, 'just a shade longer than it need have been'. Brooke was wearing a blue shirt, open at the neck, old grey longs, and sandals on his bare feet. His manner was quiet, even diffident. When he did speak, it was almost a drawl, measured and self-consciously correct – a Cambridge voice. Brooke sat down, helped himself to kidneys and bacon, followed by honey and toast. Davies went on with a rather lengthy story about 'a not wildly interesting experience he'd once had on the banks of the Mississippi'.

Sassoon was immediately rather smitten with Brooke. Most people were, men as much as women. It was not just the hair, the face, the 'sweetness and secrecy in his deepset eyes' or his often infectious high spirits: Brooke had charm. It was there in the way he put on his boots, 'frowning and groaning, with the absorbed seriousness of a child', and then looking up with a quick inclusive grin. It was there in quixotic schemes like his plan to avoid middle age by rendezvousing with friends on Basle Station on May Day 1933, and diving 'into the unknown to taste Life anew'. It was there in some of his more exhibitionist gambits. Virginia Woolf never forgot Brooke's invitation to go for a dip in Byron's Pool, Grantchester, and how he jumped naked into the water and came up with an instant erection. Sassoon was charmed, more simply but just as immediately, by the shy way Brooke shook hands.

Not that Brooke's appeal depended solely on his physical presence; his letters were equally full of 'charm-mongering', as one clear-eyed flame put it. 'It's wonderful saying *everything* to a person one absolutely trusts,' Brooke confided, charmingly but not entirely truthfully, to the actress Cathleen Nesbitt. Most charming of all was when the charm itself was sent up: 'You are the only person,' he wrote to Frances Cornford, 'who ever believed *all* my lies. Nothing (short, perhaps, of incredulity) can shake my devotion to you.' Henry James spoke for all the besotted when he described Brooke as 'young, happy, radiant, extraordinarily endowed and irresistibly attaching'.

Of course there were casualties, because, as Brooke admitted to one near-miss: 'I'm in love, in different ways, with two or three people. I always am.' Some, like the sisters Noel and Bryn Olivier, whom Brooke pursued ardently – and simultaneously – for several years, realised that the ardour was mostly an elaborate game, and wisely maintained a certain distance. Others, especially those who became lovers, like the homely Ka Cox and the naive art student Phyllis Gardner, never got over their subsequent rejection. Men found Brooke just as entrancing. Besides Edward Marsh and Henry James, the seriously smitten included Gosse, Duncan Grant, A C Benson, and James Strachey, brother of Lytton.

One of Brooke's favourite games with male admirers was to report to them ironically on the effects of his charm: 'I do my pet boyish-modesty stunt & go pink all over: & everyone thinks it *too* delightful,' he informed Marsh from Canada. 'Heaven', the poem Marsh showed Sassoon, contained a more privately charming game. Within a few lines, Brooke managed to combine a Donne-like joke about his own literary immortality with an affectionate linking of Eddie Marsh's name and his own:

> Mud unto mud! – Death *eddies* near –
> Not here the appointed End, not here! . . .
> Oh! never fly conceals a hook,
> Fish say, in the *Eternal Brook* . . . [Italics mine]

Sassoon sat charmed, surreptitiously observing Brooke at the breakfast table. He found himself thinking about Brooke's sandals and wondering whether they might conceivably be Tahitian. This led to more self-disparaging reflections on the difference between himself and Brooke: 'his idea of adventure was to go half across the world and write vividly about it, while mine was to go somewhere in Warwickshire, gallop after a pack of hounds, and stop being a writer altogether!'

Breakfast over, Davies pulled out his bulldog pipe and with Brooke
and Marsh started to talk about poetry. This, to Sassoon's disappointment, had nothing to do with the art or craft of poetry. Since
early May, he had sat at his desk a few doors down from Marsh's flat,
trying unsuccessfully to follow Marsh's and Gosse's advice to work
harder at poetic technique and dreaming about appearing in the second
volume of *Georgian Poetry*, which was already in the pipeline. What
Davies and Brooke discussed was money and strategy: which literary
editors paid the best rates, which liked what kind of poem. It probably did not cheer Sassoon up to hear Marsh confide over a final half-
cup of China tea that *Georgian Poetry 1911–1912* had now sold more than
9,000 copies. Then it was time for Marsh to set off for the Admiralty.
He left, reminding Brooke not to be late for lunch with Lady Horner
and urging Sassoon not to hurry away.

Soon after Marsh's departure, Davies too got up to go, and Nash
followed suit. Brooke and Sassoon were left alone. Brooke sat by the
window, looking out at the trees in the gardens below. The conversation did not exactly catch fire. Perhaps Brooke was tired from the
demands of Marsh's relentless social calendar which filled every unforgiving minute with literary, social and political engagements. Perhaps
he really was genuinely shy on first meeting people; Cathleen Nesbitt
thought so. Perhaps he was underwhelmed at being abandoned with
another of Marsh's literary-artistic lame ducks. He had already –
unkindly but accurately – nicknamed Spencer's *Apple Gatherers* in the
spare room 'The Bogeys'. Perhaps he just wanted a bit of time to
himself.

Sassoon made most of the conversational running, such as it was.
The two agreed that Davies was 'an excellent poet and a most likeable man'. Then Sassoon tried, rather desperately, to get Brooke to
talk about his time in the Pacific:

'What were the white people like in the places you stayed at in the
tropics?' . . .
'Some of them . . . were rather like composite characters out of
Conrad and Kipling.'
Hoping that it would go down well, I made a disparaging remark
about Kipling's poetry being terribly tub-thumping stuff.

'But not always, surely, . . . I used to think rather the same myself until Eddie made me read 'Cities and Thrones and Powers'. There aren't many better modern poems than that, you know.'

I could only admit that I had never read it.

'Composite characters out of Conrad and Kipling' was very much the line Brooke had played, writing home to friends from the Pacific. For a time he even turned spotting Kiplingesque types into an epistolary game. By the time he wrote to Gosse from Fiji on 19 November 1913, the game had taken a new and unexpected turn: Brooke had started to recognise a Kiplingesque side in himself. He acknowledged the discovery with wry, but fascinated amusement. It was true, he admitted, that 'one only finds in the South Seas what one brings there', but what he had found was a sense of duty and responsibility:

One feels that one's a White Man* – ludicrously. I kept thinking I was in the Sixth at Rugby, again. These dear good people, with their laughter and friendliness and crowns of flowers – one feels that one *must* protect them.

*Vide R. Kipling *passim*.

He was, in fact, casting himself as a character in a story Kipling never quite wrote: that of the blasé young English globetrotter of liberal views and persuasion who comes to realise that he is really 'one of us', one of the Empire in-group, after all. By April 1914, he was using Kiplingesque terms quite unironically and telling Marsh that D H Lawrence was 'a big man'.

Naturally none of this could be said to Sassoon that July morning. Nor, for his part, could Sassoon, having been so firmly put in his place, mention that actually he did like some of Kipling's poetry and even knew by heart the opening lines of 'The Return of the Children'. With poetry a non-starter, Sassoon even failed to bring up Brooke's own work. He could, for instance, have told him how much he admired 'The Old Vicarage, Grantchester'. He could even have made a joke about his gaffe with Marsh over 'Heaven' and asked Brooke what else he had been writing during his year away. Because Brooke, for all his

regular disclaimers in letters home to Marsh, had produced a clutch
of poems in the Pacific which eclipsed anything he had written before.
These new poems included not only 'Heaven' but 'The Great Lover',
several memorable sonnets and, best of all, 'Tiare Tahiti'.

The title 'Tiare Tahiti' referred both to the white-starred Tahitian
tiare flower and to the name of the boarding house in Mataia where
Brooke had stayed in early 1914. The lines were a witty and touching
celebration of Brooke's relationship with a Tahitian woman Taatamata, called Mamua in the poem. 'Tiare Tahiti' pretended to extol a
future paradise of idealised Platonic forms ('The Good, the Lovely,
and the True') in preference to the warm, human, earthly here and
now of Tahiti. In fact, it did just the opposite:

> . . . shall we wind these wreaths of ours,
> Where there are neither heads nor flowers?
> Oh, Heaven's Heaven! – but we'll be missing
> The palms, and sunlight, and the south;
> And there's an end, I think, of kissing,
> When our mouths are one with Mouth . . .

Into the poem's concluding section, Brooke wove a love-knot of echoes
from some of his favourite poets – Herrick, Milton, Shakespeare,
Marvell, Gray – together with a phrase of Tahitian:

> *Taü here*, Mamua, [My dear Mamua]
> Crown the hair, and come away! . . .
> Hasten, hand in human hand,
> Down the dark, the flowered way . . .
> Spend the glittering moonlight there
> Pursuing down the soundless deep
> Limbs that gleam and shadowy hair,
> Or floating lazy, half-asleep.
> Dive and double and follow after,
> Snare in flowers, and kiss, and call,
> With lips that fade, and human laughter,
> And faces individual,
> Well this side of Paradise! . . .
> There's little comfort in the wise.

Like Milton's Adam and Eve in *Paradise Lost*, Brooke's lovers went 'hand in hand'; but they were not expelled from Eden nor made to take 'with wandering steps and slow . . . their solitary way'. Instead they were allowed to go on enjoying Paradise, allowed to hurry 'Down the dark, the flowered way'.

But, with Sassoon ill at ease and Brooke no more forthcoming than he needed to be, there was no discussion of poetry, no impromptu recitation of the Pacific poems, no snippets of hard-won technical advice for Sassoon to store away. Nor – it goes without saying – was there any talk of more personal matters. And yet there too Brooke could probably have been of help to Sassoon.

During the same four or five years that Sassoon had been 'coming out' as a poet, he had also been coming to terms with his homo-sexuality. In 1910 he had heard from a friend about Edward Carpenter and his pioneering work *The Intermediate Sex*. By the following summer, he had read the book and started a correspondence with Carpenter. *The Intermediate Sex*, he told Carpenter, had opened his eyes and 'opened up the new life to me'. He understood now, he said, why he felt so attracted to his own sex and so antipathetic to women. He was careful to inform Carpenter that he was a virgin, as indeed he still was three years later talking to Brooke. At this point Sassoon's liber-ation was entirely literary, though probably momentous enough in his own mind. What this amounted to was the idealised admiration of the beautiful, mythological youths in his prose plays *Hyacinth* and *Amyntas, a Mystery* – though Sassoon was too cautious even to publish the latter privately – and the Housmanesque feelings for the doomed young man in *The Daffodil Murderer*.

Brooke was much more knowledgeable and experienced. He had had various sexual relationships with women, the one with Ka Cox being the messiest and the one with Taatamata the most fulfilling. His relationships with men tended to be more satisfactory, but – or more likely because – they were less physical: Brooke, like Lawrence, had a deep-seated puritanical streak. There was occasional gossip later of his homosexual encounters, but this was probably just a Bloomsbury in-joke. All that can be said for certain is that Brooke had had the usual crushes on other boys at public school and that his only known adult homosexual experience was a one-night stand with one of these former crushes, Denham Russell-Smith, at Grantchester in October 1909. When Russell-Smith died suddenly nearly three years later, Brooke sent a minutely detailed account of the whole event to James Strachey, his most faithful and besotted admirer. The letter is remarkable for its frankness, cruelty and narcissism:

> His was the woman's part throughout . . . My right hand got hold of the left half of his bottom, clutched it, and pressed his body into me. The smell of sweat began to be noticeable. At length we took to rolling to & fro over each other, in the excitement. Quite calm things, I remember, were passing through my brain 'The Elizabethan joke "The Dance of the Sheets" has, then, something in it.' 'I hope his erection is all right' – and so on. I thought of him entirely in the third person. At length the waves grew more terrific: my control of the situation was over; I treated him with the utmost violence, to which he more quietly, but incessantly, responded. Half under him and half over, I came off.

Of course Brooke and Sassoon talked of nothing so intimate or useful. Instead Sassoon, rapidly running out of conversational gambits and feeling increasingly like a junior in the presence of the head boy, rather feebly brought up the fact that the two of them must have briefly overlapped at Cambridge in the autumn term of 1906. Brooke politely agreed and mentioned his appearance as the Herald in *The Eumenides*. Again, this should have provided Sassoon with a cue since he had been to the production and – seemingly like everyone else who attended it – had carried away a warm memory of the picturesque figure with the trumpet. But again Sassoon failed to take advantage of the opportunity, and silence descended once more.

Not long after that, Sassoon took his leave and went back down the fifty-nine-step spiral stone staircase. When Brooke saw him to the door to say goodbye, he gave Sassoon the impression that 'as far as he was concerned there was no apparent reason why we should ever meet again'. That, at least, was how Sassoon later re-created the scene, even imagining that Brooke might 'have breathed a sigh of relief, as he closed the door quietly and went back to being his unimpeded self'. Brooke may have done that – equally, as one of his biographers suggests, he may have found some paper, returned to the breakfast table and started jotting down what he could recall of yet another monologue by the likeable but slightly tedious Davies:

> I've got very fond of pictures in the last two years. I've got one lovely one. It's an early Victorian landscape, oh, a very beautiful one. A friend of mine saw it in an old shop. He couldn't afford it. But he told me and I bought it. Only £2. The frame alone is worth £2; it's an awfully good frame, my friend says it's worth quite £2, and he's an artist, so it must be . . .

Sassoon went back to his half-furnished rooms and wrote Marsh a thank-you note, saying how delightful he thought Brooke and that he hoped to see him again sometime. Later, feeling lonely and loose-endish, he took himself off to Regent's Park Zoo and stared at the animals which stared back at him with 'motionless morosity'. One monkey 'looked at me as if he, at any rate, had something he would like to tell me, and then sighed and looked away, wondering why either of us was there'. The encounter, then or later, prompted a sonnet, 'Sporting Acquaintances', in which he mocked both his fox-hunting and literary selves in an imitation of Brooke's best satirical manner:

> I watched old squatting Chimpanzee: he traced
> His painful patterns in the dirt: I saw
> Red-haired Ourang-Utang, whimsical-faced,
> Chewing a sportsman's meditative straw.
> I'd known them years ago, and half-forgotten
> They'd come to grief. (But how, I'd never heard,
> Poor beggars!) Still, it seemed so rude and rotten
> To stand and gape at them with never a word.
>
> I ventured 'Ages since we met', and tried
> My candid smile of friendship. No success.
> One scratched his hairy thigh, while t'other sighed
> And glanced away. I saw they liked me less
> Than when, on Epsom Downs, in cloudless weather,
> We backed The Tetrarch and got drunk together.

Less than a month later, on the weekend of 1–2 August, England was on the brink of war, Brooke was asking Marsh whether he had 'a Brussels-before-Waterloo feeling', and Sassoon was cycling to Rye to enlist in the 1st Sussex Yeomanry.

2

Fighting the Keeper

Edward Thomas and Rupert Brooke,
8 and 18 June 1915

Rupert Brooke died on 23 April 1915 from septicaemia en route to the Dardanelles. Five weeks or so later, Edward Thomas was reviewing Brooke's posthumously published collection *1914 & other Poems*. He did the collection twice, for the highbrow *English Review* on 8 June and again ten days later for the popular *Daily Chronicle*. For all sorts of reasons, reviewing Brooke was a tricky assignment.

On the personal front, Thomas had to find the time. He supported himself, and his growing family, as a freelance writer. Back when he left Oxford in 1900, he had hoped that a writer's life would mean living in the country and composing essays about Nature in the manner of Richard Jefferies and George Borrow. He soon learnt that, for him at least, a writer's life meant living in the country in a series of not very sanitary houses and churning out non-stop reviews – topped up with £40 advances for rural travelogues and the odd critical book or literary biography.

Not that Thomas was a bad reviewer. On the contrary: he had turned himself into one of the top English literary reviewers of the Edwardian period. His trademark was the carefully weighed appraisal, in which a muted lyricism vied with a dry, sometimes glum, humour. He commented of Thomas Hardy's *Time's Laughingstocks and Other*

Poems (1909) that the collection contained 'ninety-nine reasons for not living', but also that 'The moan of his verse rouses an echo that is as brave as a trumpet'. Over the years more than 1,000 books passed through the Thomas mill, ground into around a million words. New poetry was his forte. Brooke, Walter de la Mare, D H Lawrence, W H Davies, Ezra Pound and many others were appreciatively noted on debut. When Brooke brought out his first collection *Poems* in 1911, Thomas quipped that 'Copies should be bought by everyone over forty who has never been under forty', and commented shrewdly that the poems were 'full of revolt, contempt, self-contempt, and yet of arrogance too'. He predicted a notable poetic future. When Marsh produced his first Georgian anthology, *Georgian Poetry 1911–1912*, Thomas reviewed the volume on no less than three occasions, each time finding something different to say about Brooke's contributions. He used to sell off extra and unwanted review copies to supplant his income, and one bookcase was specially reserved for volumes of unresaleable poetry, pages of which he used as spills to light his endless clay pipes.

In a good year, Thomas made £400 from his reviewing and potboiling, perhaps £25,000–£30,000 in modern terms. It was a reasonable income. A labourer earned around £50 a year and a bank clerk or curate £150–£200. But it required Thomas to stay on the treadmill full-time. Eventually the treadmill itself became a habit he couldn't give up, however much he came to despise his life as a 'writing animal', a 'doomed hack'. At times the amount of work he took on suggests both a desire to displace other anxieties and some perverse need to test himself beyond his limits. He called this 'burning my candle at 3 ends'. He broke down on a number of occasions but he never quite fell apart.

Then, with the outbreak of war, the literary market changed, and the thirty-six-year-old Thomas found himself short of work. Part of him thought he should enlist (though he was on the old side); another part thought he should join his friend Robert Frost in America. He agonised but, characteristically, could not commit himself to either course of action. He wrote articles describing the impact of the war on the rural Home Front. He started collecting material for *This England: An Anthology from her Writers*. But by mid-1915 he was pretty desperate. 'It is a fine world,' he told the poet Gordon Bottomley,

'& I wish I knew how to make £200 a year in it without sucking James Milne's –', James Milne being the literary editor of the *Daily Chronicle*.

Which was why that spring, as a last resort, he had taken on a life of the Duke of Marlborough. No one now wanted books like his *A Literary Pilgrim in England* – a volume he derisively nicknamed 'Omes and 'Aunts – but the duke's famous victories in northern France in the early 1700s at least made his biography look vaguely topical. Thomas went to some effort to point up the connections. He included a map of the 'Campagne de 1708 en Flandre', full of names with a contemporary resonance: Ypres, Armentières, Arras. He repeated these and similarly evocative names in the text: Mons, La Bassée, Namur. He devoted a chapter to the lot of the ordinary foot soldier in Marlborough's day and dropped in at least one explicit link between past and present: Sir Thomas Morgan and his men, he wrote, 'fought all over the sands and the dyked lands where the English lie now (1915)'. And he hated every minute of it.

Thomas already knew the A–Z of literary self-disgust by heart. He told Bottomley that fair-copying his rural travelogue *The South Country* was like 'returning to one's vomit, a cultivated taste I have not achieved'. But the Marlborough book was in a class of its own. It was, he claimed, 'the worst job I ever undertook'. All the same he was a pro and he forced the pages out of himself, knocking off the bulk of the biography – 75,000 words – in a twenty-six-day burst between mid-May and mid-June.

That was exactly the moment when the chance to do Brooke came up. Enmeshed in Marlborough, two quick reviews with tight deadlines no doubt had their appeal – not to mention the extra cash. In fact, with Brooke-mania sweeping the country, it was very probably Thomas who approached the *English Review* rather than the other way round. He definitely made the approach to the *Daily Chronicle* since his jibe about 'sucking James Milne's –' comes in a letter of 16 June, after he must have finished his second review. He had in any case been rereading Brooke and making rough notes towards a piece for an American journal. That idea fell through, but it meant that when he sat down to turn out around 1,200 words for the *English Review*, he already had some jottings to work on.

*　*　*

Brooke-mania gave Thomas the opportunity; it also constituted one of his main problems. In June 1915, the war was not going well. On the Eastern Front Germany was making significant gains. The Western Front in France had been deadlocked for months, hence the Admiralty's idea of getting in through the back door via the Dardanelles – but that too had quickly stalled due to bad luck, blunders and the bravery of the Turkish troops. Everywhere the casualty lists were mounting. England needed a war hero. Brooke, although not actually killed in action (his septicaemia was caused by a mosquito bite), otherwise perfectly fitted the bill. He was young, very good-looking, and – crucially – just months before his death, he had published five war sonnets in a small magazine. These sonnets were soon causing a stir. On 11 March a review in the *Times Literary Supplement* quoted two in full: number IV 'The Dead' and number V 'The Soldier'. 'The Soldier' was then read out on Easter Sunday from the pulpit of St Paul's.

This became big news. *The Times* reported the event in detail, including Dean Inge's pronouncement that Brooke would 'take rank with our great poets', and quoted the poem in full:

> If I should die, think only this of me:
>   That there's some corner of a foreign field
> That is for ever England. There shall be
>   In that rich earth a richer dust concealed;
> A dust whom England bore, shaped, made aware,
>   Gave, once, her flowers to love, her ways to roam,
> A body of England's, breathing English air,
>   Washed by the rivers, blest by suns of home.
>
> And think, this heart, all evil shed away,
>   A pulse in the eternal mind, no less
>   Gives somewhere back the thoughts by England given;
> Her sights and sounds; dreams happy as her day;
>   And laughter, learnt of friends; and gentleness,
>   In hearts at peace, under an English heaven.

The lines exactly struck the required note: insouciant self-sacrifice heavily laced with patriotic pastoralism. When, as if on cue, Brooke died soon afterwards, his death fused with the sonnet's eloquent idealisation of England and Englishness to 'match him with the hour'. The hero had been found.

Thomas, like many others, probably first learnt of Brooke's death on 26 April through Winston Churchill's eulogy in *The Times*. The First Lord of the Admiralty's grandiloquence instantly turned the dead poet into a version of Wordsworth's 'happy warrior':

> The thoughts to which he gave expression in the few incomparable war sonnets which he has left behind will be shared by many thousands of young men moving resolutely and blithely forward into this, the hardest, the cruellest, and the least-rewarded of all the wars that men have fought. They are a whole revelation of Rupert Brooke himself. Joyous, fearless, versatile, deeply instructed, with classic symmetry of mind and body, he was all that one would wish England's noblest sons to be in days when no sacrifice but the most precious is acceptable, and the most precious is that which is most freely proffered.

Other effusions quickly followed. The *Daily News* mourned Brooke as 'a part of the youth of the world'. The *Star* called him 'the youth of our race in symbol'. The *Morning Post* claimed that 'Not since Sir Philip Sidney's heroic death have we lost such a gallant and joyous type of the poet-soldier'. The five war sonnets were much reprinted.

Ironically, Brooke himself had not particularly rated the sonnets, dubbing them 'in the rough'. When he heard of Dean Inge's and *The Times*'s approval, he told a friend the poems were meant as a farewell, adding mockingly: 'Perhaps we should have put in a slip to say so; and extracted, even in these times, a few tears, a few shillings.' Not that Brooke was at all averse to being famous. Far from it. For years, he had made an elaborate game out of the prospect of his own literary immortality. Recently, in a more practical spirit, he had put one reliable friend, Dudley Ward, in charge of his letters, with an only half-ironic 'Well, I *might* turn out to be eminent and biographable. If so, let them know the poor truths'; while the besotted and even more reliable Eddie Marsh had been entrusted with the literary remains.

Brooke knew his man. The moment news of his death reached

England, Marsh, though heartbroken, at once started to curate the emerging myth. As Churchill's private secretary and as editor of the hugely successful *Georgian Poetry 1911–1912*, he was uniquely well placed. He probably lent a hand with his boss's *Times* eulogy; he certainly contributed a brief, unsigned, accompanying obituary notice in much the same key. With the obituary-machine under way – no sign there of any 'poor truths' – Marsh turned his attention to the poetry and the idea of a short memoir. He wrote to Brooke's friends, asking for anecdotes, unpublished poems, letters, and, by early June, he had rushed out advance copies of the collection Thomas would find so tricky to review.

For all Marsh's speed, *1914 & other Poems* was a carefully orches-trated volume. Facing the title page was a photograph of Brooke's head and neck caught in profile, lunging forward, poised, ready: the very image of the young hero. The collection itself was in four sections, book-ended with Englishness. The now famous five sonnets domi-nated the short opening section: I 'Peace' ('Now, God be thanked Who has matched us with His hour'); II 'Safety' ('Dear! of all happy in the hour, most blest'); III 'The Dead' ('Blow out, you bugles, over the rich Dead!'); IV 'The Dead' ('These hearts were woven of human joys and cares'); and V 'The Soldier'. Section two comprised Brooke's witty 'Pacific' poems written in 1913–14, such as 'Heaven', 'Tiare Tahiti' and 'Sonnet (*Suggested by some of the Proceedings of the Society for Psychical Research*)'. Then there was a selection of other mostly recent lyrics, before the final section brought things to a close with the nostalgic 'The Old Vicarage, Grantchester'. Marsh understood exactly what the public wanted. When the first impression of 1,000 copies reached the shops on 16 June, it immediately sold out and had to be reprinted, and reprinted, and reprinted.

At such a moment, to offer *1914 & other Poems* anything other than extravagant praise was hard. But Thomas was a reviewer with a conscience and, inconveniently, he had developed decidedly mixed feelings about the poems, particularly those sonnets. Besides, he had known Brooke personally. How much could he say?

Thomas and Brooke had been friends though never really close. All the same he knew things about Brooke that could not be put in a review. For instance, from the very beginning of their acquaintance in 1910, he had found himself embroiled in Brooke's busy love life. Brooke was then chasing, among others, the seventeen-year-old schoolgirl Noel Olivier, who was a pupil at the progressive boarding school Bedales in Hampshire. Thomas and his young family lived nearby and had strong links with the school. Brooke proposed various fantastical schemes to Noel for seeing her on her own, while making it clear that he also wanted to see Thomas. Brooke eventually combined the two objectives by persuading the Thomases to invite Noel and himself to tea. (Noel sensibly brought along a school-friend.) Predictably, matters between Noel and Brooke never really worked out – although they briefly entered into a secret engage-ment – but through the Hampshire visit Brooke and Thomas became friends.

From then on, the two met fairly regularly though Brooke made most of the running. He would read Thomas new poems, and they would talk over shared literary enthusiasms and mutual acquaintances. They certainly discussed Noel, but the more reserved Thomas is unlikely to have told Brooke that a few years earlier he too had fallen for a schoolgirl of a similar age, Hope Webb, or that at Oxford he had had serious crushes on two male undergraduates. Brooke wrote Thomas a few high-spirited letters. On setting off for America and the Pacific in May 1913, he told Thomas he left 'the muses of England' in his keeping. 'Feed the brutes', Brooke added in a cheeky half-echo of Kurtz's 'Exterminate the brutes' from Conrad's *Heart of Darkness*.

The friendship was not all plain sailing. In March 1913 Thomas was invited to one of Marsh's literary breakfasts along with Brooke. According to Marsh, Thomas was 'unforthcoming and constricted, perhaps dyspeptic' and 'seemed to look down his nose' at Brooke and his host 'as well as at the food'. The likely reasons why things went so badly wrong say a good deal about Brooke's ability to attract mutu-ally incompatible people, and also about Thomas and Marsh. Thomas could be socially withdrawn. He admitted in a letter to Edward Garnett that in company 'my only way of holding my own is the instinctive one of turning on what you call coldness and a superior manner'. This was obviously what happened at the breakfast. For his part, the sociable and donnish Marsh, with his high-pitched 'my dears', could be proprietorial in his adoration of Brooke. Thomas was never much of a 'my dearer'.

Besides, Thomas and Marsh were members of a *Poetry Review* panel about to award a £30 poetry prize, and Brooke's 'The Old Vicarage, Grantchester' was a leading contender. Marsh was not beyond a bit of literary manoeuvring, and Thomas may have wondered whether the breakfast was designed to secure his vote. (If so, the plan misfired; Brooke did win the prize, but Thomas voted for someone else.) Or perhaps the problem really was the food. To treat his depression, Thomas would periodically go on a vegetarian diet, so Mrs Elgy's standard kidneys and bacon may have been the last thing he wanted for breakfast. Whatever the reason for the fiasco, the friendship with Brooke survived, but Thomas and Marsh were always to be on edgy terms.

The edginess showed itself when Marsh wrote, asking for material for his Brooke memoir. Thomas's reply on 5 June was polite, but guarded in the extreme. Marsh had enquired after a lost herring poem of Brooke's. Thomas answered that he only faintly recalled it but did offer a possible opening line: 'What a cold life the herring leads'. He deflected Marsh's request for letters, saying Brooke had only ever sent him a few insignificant notes, and these were merely of personal interest. As for anecdotes, details, impressions, he claimed to have known Brooke 'so slightly' that he was unlikely to have anything to add. That 'so slightly' was frankly disingenuous. So too was Thomas's eager anticipation of the new poems and memoir, since by then he must have received his advance copy of *1914 & other Poems* and had almost certainly written his first review – unless the new poems referred to other pieces Marsh hoped to publish with his memoir. Finally, rather undiplomatically, Thomas put in a strong plug for Robert Frost's *North of Boston* poems, knowing that Marsh was assembling material for his second *Georgian Poetry* anthology. (Marsh did not take his advice.) Unmentionable information about Brooke, an uncomfortable awareness of the intricacies of London literary politics: these were further complications impinging on Thomas's reviews of *1914 & other Poems*.

Then there were Thomas's private reservations about the poems themselves. 'Though his death makes certain sonnets stand out,' he had told a friend in early May, 'they still seem to me rather eloquent expressions of thoughts or fancies than pure poetry; but eloquent they are in a very exceptional youthful style.' Thomas's reservations were also fuelled by the fact that he had secretly begun writing poems himself. In his own mind, he now approached Brooke not as a literary hack, but as a fellow-poet. The catalyst had been the combination of Frost's encouragement and the change in Thomas's working circumstances due to the outbreak of the war.

Frost had come to England in late 1912, pushing forty. London represented for him the literary equivalent of the Last Chance Saloon, and the gamble worked. Within months, he had published his first collection, *A Boy's Will,* and been accepted in English poetry circles. He and Thomas took to each other at once. Both were adopted countrymen of a certain age. Both were married with children, and regular refugees from domesticity. ('I run away from home every day,' Thomas told Arthur Ransome, 'but I always come back for tea.') Both were well acquainted with a sense of literary failure and with depression. Thomas had seriously contemplated suicide on several occasions and come close to it. He described himself to the writer Eleanor Farjeon, who was unrequitedly in love with him, as a 'flat grey shore which surprises the tide by being inaccessible to it'. The main difference between Thomas and Frost was that Thomas was a waverer while Frost was nothing if not decisive. Also Frost was direct, and his directness seems to have quickly overcome Thomas's deep-seated wariness – and Thomas loved Frost's poetry.

Thomas felt an immediate affinity with both Frost's rural subject matter and his literary theories. He particularly warmed to Frost's idea that poetry should use 'a language absolutely unliterary', caught 'fresh from talk'. This was a position he himself had been inching towards in his prose, trying to 'wring all the necks of my rhetoric – the geese', as he put it in a letter to Frost. When Frost's second collection, *North of Boston*, appeared in May 1914, Thomas reviewed it enthusiastically in three prominent places. His *Daily News* review threw down the challenge. 'This is one of the most revolutionary books of modern times,' he opened, and concluded: 'It is poetry because it is better than prose.'

For his part, Frost was busily convincing Thomas that he too was really a poet. The month *North of Boston* was published, Thomas made the first tentative move. 'I wonder whether you can imagine me taking to verse,' he asked Frost, adding: 'If you can I might get over the feeling that it is impossible – which at once obliges your good nature to say "I can".' Frost referred Thomas to paragraphs from *In Pursuit of Spring*, his latest travelogue, and told him that all he had to do was rewrite them 'in verse form in exactly the same cadence'. The declaration of war in August, the resultant decline in demand for Thomas's stuff and a growing sense of the England he loved being at risk also played their part. In early December 1914 Thomas produced his first poem, 'Up in the Wind', adapted from a prose sketch, and he was away.

By the time of his Brooke reviews, six months later in June 1915, Thomas had completed over seventy poems. He was even stealing time for poetry from his life of Marlborough. Some of the poems celebrated a personal notion of England, though in a rather different spirit from Brooke. Brooke's England tended to be generalised, non-specific: 'Her sights and sounds; dreams happy as her day'. It was knowingly sentimentalised: 'Stands the Church clock at ten to three? / And is there honey still for tea?' Or just knowing: 'And oft between the boughs is seen / The sly shade of a Rural Dean . . .' Thomas's England by contrast was embodied in particulars, sometimes a moment of epiphany in a specific location. In 'Adlestrop', a solitary blackbird's song heard on a hot day in an empty station turns into the song of 'all the birds / Of Oxfordshire and Gloucestershire'. In 'The Manor Farm', 'a season of bliss unchangeable / Awakened' from where it had remained 'Safe under tile and thatch for ages since / This England, Old already, was called Merry'.

Brooke's war was one of psychic plunging and purging: 'To turn, as swimmers into cleanness leaping'. Also heroic renunciation: 'These laid the world away; poured out the red / Sweet wine of youth; gave up the years to be'. Thomas's war was one in which an owl's cry heard at night spoke 'for all who lay under the stars, / Soldiers and poor, unable to rejoice'. But the war did increasingly impinge on the poems. In one, written on 13 May 1915, he described how 'the fifty faggots' he had just stacked by the hedge 'must / Light several Winters' fires', but concluded ominously:

> Before they are done
> The war will have ended, many other things
> Have ended, maybe, that I can no more
> Foresee or more control than robin and wren.

Before Brooke's death, none of Thomas's poems referred directly or indirectly to him or his work. But in the aftermath that began to change. Over two consecutive days in late May, Thomas wrote 'Sedge-Warblers'. The poem, which exists in a number of versions, rejects falsifying Romantic fantasies of Nature and advocates acceptance of the wordless song of 'the small brown birds / Wisely reiterating endlessly / What no man learnt yet, in or out of school'. On 23 May the poem seems originally to have begun:

> This beauty made me dream there was a time
> Long past and irrecoverable, a clime
> Where from such brooks shining and sunny clear . . .

Thomas then crossed out 'sunny' in the third line and substituted 'racing': 'Where from such brooks shining and racing clear'. Next he rewrote the line at the bottom of the facing page: 'Where any brook so radiant racing clear'. The following day he changed the line once more: 'Where brooklet of such radiance racing clear'. Then he replaced 'brooklet' with 'river' so that the apparently final version of the line read: 'Where river of such radiance racing clear'. Why so much tinkering? Because it seems to have struck Thomas that to put 'shining' and 'radiant' in the same line as 'brook', or for that matter 'radiance' in the same line as 'brooklet', was inevitably to evoke the already famous conclusion of Brooke's fourth war sonnet, 'The Dead':

> He leaves a white
> Unbroken glory, a gathered radiance,
> A width, a shining peace, under the night.

Punning allusions to his dead friend were not what Thomas had in mind. 'River' in place of 'brook' or 'brooklet' cancelled the possibility.

But although poems were coming regularly and friends like Frost, Bottomley and Walter de la Mare were encouraging, Thomas had drawn a complete blank with the literary magazines. He would probably have fared better had he sent the poems out under his own name, but typically he did nothing so straightforward: instead he used the pseudonym 'Edward Eastaway'. He told friends it was to ensure the poems were read on their own merits. Perhaps. Perhaps too he wanted to keep his newly released poetic self separate from that of the literary hack. (In one early poem, 'The Other', he cast himself as a *Doppelgänger* unsuccessfully but compulsively pursuing an improved, more admired version of himself.) He may simply have thought a pseudonym would make rejection easier to bear. Whatever the reason, the stratagem entirely failed. By the summer of 1915, Thomas had collected nothing but rejection slips. And here he was reviewing the suddenly popular Brooke. How was he to tackle it?

Thomas opened quietly, simply giving the facts, as these were then generally thought to be: 'On 23 April the poet Rupert Brooke died of sunstroke at Lemnos in his twenty-eighth year. He was a second lieutenant in the Royal Naval Division, on his way to the fighting in the Dardanelles.' Next, more conventionally, he reproduced the commonplace of Brooke's cut-down promise: 'No poet of his age was so much esteemed and admired, or was watched more hopefully.' But in the third sentence Thomas unobtrusively introduced a more equivocal note: 'His work could not be taken soberly, whether you liked it or not.' At that moment to raise in public the idea of not liking Brooke's poems was reasonably courageous. Harking back to his review of *Poems* and to private letters to friends, Thomas then emphasised again what could be put positively – the youthfulness of Brooke's poetry: 'It was full of the thought, the aspiration, the indignation of youth; full of the praise of youth.' At the same time, Thomas added apparently casually, there was the unavoidable effect of Brooke's personality: 'Many people knew the man or the reputation of his personal charm.'

So far Thomas had remained coolly detached. Now momentarily the tone flickered with irony: 'Wherever he went he made friends, well-wishers, admirers, adorers.' The irony lay in the sequencing of the careful list, the way 'friends' was hived off from the disquieting crescendo of 'well-wishers, admirers, adorers'. But then Thomas tilted the picture again. Brooke, he insisted, 'was himself a friendly man, with humour and good humour added', someone who generated an atmosphere of laughter and geniality, the Brooke whose lively company had made Thomas a friend and, mostly, a well-wisher.

Again more matter-of-factly Thomas spelt out Brooke's dream run: good at work and games at Rugby; awarded a fellowship at King's; revered as the Young Romantic Poet: 'he was celebrated as a golden young Apollo, in Mrs Cornford's phrase, "Magnificently unprepared / For the long littleness of life"'. And yet, with all his success, said Thomas generously, Brooke's 'attractiveness included modesty and simplicity'. Then, as though that made Brooke sound too impossibly good and himself too much like an admirer or adorer, he once more subtly readjusted the focus. In a single sentence Thomas managed to suggest Brooke's sociability and responsiveness, but also a certain poseyness: 'He stretched himself out, drew his fingers through his waved, fair hair, laughed, talked indolently, and admired as much as he was admired.' The fact was, Thomas continued, that, if you knew Brooke, it was hard to separate the person from the poetry: 'not that they were the same, but that the two inextricably mingled and helped one another.' Which silently begged the question of how good, taken on its own, the poetry really was.

Thomas next offered a memorable close-up of Brooke's physical presence, manner and looks, obviously drawn from life:

> He was tall, broad, and easy in his movements. Either he stooped, or he thrust his head forward unusually much to look at you with his steady, blue eyes. His clear, rosy skin helped to give him the look of a great girl.

The snapshot was a conscious reaction against the newspaper accounts. These, as Thomas dryly noted, had almost all talked about Brooke's '"beauty", his good looks, his "glamour", one said that he was one of the handsomest Englishmen of our time'. By contrast, Thomas deliberately highlighted the unmanly aspects: 'His clear, rosy skin helped to give him the look of a great girl.'

Up to now, Thomas had created a mostly appreciative portrait of his younger friend with small lacunae of irony and silence for those who could read between the lines. But he had said little about the poetry. There clearly had to be some reference to the famous war sonnets. Thomas brought them in abruptly with a simple 'And': 'And just before he died it happened that one of his last-published sonnets

was quoted in St Paul's Cathedral by the Dean'. Thomas then
quoted 'The Soldier' in full but entirely without comment. This was
a cunning way of leaving a space for private reservations without
actually spelling them out. Most readers would naturally assume
that so obviously celebrated a poem rendered comment superfluous,
while the discerning few could be safely left to ponder the echoing
silence.

Thomas instead, and tellingly, assessed the effect of such a poem
on Brooke's posthumous reputation: 'So, instantly he took his share
of the fame that comes to young poets dying conspicuously and
unexpectedly, but not unprophesied by themselves.' This was as openly
wry as Thomas was prepared to be. While implicitly placing Brooke
in the company of Shelley, Keats and Byron, Thomas also managed
to hint that there was something slightly spurious about fame of this
type: 'dying conspicuously' suggested that such deaths were almost
a form of showing-off; as did the laconic 'but not unprophesied by
themselves'. Here Thomas came closest to raising the reservations
of his May letter: 'his death makes certain sonnets stand out'. He
was acknowledging the impossibility already of rescuing any real
sense of Brooke the person and poet from the hardening carapace
of myth.

The last two thirds of the review mostly settled for what could be
said without completely forfeiting Thomas's critical soul. He spelt out
the slimness of Brooke's published *oeuvre*: one previous volume of
poems, journal essays on Donne and Webster, further poems in magazines, newspapers and *Georgian Poetry*. He reiterated his earlier point
about the poetry's youthfulness. He exhumed older poems like 'Dust'
and 'The Hill', but picked out 'The Funeral of Youth', 'The Great
Lover' and 'Tiare Tahiti' for particular attention and quotation. He
cast Brooke as a latter-day, if apolitical, Shelley – eager, despairing and
metaphysical – with something distinctly 'fishy' about his metaphysical examples: 'One of his poems was the result of an effort to look
at the world, another to see God, like a fish; while a third spoke of
the cold life of the herring, but ended: "He has his hour, he has his
hour."'

Thomas approved of 'The Great Lover' with its celebration of
'tea-cups and peeled sticks as well as rainbows'. Brooke, he implied,
was growing up, 'beginning not only to enjoy things as mortals do,

but perhaps to be content to do so'. He paid back Brooke's own compliment about Donne's humour in his love poems and quoted in support the closing lines of 'Tiare Tahiti':

> It had long been true of him what he said of Donne: that 'humour was always at his command. It was part of his realism, especially in the bulk of his work, his poems dealing with love.' He turned to

> > . . . lips that fade, and human laughter,
> > And faces individual,
> > Well this side of Paradise . . .

> and remarked 'There's little comfort in the wise.'

Reverting again to Shelley, he claimed that Brooke might have failed to reach the 'Shelleyan altitude where words have various radiance rather than meaning' but he had at least aspired to that altitude. His real achievement, Thomas reiterated, and a 'rare and considerable' one, was 'to have expressed and suggested in so many ways the promise of youth'.

Thomas was now ready for his finale and delivered at least a Forsterian two cheers. The war had, he claimed, given Brooke a fresh existence beyond 'all the little emptiness of love', and in support he quoted the whole sestet of 'Peace'. A phrase from another of the war sonnets, coupled with a further echo of Frances Cornford, allowed Thomas to sign off with his own mythologising gesture:

> He felt safe, 'and if these poor limbs die, safest of all'. His reputation is safe: it was never greater than now, when he stands out clearly against that immense, dark background, an Apollo not afraid of the worst of life.

The review was an impressive achievement: appreciative, at times vivid, and, all things considered, not overly reverential. Typically Thomas was soon unhappy with it – not least because he now had to do it all over again – but somehow slightly differently – for the *Daily Chronicle*.

He wrote the second review, nearly 1,000 words this time, on the evening of Friday 11 June. It appeared in a single column a week later under 'Books of the Day'. On the same page were advertisements for

Florence L Barclay's *My Heart's Right There: A Patriotic Story of the War* and *The Long Retreat*, a shilling book of soldiers' doggerel, telling 'in the language of Thomas Atkins the story of the retirement from Mons, a military episode as glorious as Corunna'. Under 'Miscellaneous', the Antient Society of Cogers announced the commemoration the following day of the centenary of the Battle of Waterloo at the Salisbury Hotel off Fleet Street.

Thomas seems to have rattled off his second review fairly smartly, recycling where he could. But he still tried to work in a couple of unexpected points. After quoting 'Peace' in full, he noted that it 'expresses self-denial as if it were the supreme self-indulgence'. These sonnets, he went on, were probably not nearly as personal as people seemed to assume. Although the phrase 'all the little emptiness of love' would instantly recall Brooke to old friends, the impersonality of the lines was, he suggested, more striking. In fact, to see what Brooke had really given up, you had to look at 'The Great Lover', where the ordinary was cherished as the special: 'white plates and cups, clean-gleaming'; 'the musty reek that lingers / About dead leaves and last year's ferns'. 'It is because those things are surrendered', Thomas insisted, 'that, to those who knew him, "Peace" is such a moving poem.'

This time there were no Shelleyan altitudes. The Brooke served up to *Daily Chronicle* readers (who included the young Ivor Gurney) fluctuated intensely between thinking and enjoying. Until the war and those sonnets, that is. Thomas then quoted 'The Soldier' in full. Here, he claimed, Brooke had risen above being either 'metaphysician or aesthete': 'He embraces England and eternity, unites the "kindred points of heaven and home", and shows them to be one.'

It did the job, but a couple of days later, on Sunday 13 June, he let out his dissatisfaction in a letter to Frost, unpicking a good deal of what he had said in the second review:

> I wish I hadn't to say more about poetry. I wished it on Friday night particularly as I had to spoil the effect of your letter by writing 1000 words about Rupert Brooke's posthumous book – not daring to say that those sonnets about him enlisting(?) are probably not very personal but a nervous attempt to connect with himself the very widespread

idea that self sacrifice is the highest self indulgence. You know. And I don't dispute it. Only I doubt if he knew it or would he have troubled to drag in the fact that enlisting cleared him of

All the little emptiness of love?

Well, I daren't say so, not having enlisted or fought the keeper.

The idea that the famous sonnets might not have been very personal: well, he had more or less said that. But he had not dared to pitch his more heretical insight that there was something willed, rhetorical, about the sonnets' heroic surrender, that they were really 'a nervous attempt to connect with himself the very widespread idea that self sacrifice is the highest self indulgence'. That could not be said publicly but it was not simply or even primarily Brooke-mania which restrained Thomas. Brooke had at least enlisted. He had dared to die for his words. For Thomas, only someone who had similarly dared had the right openly to criticise the poems and the motives behind them.

The reference to 'fighting the keeper' reinforced the point. Frost would have immediately known what he meant. In August 1914, the Thomases and Frosts had holidayed together in the West Midlands. Out walking one day, Thomas and Frost had been menaced by a gamekeeper with a shotgun. Frost had stood up to the bully and duly received an apology from the local landowner. Thomas felt he himself had behaved in a cowardly fashion. The phrase (meaning something like 'purposefully confronting life's threats') became a piece of shorthand code in Thomas's letters to Frost, and he included it in one of his first poems, 'An Old Song': 'Since then I've thrown away a chance to fight a gamekeeper'.

Within a month of his punch-pulling reviews of Brooke, the thirty-seven-year-old Thomas made his big decision. He would not be joining Frost in America; he would fight the keeper and enlist. On Friday 9 July 1915, he went to the Artists Rifles HQ to make enquiries. On Wednesday 14 July he passed his medical and was accepted. The following day he described the occasion to Frost; his relief was palpable:

Seven of us were examined together, stripped & measured & made to hop it round the room on each foot. I suppose I was too excited & he kept sounding my left side & asking me if I had ever had rheumatic fever. There was one man of my age, the rest boys, mostly clerks.

Brooke and the difficulty of writing honestly about his *1914 & other Poems* was not the only reason, or the main reason, why Thomas enlisted. But it seems to have tipped the balance.

3

Rupert Brooke Must Have Been Rather Like You

Vera Brittain, Roland Leighton and Rupert Brooke, 29 July 1915

On Thursday 29 July 1915 Vera Brittain sent Roland Leighton a copy of Rupert Brooke's posthumously published volume *1914 & other Poems*. She was at home in Buxton, nursing at the Devonshire Hospital; he was a lieutenant in a territorial battalion of the Worcestershire Regiment (the 1/7th), stationed in the Armentières sector in northern France. For both of them it was to prove a significant gift.

Vera had first encountered Brooke's war sonnets on 12 May. She was in the summer term of her first year at Oxford, reading English. Her college, Somerville, had recently been turned into a military hospital, and the members of the college had shifted to Oriel College in the centre of town. With a few other women undergraduates, she now occupied a room at Micklem Hall, an old house down a side street with its own garden. Her tutor Helen Darbishire lived upstairs.

That Wednesday evening it was chilly, and Darbishire invited Vera and another undergraduate Marjorie Barber up to her sitting room to enjoy her fire and to look at her facsimile Milton manuscripts – 'an immense privilege' as Vera noted in her diary. They talked about scholarship candidates, and Vera recalled some blunder she

Left: Vera Brittain as a VAD nurse
Right: Roland Leighton, December 1914

had made about Blake in her scholarship interview. (This had not
stopped the college awarding her one of two exhibitions of £20 per
annum.) Then the talk turned to the war and to poetry about the
war, and Vera asked her tutor to read them Rupert Brooke's war
sonnets.

The poems instantly seared themselves into her imagination. They
were 'all sad & moving, in spite of their spirit of courage & hope,'
she noted, '& through them all ran a strangely prophetic note, a
premonition of early death.' Hearing the lines read in her tutor's
'grave, deliberate voice', Vera could barely keep back the tears. Poems
and dead poet immediately and inextricably fused themselves with the
man she was in love with, Roland Leighton. She went to bed that
night 'sorrowful & heavy-laden with the thoughts of Roland & Rupert
Brooke's sonnets mingled in my mind'.

At Uppingham School, Roland Leighton had been one of the closest
friends of Vera's adored younger brother Edward. With Victor
Richardson, the trio had been known as The Three Musketeers, but
there was no doubt that Roland was chief musketeer. His school nickname was not Monseigneur for nothing. He was a golden boy from
a literary and artistic family, who had carried off an unprecedented
seven prizes at his last Uppingham speech day in July 1914 and gained
the Senior Open Classical Postmastership at Merton College, Oxford.
He was not exactly good-looking, as Vera later noted: 'hair like a
brush & a mouth too resolute for the smallest degree of beauty'. But
he did have 'deep intelligent eyes', and he wrote poems. The other
musketeers, Victor and Edward, used to tease him about his Quiet
Voice, a superior tone he was prone to adopt.

Life had come easily for Roland, less easily for Vera. A feminist in
the making, she was an admirer of Olive Schreiner's *Woman and Labour*
(1911), a supporter of women's suffrage and a despiser of 'mean, fault-
finding' Buxton. At boarding school she had dreamed of going to
Oxford but had to wear down stiff opposition from her papermill-
owning father in order to sit the two entrance exams. He used to call
her Jack or John, because he had hoped she would be a boy, also
perhaps because she often talked and acted like one. She was petite
and feisty with a pretty face under dark hair. Roland would later
comment on her '"wet" eyes'.

That speech day, Saturday 11 July 1914, and the days immediately surrounding it marked a major advance in Vera's and Roland's acquaintance. They had intense debates about Olive Schreiner's *The Story of an African Farm* (1883), fickleness in friendship and Kant. There was also a good deal of sparring and banter. On the evening of her arrival, Vera tried her best to tease Roland about all the prizes he was to receive the following day. 'I shall look out for every atom of conceit when you get them to-morrow,' she told him, 'and as soon as I see the least symptom, I mean to squash it flat.' But Roland, not at all fazed, neatly capped her attack:

> Well . . . you won't be so very original, after all. One of the housemasters' wives was asked the other day what she thought of the boy who was taking so many prizes, and she said she knew nothing about him except that he was the biggest mass of conceit in the whole of Uppingham.

At the prize-giving ceremony, Vera was struck by the headmaster's short preliminary speech, the climax of which was that 'if a man could not be useful to his country he was better dead'. She left after the weekend, admiring and impressed and well on the way to being in love. Roland, she told her diary, 'seems even in a short acquaintance to share both my faults & my talents and my ideas in a way that I have never found anyone else do yet'.

Now, nearly a year and several more encounters later, he was out in France, she at Oxford. Their relationship flowered through their regular letters. His gave a vivid, realistic account of life in billets and the trenches. Dug-outs were called 'bug-hutches', he told her. In the trenches, officers had to do their rounds 'every three hours or so', day and night. You had to be fully dressed at all times, including boots; so you used a bayonet to get off as much mud as you could, encased 'each foot in a small sack' and wriggled into your sleeping-bag 'boots and all'.

He described going out at night into no man's land and, hearing German soldiers 'about sixty yards' away, thinking how 'extremely youthful' they sounded. One day in Ploegsteert Wood (Plug Street Wood, as the English called it), he found a long-dead British soldier submerged in the swampy ground 'so that only the toes of his boots'

were visible. At the time he did not mention the semi-villanelle he
wrote for her about the discovery, 'Violets from Plug Street Wood':

> Violets from Plug Street Wood,
> Sweet, I send you oversea.
> (It is strange they should be blue,
> Blue, when his soaked blood was red,
> For they grew around his head;
> It is strange they should be blue) . . .

But he did add a telling postscript to that 20–21 April 1915 letter. There
was 'nothing glorious in trench warfare,' he observed despondently.
'It is all a waiting and a waiting and taking of petty advantages – and
those who can wait longest win. And it is all for nothing – for an
empty name, for an ideal perhaps – after all.' A month after going
out, the realities of war were already proving very different from his
idealistic expectations of honour and glory. Vera was probably also
holding back on the poems she had started to write. One, 'August
1914', written after she went to Oxford, angrily claimed that the war
was God's punishment on mankind for forgetting him, only for the
punishment to backfire:

> But where His desolation trod
> The people in their agony
> Despairing cried, 'There is no God.'

  She found Roland's letters 'most thrilling', she told her brother. Her
own side of the correspondence gave snippets of vacation life in Buxton
and student life in Oxford. After her first-year exams, she planned to
suspend her studies and train as a VAD (Voluntary Aid Detachment)
nurse – so as to play a more active role in the war and feel closer
to Roland (and her brother and Victor who had also joined up).
With this in view, she worked part-time during the Easter vacation at
the Devonshire Hospital in Buxton. She mentioned the nursing in
her letters to Roland but not how reading the love scenes between
Elena and Dmitri in Turgenev's On the Eve made her 'wild with desire'
for him. Back in Oxford, she described getting up before dawn on
May morning and hearing the traditional Latin hymn sung at sunrise

from Magdalen tower. 'I could quite easily have wept at the beauty & pain of it', she told him. She picked up on his disillusioned remarks about trench warfare ('Is it really all for nothing, – for an empty name – an ideal?') and reminded him that at their last meeting that was exactly what she had said to him, and he had disagreed. What did he 'really think'? She urged him to tell her.

In their letters the two became increasingly forthcoming about their feelings. At times, however, both were aware that each was becoming something of 'a dream' to the other.

After the evening with her tutor, Brooke's glamorous image firmly lodged itself in Vera's mind. In him, she found the epitome of the doomed warrior-poet. In his war sonnets she found a voice which both thrilled her and aroused her pity. From the start this crush was intertwined with her feelings for Roland. On 18 May she wrote, asking whether he knew the war sonnets, quoted some in her letter and remarked: 'Somehow I feel that Rupert Brooke must have been rather like you.'

Roland replied promptly. Yes, he too was 'very fond' of the war sonnets, he said, some but not all of which he already knew. He made no comment on his supposed similarity to Brooke, but brought the poems and his own military experience into close alignment. He was currently in billets near the front, sitting in a field in the sun. Nearby, making Brooke's 'two poems on "The Dead" more real than ever', were the graves of a private in the Somerset Light Infantry and a major of the 19th Hussars. 'What a pity it is,' he reflected, with himself in mind rather than the dead major and private, 'that the same little piece of lead takes away as easily a brilliant life and one that is merely vegetation. The democracy of war!'

From the beginning of their acquaintance Vera and Roland had used particular books in this way as touchstones of authentic feeling and thought, particular phrases operating like an intellectual and emotional shorthand. Schreiner's *The Story of an African Farm* had been the first of these, and remained the most important. On an Easter holiday visit to the Brittains in 1914, Roland had enthused about the novel and likened Vera to Lyndall, Schreiner's self-determining heroine and his own model of what a woman should be. When he sent her a copy, the novel quickly became established as *their* book: much referred to in conversation and letters and intimately connected to their burgeoning relationship. On 23 May 1915, for instance, Vera speculated about a recent semi-dream in which Roland had unexpectedly appeared to her. Was confessing 'the need of someone's personal presence,' she wondered, 'to confess a human weakness too'? She thought it might well be and automatically turned to Waldo's letter to Lyndall in Schreiner's novel for her notion of 'the highest of all human relationships': 'Sometimes such a sudden gladness seizes me when I remember that somewhere in the world you are living and working.' Vera concluded that, as far as she was concerned, one could feel both the Waldo ideal and 'the personal need'.

The couple employed other forms of code in their correspondence. Roland used a system of dots under the letters of particular words to let Vera know approximately where he was in France. Similarly, to warn her that he was likely to be going into action, he would slip in the Latin phrase 'Hinc illae lacrimae' (literally, 'Hence those tears'). Vera soon adopted Brooke's *1914 & other Poems*, especially the war sonnets, as part of this private code, and the collection became for her a sacred book second only to Schreiner's novel. When she sent Roland the copy of the poems on 29 July (perhaps partly in response to a 'Hinc illae lacrimae' from him), her accompanying letter described the collection as by 'your brother-spirit, Rupert Brooke'. She imagined Roland would warm to all the poems, not just the war sonnets, 'though they are perhaps the most beautiful'.

And so at first he seemed to. Writing to her on 2 August, he mock-apologetically began 'Dear Child' (a very Brookeian form of address in both poems and letters). He then thanked her for the poems which he told her he had immediately read from cover to cover. But whereas Vera thought of Brooke's poetry as enshrining and affirming a shared view of life and particularly the war, it had a more troubling effect on Roland. The poems made him feel dissatisfied rather than uplifted or even inured. They made him want to 'write things myself', he told her, 'instead of what I have to do here'. They reminded him of an imaginative life away from the boredom of the billets and the danger of the trenches. The poems brought back 'old forgotten things' and made him 'so, so angry and impatient with most of the soul-less nonentities one finds around here'.

Reading the poems also prompted in Roland a reaction deeper

than dissatisfaction – the disillusionment he had touched on in his 20–21 April letter. He too had once talked about 'the Beauty of War', he admitted to Vera, but not now. War, he assured her, was only beautiful 'in the abstract'; modern soldiering was really no different to being a greengrocer. Occasionally, he conceded, an individual might 'rise from the sordidness to a deed of beauty: but that is all'. The repudiation, the disgust, were directed at his own former naive aestheticising and idealising of war. Brooke and his sonnets were not explicitly arraigned, but the implication was there.

Later in August Roland was back in England on a week's leave. Not surprisingly, he and Vera failed to reach in person the level of intimate connection and easy exchange they had developed in their letters. Things got off to an unpromising start at St Pancras, where they barely recognised each other: he because of his short sight and 'inward abstraction', she because he looked thinner, older, very military in his uniform, and had acquired a 'premature air of having knocked about the world'.

Shyness, reserve, a certain aloof reticence on his part, a certain wilful coolness on hers: these persisted for much of his leave. Even when he proposed to her that first day on the train to visit her parents, and she eventually accepted him the following day on the train to visit his parents in Lowestoft, a barrier remained. There was a lunch in London with the other two musketeers, Edward and Victor, neither of whom had yet seen action. Vera listened fascinated as Roland, quizzed in great detail by the others about life at the front, discussed unmentionable subjects such as sentries being shot for falling asleep on watch and subsequently listed as 'Died'. On another day, shopping in London, he bought 'a vicious-looking steel dagger', which he examined with cold-blooded expertise, 'wondering whether it would do for getting between someone's ribs'. Again Vera observed him, fascinated but depressed, telling him, as he wrote the cheque, that it seemed 'very incongruous that a person with such artistic handwriting should have use for a thing like that'.

At the Leightons' clifftop house in Lowestoft, there were several heart-to-hearts with Roland's gushingly doting mother. (Vera found the whole atmosphere remarkably casual and easy after the fussy decorum of Buxton.) Mrs Leighton told Vera that *The Story of an African*

Farm had changed her own life and that when she heard Roland had given it to Vera she 'felt instinctively that [their] fate was decided'. As for Roland, he might have broken the news of their engagement to his mother with an insouciant *'Je suis fiancé; c'est la guerre!'*, but throughout the weekend he seemed mostly withdrawn towards Vera herself. She too was ill at ease.

There were occasional moments of closeness. One was when, after some prompting, he finally showed her 'Violets from Plug Street Wood'. Another was when he invited her for a walk in the moonlight along the cliff. They sat down 'on a soft dry bed of heather' and looked out at 'the vast grey shadow' of the sea. After a while, Roland 'suddenly put his arm round me and drew me close to him – closer than I had ever been before'. He played with her wind-blown hair, 'rested his head against my shoulder & we became quite silent'. For Vera it was 'the sweetest hour of my life' but, characteristically, she tried to break the mood by asking him the time. Telling her they could stay a bit longer, he kissed her. It was, for her, an experience of 'agonising joy' and revelation. 'There, on that dark heather-covered cliff beside the sea,' she told her diary, 'I realised the depth & strength of my own passion – realised it & was afraid.'

Roland might have appeared withdrawn, but the experience of seeing Vera again had been momentous for him too. One side of him welcomed the simplified exigencies of army life, enjoyed being the professional who knew about trench-wire and suitable daggers. But the visit had reawakened his intellectual and artistic side and what Vera called his feminism. When he saw her off at St Pancras, the military mask slipped: 'He said very bitterly that he didn't *want* to go back to the front, and this glimpse of England and real life had made him hate France more than ever.' At the station they confirmed their engagement to each other. She reminded him sadly of a line from one of his letters after their previous parting: '"Someday we shall live our roseate poem through – as we have dreamt it."' He said: 'We must – we *shall*.' The whistle blew. He kissed her passionately. She kissed him back and whispered goodbye. The train pulled out. He walked away without a backward glance, sat in a taxi cab in Russell Square, wrote her a note. It began: 'I could not look back dear child – I should have cried if I had.'

★   ★   ★

Vera nursing in Buxton and Roland back in France tried to keep up the emotional momentum through letters. In fact, the return to letter-writing was probably something of a relief, given the awkward-nesses and blank spots of the days they had spent together. Vera still found Roland in himself elusive and intangible, and even his face was already hard to recall. She clung, however, to the memory of his 'queer bristly head against my shoulder'. That, she told him, had been 'the sweetest hour of my life. And it belonged only to you.' Not only was it a struggle to recapture her interest in nursing, but the frustrations of life in her parents' oppressive household only reminded her how much she missed, and valued, Roland's capacity to see things 'from a woman's point of view'. When she informed her parents that she and Roland were engaged, her father told her 'with his usual tactfulness' that 'it seemed very ridiculous because of course Roland wouldn't come back'. To which, Vera retorted that in that case there was 'all the more reason for being engaged to him while he *did* exist'.

Roland too had found it hard to slot back into army life. In a note written just before leaving England, he had reanimated their Brooke code with an aptly nostalgic phrase from 'The Old Vicarage, Grantchester': 'Oh, damn, I know it'. He agreed that in letters they both seemed more open, more their 'real selves'. But by early September his 'old interest in what happens out here' was quickening again, and he was telling her that for him in France it was 'perhaps easier to forget'. Then, as though anticipating her reaction, he added: 'to forget not what one has known & has felt, but the pain that accompanies the memory.' He was returning to the trenches (at Hébuterne between Amiens and Arras), and was now mess president. He looked forward to her giving him cooking lessons. He sent his sympathy for her problems at home and stuck on another 'Oh, damn, I know it'.

On 6 September he confessed that she and England seemed extremely remote. He was now in the trenches and feeling very low, his mood embodied in a poignant description of that particular section of the front. Nothing, he told Vera, was 'more melancholy & depressing than an old trench, disused and overgrown with grass, with dug-outs fallen in or wrecked by shells, and here and there a forgotten grave and a rusty bayonet'. The following day his mood had swung, and he

was seriously wondering whether he was really 'a man of action with
lapses into the artistic, or an artist with military sympathies'. Should
he perhaps take a Regular commission? Three days later he was fanta-
sising about Vera suddenly appearing along the trench and entering
the twilight of his dug-out. How he would just look at her 'like a very
shy child at his first party', and she would look at and through him
with her '"wet" eyes'. And, the intimacy of their letters lost, nothing
would happen.

On 11 September he delivered his most disillusioned condemnation
of the war. This pointedly included a denunciation of Brooke's third
war sonnet (the first of the two entitled 'The Dead') in which Brooke
deliberately struck the grand attitude, the Elizabethan note:

> Blow out, you bugles, over the rich Dead!
>   There's none of these so lonely and poor of old,
>   But, dying, has made us rarer gifts than gold.
> These laid the world away; poured out the red
> Sweet wine of youth; gave up the years to be
>   Of work and joy, and that unhoped serene,
>   That men call age; and those who would have been,
> Their sons, they gave, their immortality.
>
> Blow, bugles, blow! They brought us, for our dearth,
>   Holiness, lacked so long, and Love, and Pain.
> Honour has come back, as a king, to earth,
>   And paid his subjects with a royal wage;
> And Nobleness walks in our ways again;
>   And we have come into our heritage.

Here Brooke presented the dead as heroic self-sacrificers, redeeming
both themselves and the country as a whole, restoring lost chivalric
values of Holiness, Honour, Nobleness. After his experiences at the
front, Roland would have none of this uplift, these capitalised abstrac-
tions and elevated consolations. In a bitter, almost unpunctuated
diatribe, he contrasted the Brookeian view (quoting the phrase 'red
sweet wine of youth') with the physical reality. He had been on the
go since four in the morning, supervising repairs to smashed dug-outs
and dismembered wire:

in among this chaos of twisted iron and splintered timber and shapeless earth are the fleshless, blackened bones of simple men who poured out their red, sweet wine of youth unknowing, for nothing more tangible than Honour or their Country's Glory or another's Lust [for] Power.

He likened those, like Brooke, who fervently 'roll forth stirring words of exhortation, invoking Honour and Praise and Valour and Love of Country', to 'the priests of Baal'. He invited them, looking at 'a little pile of sodden grey rags that cover half a skull and a shin bone', to 'realise how grand & glorious a thing it is to have distilled all Youth and Joy and Life into a foetid heap of hideous putrescence'.

Vera had been trying to move to a London hospital and had heard that this was now a certainty. She was dismayed at the idea that Roland might take up the army as a career. She had just been admiring the 'literary beauty' of his letters in her diary and, ironically echoing the same Brooke sonnet Roland was about to excoriate, called them 'gifts of "a rarer sort than gold"'. Writing to Roland, she reaffirmed her own anti-militarist beliefs and her faith in his artistic destiny. But she was aware of a kind of grey area in her thinking: 'Of course, much as I always detested the Army before the War, I would rather have you as a soldier than not at all. At least, I think so.'

She said she empathised with his bitterly disillusioned feelings, that the only justification of the war was 'if it puts an end to all the horror & barbarism & retrogression of War for ever'. But for all her hypersensitive reading of his letters, Vera had not fully grasped the inner conflict he was struggling with, or chose not to. Vera merely copied out his swingeing repudiation of Brooke, commenting that it was 'a fine if somewhat morbid description of the charnel-house condition of his present trenches – poor darling!' She was soon staunchly quoting 'War knows no power' to him from the second of the war sonnets. When she received another 'Hinc illae lacrimae' letter, it was to 'The Soldier' she turned for comfort in her diary, imagining that by then all that remained of Roland might be just 'some corner of a foreign field / That is for ever England'.

Much to Roland's exasperation, his section of the line was not involved in the costly and inconclusive battle of Loos in late September and early October. This was the battle in which the young poet Charles

Sorley was killed. Another casualty, and one which Vera sadly noted, was Rudyard Kipling's son. During October Roland reimmersed himself in his military world, and his letters became more intermittent. As he told Vera on 18 October, 'It is the only way to stifle boredom and regrets.' That was the same day she moved to London to take up nursing duties at the 1st London General Hospital, Camberwell, and was soon trying to displace her anxieties by immersing herself in her new world. She was anxious not only about Roland but also about her brother who seemed finally on his way to France (though, in fact, this proved another false alarm). Trying to connect her experience of first-hand horrors with Roland's, and to assert her own professionalism, she told him that alleviating a patient's pain was now 'nothing but a matter of business'. She might have 'lofty thoughts' while off duty but not at work. All the same – showing that she really had not grasped the point of his anti-Brooke letter – she told him she constantly found herself thinking of Brooke's lines, 'These cast [sic] the world away, poured out the red / Sweet wine of youth, gave up the years to be / Of work and joy', as she gazed at 'the rows of poor permanently shattered people on either side of the long ward'.

November produced an epistolary spat or perhaps something more serious. On the 3rd, Roland wrote Vera a very detached, cool letter. He wondered if her metamorphosis into full-time nurse had been as total as his into 'an incipient martinet', the last person anyone would connect with 'prizes on Speech Day or poetry or dilettante classicism'. He had been enjoying a stint as temporary adjutant, had been just too busy to write letters even to his mother. He was returning to the front the next day.

Vera weighed in with a 'Most estimable, practical, unexceptional Adjutant' and started to tick him off in no uncertain terms. His letter, she told him, was 'very much like an epistolary expression of the Quiet Voice'. Then, remembering that he would already be in the trenches – might even be dead, she reined in her indignation and gave him the latest instalment of hospital life. At the end, however, she could not resist a final swipe and suggested that perhaps rather than a spell of leave he now preferred 'a sensible business-like life where one doesn't have to bother about little things like Poetry or Art or dilletante [sic] classicism'. His apology was suitably abject – 'I have been a perfect beast, a conceited, selfish, self-satisfied beast'

– and was punctuated by two 'Oh, damns', reaffirming their Brookeian code.

From this point on (22 November), most of his letters were warmly affectionate and considerate. He reverted to calling her 'dear child'. He was keen to reassure her that he had not entirely lost his aesthetic side and larger sympathies:

> I have been looking at a bloodred bar of sky creeping down behind the snow, and wondering whether any of the men in the trenches on the opposite hill were watching it too and thinking as I was what a waste of Life it is to spend it in a ditch.

But hearing that Vera had been talking with his mother about their relationship and, in particular, about what his mother called his 'Lyndallesque Romanticism' – his identification of Vera with his ideal woman Lyndall in Olive Schreiner's novel – he was understandably 'just a little bit bad tempered'. It was, he crisply pointed out, 'quite possible to love an ideal crystallised in a person, and the person because of the ideal: and who shall say whether it is not perhaps better in the end?' To which he added a little tetchily that 'it must be very trying to be the incarnation of an ideal – very trying'. He clearly had her primarily in mind as an incarnation of Lyndall, but there may well have been a tacit side-glance at her idealisation of him: you Lyndall, me Rupert. Each seriously tried to live up to the other's high expectations, but at times needed to assert more ordinary human frailties and limitations.

Another short leave in late December was on the cards, and then confirmed for 24–31 December. He would be landing in England on Christmas Day. On 6 December, a morning walk of 'racing clouds in a pure rainwashed sky' after a night shift reminded Vera of the opening lines of Brooke's second war sonnet, 'Safety', and she was soon busily arranging to take leave to coincide with Roland's. Her parents had temporarily taken up quarters in the Grand Hotel in Brighton, and his parents were also to be close by; so they would be able to divide the time between the two. Vera's letter to Roland on 15 December concluded: 'But somehow I feel the end is not destined to be here and now' – carefully melding an echo of Brooke's 'Heaven', 'Not here the appointed End, not here!', with a treasured line of Roland's: 'Someday we shall live our roseate poem through.'

On the morning of Sunday 26 December, Vera was told there was a telephone call for her. She 'sprang up joyfully', expecting it to be Roland. It was his sister Clare. The Leightons had had a telegram redirected from Lowestoft. It was from the 'Colonel of Territorial Force, Records, Warwick'. It said simply that Roland had died of wounds on 23 December and, in a stock phrase, that Lord Kitchener sent his sympathy.

What seems to have happened was this. On the night of 22 December, Roland and his platoon were detailed to repair the wire in front of their trenches. There was a bright moon. Around midnight, Roland, like the dutiful officer he was, went ahead to do a recce along 'a concealed path which led to No Man's Land through a gap in a hedge'. The Germans, only a hundred yards away at this point, knew of the concealed path, were on the look-out and fired as soon as he reached the gap. A single machine-gun bullet hit him in the stomach. He collapsed 'gesticulating wildly, in full view of the company'. Brought back to the trench, he was heavily dosed with morphine, and stretchered ten miles to the casualty clearing station at Louvencourt. There he was operated on at 10 a.m., though with little chance of survival. 'In a state of mazy contentment', he was given extreme unction – and, later, absolution – by the Roman Catholic chaplain. He was apparently quite unaware throughout that he was dying and was kept ignorant of the fact. His last coherent words, spoken to the chaplain, were 'Lying on this hillside for six days makes me very stiff'. He died peacefully at 11 p.m. that night and was buried in the Louvencourt military cemetery on Sunday the 26th, the day Vera received the phone call.

The story of Roland's death, as she was later able to piece it together from various sources, left Vera with some puzzling questions. These were further complicated by the arrival of his clothes and other effects, including the copy of 1914 & other Poems she had given him. Why had Roland not told her, or indeed his mother, of his conversion to Catholicism? What of their conversation on the tennis court at Lowestoft that August about immortality in which he – apparently by then a Catholic – had argued that human beings were 'probably entirely physical' and that 'personality depended in no more than the more or less of grey matter that composed the human brain'? Had his death really been necessary? Why had he taken the risk on a moonlit night so near his leave? Why had he left no final message to help her through the years ahead? What did he mean by 'Hédauville, November 1915', a new poem she had not seen before?

His secret Catholicism she was soon able to accept (such conversions were not unknown during the war). Although an agnostic herself, she felt 'the Roman Catholic Church holds out a fairer and surer hope of a Life hereafter than any other faith in the world'. She even took to attending the occasional mass. The other questions were harder to resolve. Another musketeer, Victor, was more or less able to reassure her that, bright moonlight and leave or not, the wire would have needed repairing, and Roland would have taken the lead because 'His was not the nature to allow another man, especially an inferior, to run a risk that He would not take Himself'. (Victor, following Vera's lead, always used a reverential capital 'H' in letters when referring to Roland.) Of course nothing could ever entirely cancel out the appallingly bad timing of Roland's death, made all the more acute in late January by a letter offering him a safe Headquarters Staff position in Salonika.

Vera never did come to terms with the lack of a final message from Roland, though her experience as a nurse might have helped her there. The obvious answer lay in the 'mazy contentment' with which he received extreme unction and his fantasy about lying on a hillside for six days. He was quite simply 'high' from the morphine and had absolutely no idea where he was or what condition he was in.

Then there was 'Hédauville', Roland's most ambitious and successful poem – and probably his last, the one that suggested he really might have had a literary future:

> The sunshine on the long white road
> That ribboned down the hill,
> The velvet clematis that clung
> Around your window-sill,
> Are waiting for you still.
>
> Again the shadowed pool shall break
> In dimples round your feet,
> And when the thrush sings in your wood,
> Unknowing you may meet
> Another stranger, Sweet.

And if he is not quite so old
As the boy you used to know,
And less proud, too, and worthier,
You may not let him go –
(And daisies are truer than passion-flowers)
It will be better so.

Sending this to her brother Edward on 14 January 1916, Vera called it 'perhaps the most beautiful' of Roland's poems, echoing a phrase she had used to Roland about Brooke. She went on: 'I wonder if he was prophetic in that – and I wonder quite what he meant.'

'Hédauville' had been written during the couple's epistolary spat. Its tone – rueful? resigned? desolate? – was not easy to catch. Presumably Vera wondered – feared – that the poem prophesied Roland's own death, imagined his successor and gave her permission to find new happiness. Alternatively, and worse, the poem might imply his sense that the relationship was already weakening and tried to foresee the inevitable next stage. Neither interpretation was what she was looking for in this message from the grave. Some version of her fears may well have been justified. Roland had lifted his stanza form – with an extra delaying line in the last verse – from Brooke's 'The Chilterns'. Brooke's poem ended:

And I shall find some girl perhaps
And a better one than you,
With eyes as wise, but kindlier,
And lips as soft, but true.
And I daresay she will do.

Roland's lines, though far gentler and more imaginatively sympathetic, could be read as a variation on Brooke's brisk brush-off.

No wonder she told her brother: 'Oh! there are millions of things I want to ask him – now.' It was more comforting to imagine Roland, in death as in life, as the Brooke of the war sonnets. And that is initially what she did, reassuring herself that the much-loved lines from Brooke's second war sonnet which she had inscribed in Roland's copy of *1914 & other Poems* were 'still true':

We have built a house that is not for Time's throwing.
We have gained a peace unshaken by pain for ever.
War knows no power.

Her poem 'Perhaps –', written a few weeks later in February 1916, gave a starker picture of her grief. It offered an answer of a kind to Roland's 'Hédauville': she might perhaps recover in time, but her heart never would. After the vigour, eloquence and allusiveness of Vera's diary and letters, the blankness of her lines, their numbed banality, remains moving:

Perhaps some day the sun will shine again,
    And I shall see that still the skies are blue,
And feel once more I do not live in vain,
    Although bereft of You . . .

But, though kind Time may many joys renew,
    There is one greatest joy I shall not know
Again, because my heart for loss of You
    Was broken, long ago.

4

A Big Blot Has Hid Each Yesterday

Siegfried Sassoon, Robert Graves, Charles Sorley, 28 November 1915

Siegfried Sassoon and Robert Graves first met on 28 November 1915 in northern France. They met in the mess of C Company, 1st Battalion, Royal Welch Fusiliers, stationed near Béthune. Graves, at twenty, was already a captain, Sassoon, nine years older, a second lieutenant. Two dead poets and a dead friend cemented their friendship.

Sassoon had spent the initial months of the war as a gentleman-ranker, a trooper in the Sussex Yeomanry. But by early April 1915, frustrated that the war proper was passing him by, he applied for a commission in the Special Reserve and was posted to the Royal Welch Fusiliers. Now, after preliminary training in Litherland and Cambridge, he had reached France as a subaltern in C Company and was at last within distant earshot of the front-line guns. Amongst his reading matter were *A Shropshire Lad*, *Nostromo* and a volume of essays. He had started a diary and, with his recently dead brother in mind, was telling himself: 'I must pay my debt. Hamo went: I must follow him. I will.'

Graves, like Sassoon, had immediately enlisted on the outbreak of war; in fact, he had only days earlier left Charterhouse at the end of his final term. For him the choice of the Royal Welch Fusiliers was also somewhat arbitrary, their regimental depot happening to be the

Left: Siegfried Sassoon, *c.*1916
Right: Robert Graves, 1915

nearest to the Graves holiday home in Harlech. One major difference between Sassoon and Graves when they met was that the considerably younger Graves had been out in France since April 1915 (with Keats, Homer and the novelist Samuel Butler in his knapsack) and was already an experienced campaigner. He had seen action in the trenches in May, and again in September–October at the battle of Loos. He knew what it was like to be under fire and gas attack, and to put your hand on 'the slimy body of a dead corpse' in no man's land. He had seen his share of horrors, kept himself going on a bottle of whisky a day, and just about managed to hold his nerve. He had recently been posted to A Company of the 1st Battalion of the Royal Welch Fusiliers.

When Graves walked into C Company mess on 28 November 1915 on some errand, he noticed an unexpected book on the table. It was a copy of *Post Liminium*, a collection of essays by the late nineteenth-century poet Lionel Johnson. The army was not noted for its Lionel Johnson readers; a 'military text-book or a rubbish novel' were more the order of the day. Graves took a discreet look at the name on the flyleaf. A glance round the mess was enough to indicate 'Siegfried Sassoon': the tall, lanky, shy subaltern. Graves, also tall but anything but shy, quickly struck up a conversation. Both being off duty, the two were soon walking into Béthune for cream buns, busy talking poetry.

Sassoon and Graves were drawn to each other, but both had reservations, particularly Sassoon. 'An interesting creature, overstrung and self-conscious, a defier of convention' was his verdict after that first meeting. He also noted that Graves was 'very much disliked'. In the mess they said things like 'I was . . . with him last month, and he fairly got on people's nerves with his hot air about the battle of Loos, and his brainwaves about who really wrote the Bible'. Graves probably mentioned his unpopularity himself. 'I'm very much disliked' was just the sort of remark he used to make; it was almost a boast. He had said as much in a recent letter to Eddie Marsh:

> The Captain who commands my company is a regular with some considerable service and can't see the use of 'a man like Graves who never goes with a woman or gets tight [this despite the daily bottle of whisky] or shows any interest in hunting or racing or the stage and can't even play Auction'.

Graves was bumptious, untidy, a bit of a prude, and 'a positive expert at putting people's backs up unintentionally'. Even if you did like him, there was almost bound to be a quarrel: sometimes you made it up, sometimes you didn't. Sassoon was more of a brooder and a smoulderer; he nursed both his admirations and his antipathies. His shyness drew him to those, like Graves, who were more ebullient or socially confident. It was not long before he was cosily informing one of his mentors, Edmund Gosse, that 'Robert G. is quite a dear; they don't appreciate his qualities out here, he has too much brains for them'.

Poetry sparked the friendship but, ironically, neither at first thought much of the other's poems. Graves was putting together a collection for publication and lent Sassoon the manuscript. Sassoon probably read it with some trepidation. Graves might be the more experienced and higher-ranking officer, but, in literary terms, he definitely reckoned himself the senior of the two. It was true that his own poems had appeared almost exclusively in small, privately printed editions, paid for by himself; but he had had a modest *succès d'estime* with his Masefield pastiche *The Daffodil Murderer*. Graves's only publications were in his school magazine, *The Carthusian*. Both counted themselves as among Eddie Marsh's up-and-coming protégés, but Graves had only been promised a meeting with the late and now great Rupert Brooke; Sassoon had actually had breakfast with him.

All the same, Sassoon still lacked literary self-confidence. He considered himself 'one of the mugs who only find a method by long years of groping'. So it must have been a relief to find Graves's poems underwhelming. Some were 'very bad, violent and repulsive. A few of promise and real beauty,' he told his diary on 2 December, adding a trifle snootily: 'He oughtn't to publish yet.'

It was presumably Graves's clutch of war poems which Sassoon thought 'violent and repulsive'. These had Made in the Trenches stamped all over them, and their imagery was far more graphic than anything Sassoon had written. 'Through the Periscope' referred to 'Trench stinks of shallow-buried dead'. 'Limbo' included 'hideous cries' and 'reek/Of death', 'roars and whirs and rattles' and rats 'big as kittens'. There was a squib in which the trenches were imagined as seams on a 'Greyback Shirt' and the troops as lice briefly 'Wriggling about' in the seams. 'The Morning Before the Battle' began 'To-day the fight:

my end is very soon', which considerably upped the ante on Brooke's 'If I should die, think only this of me'. Where Brooke consolingly pictured his dead self as a 'pulse in the eternal mind', Graves grimly imagined meeting his own ghost: 'His head all battered in by violent blows'. These were the 'violent French lyrics about lice and corruption' which, Sassoon told Nellie Gosse, had shocked Graves's father. He omitted to mention how much they had shocked him. But when he not very subtly hinted to Marsh that the latter should dissuade Graves from publishing, Marsh, to his credit, would have none of it.

The fact was Sassoon did not think war should be written about in a gruesome, realistic way. His own poems were still full of images of 'hooded night', of mornings glimmering 'out of dreams', larks ascending, and trees 'blown to music by the ruffling breeze'. To date, the war itself had hardly impinged on his poetry at all; and, when it did, it was only indirectly. In 'Storm and Sunlight', after the storm had finished riding 'a hurtling legion / Up the arched sky', Sassoon improbably invited the troopers of the Sussex Yeomanry to 'come forth to stand / A moment simple in the gaze of God', as though they had all suddenly stumbled into one of Coleridge's minor poems of the 1790s.

The one partial exception was the recent 'Absolution'. Sassoon had started the poem the previous April when putting in for the Special Reserve and finished it in September shortly before going out to France. Like almost everyone else, he was by then steeped in Brooke's war sonnets, and it showed. 'Absolution' made all the right Brookeian noises. Edward Thomas had accused Brooke of trying to connect to himself the widely held idea of redemption through self-sacrifice. Had he read 'Absolution', he would probably have said the same of its willed camaraderie and would-be insouciance. 'We are the happy legion,' Sassoon exhorted his fellow combatants, 'for we know / Time's but a golden wind that shakes the grass.' Two key Brookeian words – 'heritage' and 'heart' – alliteratively underwrote the afflatus of the concluding quatrain:

> There was an hour when we were loth to part
> From life we longed to share no less than others.
> Now, having claimed this heritage of heart,
> What need we more, my comrades and my brothers?

No wonder Graves was soon telling Marsh that, 'very nice chap' though
Sassoon was, 'his verses, except occasionally, don't please me very
much'. What he apparently told Sassoon himself was that, after a spell
in the trenches, 'he would soon change his style'.

One poem of Graves's that Sassoon would certainly have thought 'full
of promise and real beauty' was '1915', especially the second stanza:

> Dear, you've been everything that I most lack
> In these soul-deadening trenches – pictures, books,
> Music, the quiet of an English wood,
> Beautiful comrade-looks,
> The narrow, bouldered mountain-track,
> The broad, full-bosomed ocean, green and black,
> And Peace, and all that's good.

He would have spotted that, for all the heterosexual smokescreen of
'broad, full-bosomed ocean', the 'Dear' here was not a female sweet-
heart but a young man. And so he was. The 'comrade-looks' belonged
to George ('Peter') Johnstone, a boy four years younger than Graves.
    Graves had fallen in love with Johnstone at Charterhouse and after
he left continued to worship him in an extravagantly pure fashion.
Johnstone, Graves told Marsh, was 'my best friend, a poet long before
I'll ever be, a radiant and unusual creature . . . and though now in the
first half-dozen of the Sixth Form at Charterhouse he's still wholesome-minded and clean-living'. The last bit about Johnstone being
'wholesome-minded and clean-living' was bunk, as Graves well knew
by this point, having been put right in no uncertain terms by a
Carthusian cousin. But he put it in to cheer himself up. Also it was
exactly the kind of thing the celibate Marsh liked to hear.
    Sassoon would have got '1915' straightaway. His prose plays *Amyntas,*
a Mystery and *Hyacinth* were also codedly homo-erotic though in a more
'90s manner. Once sure of Graves's sympathies, he could respond in
kind, because for the last six months he had been in love too. The
object of his affections was David Thomas (Tommy), a fair-haired
fellow-subaltern in the Fusiliers, with whom he had shared rooms in
Pembroke College, Cambridge during his military training. Sassoon
later noted that the previous occupant of the rooms had been someone

called Paradise; this was both a wistful joke and, the college records show, literally true. Sassoon no doubt saw his friendship with Thomas in the same idealised light as Graves saw his with Johnstone: that is, as sanctioned by 'Plato, the Greek poets, Shakespeare, Michael Angelo and others, who had felt the same way'. Their situations, however, were significantly different. Johnstone understood Graves's feelings, up to a point reciprocated them and was himself homosexually active: in 1917 while still at Charterhouse, he was arrested for propositioning a Canadian corporal stationed near the school. David Thomas too seems to have understood Sassoon's feelings: after reading *Hyacinth*, he told Sassoon he recognised 'old Sassons himself' in the play 'as things are introduced which I know to be your own experience'. But he himself was not homosexual and apparently valued Sassoon – 'Sassons', as he affectionately nicknamed him – simply as a close friend.

So Sassoon and Graves had a good deal in common. Both were conventionally unconventional public school products, trying to turn themselves into competent army officers and into the kind of poets Eddie Marsh would publish in his *Georgian Poetry* anthologies. Both, anxious about being insufficiently manly, had cultivated a tougher, sportier side: Sassoon through fox-hunting and cricket; Graves through boxing – he had been the school middleweight champion. Both were lonely and in love. Both were almost certainly still virgins.

The friendship necessarily developed in fits and starts, and owed some of its intensity to that. Long conversations, the uninterrupted exchange of poems and confessions, were a rare luxury. Graves gave Marsh a humorous but probably not very misleading account of their difficulty 'in talking about poetry and that sort of thing': 'If I go into his mess and he wants to show me some set of verses, he says: "Afternoon Graves, have a drink . . . by the way, I want you to see my latest recipe for rum punch."' He also made it pretty clear to Marsh that it was not just poetry they had to be careful about discussing openly: 'I don't know what the CO would say if he heard us discussing the sort of things we do . . . His saying is that "there should be only one subject for conversation among subalterns off parade." I leave you to guess it.'

There was obviously a secret thrill in these surreptitious exchanges, a sense that Graves and Sassoon were like two naughty schoolboys, hoodwinking their peers and those in authority.

* * *

If Lionel Johnson brought Sassoon and Graves together, a much more recently dead poet helped to seal their friendship.

Charles Sorley was Graves's discovery. He had been a captain in the 7th Suffolk Regiment and had died at the battle of Loos in October 1915, the month before Graves and Sassoon first met. In January 1916, Sorley's parents brought out a collection of his poetry, *Marlborough and Other Poems*. On 24 February, Graves was writing to Marsh in ecstatic terms. He had, he said, totally fallen for the dead poet: 'he seems to have been one so entirely after my own heart in his loves and hates, besides having been just my own age and having spent just the same years at Marlboro' as I spent at Ch'house.' Sorley, too, had gained a classical scholarship to Oxford, and Graves claimed to 'half-remember meeting him' when the two of them were up for interview in late 1913.

But what really bowled Graves over was the poetry, and Sassoon quickly became a convert. Sorley was one of them, his work a shared possession. By May 1916 Graves had even persuaded himself from a lack of 'conventional love-lyrics' that, like himself and Sassoon, Sorley must also have been 'so' – that is, homosexual. They saw him as a Georgian *manqué*, a missing link between themselves and Brooke. That at least was how Graves recommended Sorley's work to Marsh, well aware of the pulling power of Brooke's name. He quoted three stanzas of 'All the hills and vales along' with its disconcerting blend of celebration and fatalism ('So be merry, so be dead'), and suggested that Sorley had been 'under Rupert's influence rather in his method'. As evidence, he quoted, actually very slightly misquoted, the reversed octave from the second of 'Two Sonnets':

> Victor and vanquished are at one in death:
> Coward and brave: friend, foe. Ghosts do not say
> 'Come, what was your record when you drew breath?'
> But a big blot has hid each yesterday
> So poor, so manifestly incomplete.
> And your bright Promise, withered long and sped,
> Is touched, stirs, rises, opens and grows sweet
> And blossoms and is you, when you are dead.

Marsh showed no sign of being impressed. Nor, ironically, would Sorley himself have been. Like Edward Thomas, he thought Brooke had been 'far too obsessed with his own sacrifice', when enlisting was 'merely the conduct demanded of him (and others) by the turn of circumstances'. Brooke 'clothed his attitude in fine words', Sorley told his parents in a letter, but had taken 'the sentimental attitude'. His own final poem, a sonnet written in pencil found amongst his kit after his death, was a tough and deliberate repudiation of the Brooke stance:

> When you see millions of the mouthless dead
> Across your dreams in pale battalions go,
> Say not soft things as other men have said,
> That you'll remember. For you need not so . . .
> Say only this, 'They are dead.' Then add thereto,
> 'Yet many a better one has died before.'
> Then, scanning all the o'ercrowded mass, should you
> Perceive one face that you loved heretofore,
> It is a spook. None wears the face you knew.
> Great death has made all his for evermore.

It was the word 'spook' – so utterly unromantic, almost comic – which undercut any pretensions to the 'sentimental'.

However, that was not at all how Sorley struck Graves and Sassoon at the time. A claim like 'Victor and vanquished are at one in death: / Coward and brave: friend, foe' obviously seemed to them in the same vein as Brooke's 'And the worst friend and enemy is but Death'. What Graves saw in Sorley was not Brooke's supplanter but another of his apprentices. On New Year's Day 1916, he had written to Marsh about Brooke's contributions in *Georgian Poetry 1913–1915*: 'I feel in reading them that his is exactly the language I'm floundering to catch, musical, restrained, refined & not crabbed or conventionally antique, reading almost like ordinary speech.' He could just as easily have been describing the language of Sorley's poems. The Sorley who wrote 'Is touched, stirs, rises, opens and grows sweet' had learnt to run verbs in a typically Brookeian manner.

Graves and Sassoon found Sorley's bleak attitude towards death and the war sympathetic, but no Brooke-threatening revelation. Graves later wrote a poem called 'Sorley's Weather' in which Shelley was discarded for the 'rain-blown hill / And the ghost of Sorley', but neither

he nor Sassoon ever tried to imitate Sorley's blanker vision. Sorley
was special because they had discovered him. Like Brooke, he was
someone whose work could be put against the fear and the dark. He
was another poetic forerunner on the path on which they had already
set out. Graves had started the previous year. Sassoon, following him,
had begun in the early weeks of 1916, even before encountering
Sorley.

At first, being in France had brought Sassoon a sense of release. 'I
am happy, happy,' he wrote in his diary on 17 December; 'I've escaped
and found peace unbelievable in this extraordinary existence which
I thought I should loathe.' For one thing, his new life kept him extraordinarily fit. When he was not marching or on working parties to
dig fresh trenches, he rode regularly in the surrounding countryside,
prompting diary entries such as: 'The ghost of Apollo is on these
cornlands'. There was also the daily presence of his adored David
Thomas in the same company, and when Graves was around, the trio
became a close-knit group – with Graves too calling Sassoon 'Sassons'.
'To Victory', in early January 1916, might bewail the absence of
'colours that were my joy' and 'hours that move like a glitter of
dancers'; but, in general, Sassoon felt 'soaked in the glory of sunlight
and past seasons – "sleep, and sunshine [sic], and the autumnal earth"
as R.B. says'.

In late January 1916, all that began to change. The battalion moved
to Morlancourt only five miles or so from the front line. On 2 February,
Sassoon, accompanying the rations, had his first real taste of the
trenches: 'only sixty yards from the enemy in places and many mine-
craters between'. Three days later, he was again briefly sent up the
line and found his fellow-officers 'Greaves, Stansfield, Orme, and Wadd
all serene, and no one hurt, though they had been peppered with
trench-mortars etc from 8.30 to 3.30'.

Something had hit home. On 10 February, Sassoon wrote his first
realistic war poem. It was called 'In the Pink' and, like his Masefield
take-off of three years earlier, it was written in a colloquial, demotic
style. Again, as with The Daffodil Murderer, 'In the Pink' happened
because for once Sassoon was not thinking about his own experience
but trying to empathise with someone else's. 'To Victory' had appeared
in The Times on 15 January above the initials 'SS' and been mistakenly

glossed: 'By a Private Soldier at the front'. Now Sassoon really was trying to imagine being just such a private – a Welshman called Davies, in a cold barn, writing home, temporarily warmed by 'rum and tea', yet knowing that the next day he would 'trudge / Up to the trenches' in 'rotten' boots. Davies was another doomed Shropshire lad: 'To-night he's in the pink; but soon he'll die. / And the war goes on – he don't know why.'

When he wrote this, Sassoon probably had little more idea of the big picture than his Davies did – or the thousands of Davieses soon to be called up under the Military Service Act: national conscription for single men and childless widowers between the ages of 18 and 41. But you did not have to be clairvoyant to sense that the Allies' war effort was faltering. In January 1916, the last British troops had been evacuated from Gallipoli, signalling the end of that ill-fated venture which had cost over 110,000 Allied and Turkish lives. The same month Austria overran Montenegro. Both in the air and on the sea, Germany held the advantage. The Eastern Front was deadlocked. So too was the Western Front, although here both sides were planning major offensives designed to end the war. In February a vast German force struck at the enormously symbolic French fortress of Verdun. The aim was to bleed the French army dry, and by the end of the ten-month siege a million French and German lives had been lost. Meanwhile the British and French were preparing for an equally big summer push at the Somme.

The day Sassoon wrote 'In the Pink', he had also been writing to Marsh. How to describe the war accurately and realistically was suddenly very much on his mind. 'I put "angry guns that boom and flash" in my poem ['To Victory'],' he told his mentor, 'but really they flash & thud.' He then gave a rhapsodic account of the evening he had visited Greaves & Co:

> there was an evening sky overhead with all the stars on parade & the young moon in command, (on her back!) & some owls flitting across the lines. It seemed so strange, with the men ancle-deep in clay peering from under the round steel caps, very tired after a day of strafing with trench mortars & 'oil-cans', & the rattle of machine guns on the left in the luminous dark –

At which point he pulled himself up with a 'But this is fine writing. I must stop it.' Fine writing was always Sassoon's 'fatal Cleopatra'. 'In the Pink' was his first attempt to 'stop it' and produce something sharper.

An officer companion piece to 'In the Pink' was 'A Subaltern'. This sonnet about David Thomas was also Sassoon's complement to Graves's '1915':

> He turned to me with his kind, sleepy gaze
> And fresh face slowly brightening to the grin
> That sets my memory back to summer days,
> With twenty runs to make, and last man in.

Behind those opening lines were the idyllic weeks in Cambridge when Sassons and Tommy had shared rooms. A few lines later the subaltern admitted he had been having 'a bloody time / In trenches', but the speaker's 'stale philosophies' had apparently 'served him well' – at any event gratifyingly better than 'Dreaming about his girl' which just 'send his brain / Blanker than ever'. Pulling back, Sassoon topped off his Shakespearean sonnet with a jaunty couplet: '"Good God!" he laughed, and slowly filled his pipe, / Wondering "why he always talks such tripe".'

Graves was jubilant. 'I think S.S.'s verses are getting infinitely better than the first crop I saw,' he told Marsh on 15 March, 'much freer and more Georgian.' He picked out 'A Subaltern' for special praise – 'A perfectly ripping one' – knowing it would appeal to Marsh. Graves, who was by now near collapse, had obviously been urging Sassoon to send his recent work to their mentor. Sassoon wrote in edgy fashion the following day: 'O Eddie, you *must* get my poems printed soon; it will be such fun to think of them when everything becomes horrid and people begin to be sent away hurt.'

'Begin to be sent away hurt' – or die. Because two days later David Thomas was dead. He had been hit in the throat 'by a stray bullet'. Sassoon had last seen him on the evening of the 16th. He had been reading a recent poem of Sassoon's; they had said good night 'in the moonlit trenches'. Sassoon was devastated. He rode off to some nearby woods above Sailly-Laurette to be alone with his grief. He lay sobbing under a beech-tree. He could hear his horse stamping its feet, birds in the trees, the 'distant mutter and boom of guns'. He lay there, 'wondering, and longing for the bodily presence that was so fair'. Grief – he tried to persuade himself – 'can be beautiful, when we find something worthy to be mourned'. He inscribed Thomas's name 'in chalk on the beech-tree stem'. In a fey but touching gesture, he 'left a rough garland of ivy there, and a yellow primrose for his yellow hair and kind grey eyes'. Recording the moment in his diary, he allowed himself to say the words he had probably never allowed himself to say to Thomas in life: 'my dear, my dear'.

Sassoon's diary account of David Thomas's burial was a model of restraint:

> In the half-clouded moonlight the parson stood above the graves, and everything was dim but the striped flag laid across them. Robert Graves, beside me, with his white whimsical face twisted and grieving. Once we could not hear the solemn words for the noise of a machine-gun along the line; and when all was finished a canister fell a few hundred yards away to burst with a crash.

The feeling was in the detail: the 'half-clouded moonlight', the machine-gun that briefly obliterated the words of the funeral service, the crash of the canister. Also in what was inferred – Sassoon's own grief reflected in the description of Graves's face – and understated: 'when all was finished'. As much as anything, it was the economy of keeping a diary and writing letters to friends like Marsh that helped to make Sassoon the poet he became. Only at the end of his entry did he allow himself a final elegising, idealising touch: 'So Tommy left us, a gentle soldier, perfect and without stain. And so he will remain in my heart, fresh and happy and brave.'

After David Thomas's death, the war was never the same for Sassoon or Graves. Sassoon tried to sanctify his death: 'dawn and sunset flame with my spilt blood'. Graves, playing on Thomas's Christian name, cast him as an exemplary victim of the war machine: 'Steel-helmeted and grey and grim / Goliath straddles over him.' Sassoon got himself transferred to the trenches and deliberately risked death in a series of hair-raising night patrols in no man's land. His company nickname had been 'Kangaroo'; to this was now added 'Mad Jack'. Both were lucky to miss the opening day of the Somme, 1 July 1916, with its 57,000 casualties (20,000 killed), although Graves's death was mistakenly reported in *The Times* three weeks later. Both, as 'A certain cure for lust of blood', continued to write the first modern war poems.

5

Gathering Swallows

Edward Thomas and Wilfred Owen, Sunday 20 February 1916

Lance-corporal Edward Thomas and officer-cadet Wilfred Owen both enlisted in the Artists' Rifles in 1915: Thomas in July, Owen in October. Both arrived at Hare Hall Camp, Romford, Essex in mid-November and were based there until mid-May 1916 when Owen left to take up a commission in the 5th (Reserve) Manchester Regiment.

The camp, in the grounds of an eighteenth-century country house and a mile or so from the town centre, was new. Its forty-odd wooden huts housed around thirty cadets each under the supervision of one or more NCOs, one of whom was Thomas. There was also a canteen, sergeants' mess, hospital, lecture room. Officers were quartered at the hall.

On his arrival Thomas described the location as 'the dullest flattest piece of a beautiful piece of country'. Owen merely remarked: 'All very nicely set out here.' He found himself with twenty-nine others in Hut 6a and a week after his arrival sent a picture postcard of most of its occupants to his brother Harold and cousin Leslie Gunston. The twenty-four officer cadets are in three rows, the front row seated. An NCO stands on the extreme left of the second row. There is a pleasantly relaxed air to the photograph. Many of the cadets are smoking pipes or cigarettes. Some of those in the front row have their

Left: Edward Thomas, sketched by John Wheatley, 1916
Right: Wilfred Owen, Hare Hall Camp, November 1915

arms folded; some have their legs crossed. All are in uniform, but three are bareheaded, and two wear camp comforters. One of these even has his right thumb raised in the time-honoured gesture.

Owen is in the back row, second from the left. He has a moustache, a cigarette in his right hand and looks faintly pleased with himself. At five foot five, his lack of height would have debarred him from the army earlier in the war but not now. By contrast, the NCO at the end of the second row is a tall man. He stands at ease, but his body is slightly braced, legs apart, arms at his side, hands bunched. His right hand curls in a fraction. He too has a pipe in his mouth and a small moustache. There seems an outside chance that the NCO is Thomas; at least what can be seen of the long, narrow face and prominent cheekbones under the peaked cap is a possible fit. 'I wonder would you recognise me with hair cropped close and carrying a thin swagger cane,' Thomas wrote his friend Robert Frost, 'many don't who meet me unexpectedly.'

Even if it is Thomas in the photograph, he and Owen could only have shared a hut very briefly. Thomas's letters between November 1915 and July 1916 show him attached to A and D Companies (Owen was in C Company) and moving between no fewer than eight different huts. Owen himself stayed in the same hut until March 1916, except for a couple of weeks in Isolation Hut B11 during a measles outbreak in February. In March, he moved to the nearby Cadet School in Balgores House.

The chances of some sort of encounter are high. Thomas was an assistant map instructor, and one of his duties was to take contingents of ten to a dozen cadets out into the surrounding countryside for five-day exercises. The object, he reported, was to teach them 'the elements of map-reading, field sketching, the use of compass and protractor, and making maps on the ground with and without the compass'. There was a weekly turnover of these contingents, so Owen could easily have been in one of Thomas's batches. If not, he might well have attended some of the lectures Thomas regularly gave. Thomas was typically diffident about his lecturing abilities:

As soon as I stand up and look at thirty men I can do nothing but crawl backwards and forwards between the four points I can still remember under the strain. It will mean a long war if I am to improve.

If Thomas was one of Owen's instructors, the latter did him proud, gaining high marks in his Reconnaissance exam. A few days after his arrival, Owen proudly told his mother that he was one of only three out of 700 at the camp to have taken a cold shower at six o'clock that morning. Thomas is unlikely to have been one of the other two, but they could well have shared daily drill, guard duty, route marches. At the very least, one can imagine the two sitting near each other in the crowded canteen or passing each other in the grounds. A quick salute, perhaps a glance.

If there was some more substantial encounter, it could have occurred during a field exercise or, as I am imagining here, on a Sunday afternoon, perhaps Sunday 20 February when both men seem to have been in camp. Owen had just been released from quarantine in Isolation Hut B11, and his naval younger brother Harold had paid him a visit the previous day. In his autobiography, *Journey from Obscurity*, Harold's portrait of his brother was to come close to Aldous Huxley's definition of 'vindictive hagiography': 'malice expressed in terms of worship'. His account of that February 1916 visit was fascinatingly peculiar and well up to par: he claimed that his brother had gauchely tried to fix him up with a local waitress.

It is a wet afternoon; Thomas is alone in Hut 16. Some errand brings Owen to the hut. Thomas has been brooding about his delayed promotion to corporal. He has vaguely noticed Owen about the camp as rather dapper-looking. He had hoped to write this afternoon, not having written any poems for five or six weeks. But he cannot help thinking about that promotion. Distraction is welcome. What might they talk about? Or, more specifically, what would one like them to talk about? Here are the outlines of three imaginary conversations.

Thomas would probably have initiated any exchange. As he told Robert Frost:

> here I have to like people because they are more my sort than the others, although I realise at certain times they are not my sort at all and will vanish away after the war. What almost completes the illusion is that I can't help talking to them as if they were friends.

His favourite ploy with cadets was to establish an area of England they both knew and encourage the other to talk about it. As he observed: 'There isn't a man I don't share some part with.' With Owen, the link was Shrewsbury. His family, Owen tells Thomas hesitantly at first, moved there from Birkenhead in 1907 when he was nearly four-teen. Father in the railways. He was enrolled at the local pupil-teacher centre and stayed there for four years. Pleasing country, observes Thomas in his husky mellow voice. Which gives Owen the chance to enthuse about taking the little ferry across to Haughmond Hill for family picnics and bicycle rides to collect shards from the Roman remains at Wroxeter (Uriconium). Thomas seems kindly, but Owen says nothing about the ode he wrote three years ago about Uriconium though some lines suddenly flash into his head:

> If thou hast ever longed
> To lift the gloomy curtain of Time Past,
> And spy the secret things that Hades hath,
> Here through the riven ground take such a view.
> The dust, that fell unnoted as a dew,
> Wrapped the dead city's face like mummy-cloth:
> All is as was: except for worm and moth.

Not very good, he thinks with his crooked smile, though he is pleased by the way 'hath' half-rhymes forward with 'cloth' and 'moth'. Nor does Thomas mention that he has written about Shrewsbury in his as yet unpublished *A Literary Pilgrim in England*. If he knew Owen better, he could ask him if he knows the story of the young Hazlitt walking from Wem to Shrewsbury to hear Coleridge preach and then walking back again with his hero a few days later. But then if Owen turns out to be literary – he has taken his cap off to reveal a careful centre parting – he would probably know the story, and jump to con-clusions. Which might lead to an excited 'Are you by any chance Mr Edward Thomas, the well-known critic and essayist?' And what would he say then?

And after Shrewsbury? asks Thomas. After Shrewsbury, says Owen, lighting a cigarette, came Dunsden and – taking the plunge – becoming a parish assistant. Thomas makes no response to this; his long, narrow face retains the same look, not unfriendly, but rather distant and detached. Dunsden should have been called Dullsden, Owen continues, tapping his cigarette, but visiting the poor was an education in 'the

Book of Life'. He smiles at the phrase, which he remembers once using rather sententiously in a letter to his sister. And then? prompts Thomas, more interested in this short young man than he had expected to be. And then there had been the failure to get into University College, Reading, but Owen does not want to think about that and talks engagingly about his time as an English teacher and tutor in Bordeaux and the Pyrenees. Which was where he was when the war broke out. An unspoken 'But plainly you did not hurry back to answer your country's call?' hangs in the air. And a year later, says Owen, I said to myself 'I don't imagine that the German War will be affected by my joining in, but I know my own future Peace will be.' So here I am, he concludes. Yes, says Thomas slowly, one could not keep out any longer. He taps his pipe against his boot. The conversation is over, and Owen realises he has done almost all the talking and still knows next to nothing about Lance Corporal P E Thomas.

The second imaginary conversation starts similarly with Thomas getting Owen to talk about Shrewsbury. This time, however, Thomas is feeling less guarded. From something Owen lets slip, it is clear he has literary leanings. Suddenly Thomas has a longing to talk about books. Mostly he rather enjoys the way army life prevents him thinking too much, but every now and then he misses those literary lunches at the Mont Blanc in Gerrard Street with Garnett and Hudson. Or tea on the top floor at St George's in St Martin's Lane, where he first met Frost and they nicknamed him 'The Iambic' because he was such a regular attender. The only literary type he has come across so far in camp is Edmund John, a writer of amorous, out-of-date verses and wearer of great rings, who had to have a fortnight's sick leave after a day digging trenches.

So Owen at least seems a better bet than Edmund John. Close up, you can see he already has flecks of grey in his hair though he must still be only in his early twenties. Anyway Thomas decides to risk the Hazlitt–Coleridge story and is rewarded by a marked increase in Owen's attention. And did Thomas know that Keats's friend Reynolds came from Shrewsbury? asks Owen. Once he has started on Keats, it soon becomes apparent that the young man is besotted with him. He pronounces Keats's name with such reverential awe that for a moment Thomas almost regrets having embarked on the conversation. But he

recalls how diffident and proud he himself was once, and asks the
obvious question: And you write poems yourself?

Yes, Owen admits, he does write poems though here at camp there
is no time, no private place. But he makes it clear that for the last six
years he has consciously apprenticed himself to Keats, reading and
studying his work like an army manual. He confesses, a little sheep-
ishly, that he has scoured biographies of Keats for details which mirror
his own life. Once he even went to the British Museum manuscript
section to compare his handwriting with Keats's and found it rather
large and sloped like his own. So, says Thomas, what is a follower of
Keats doing in the army? Didn't Keats think soldiers were 'cheated
into an *esprit de corps* by a red coat, a band, and colours'? I used to
believe, says Owen, that what would hold me together on a battle-
field was the sense that I was perpetuating the language in which
Keats and the rest of them wrote. But now I find myself wondering
what Keats has to teach me about rifle and machine-gun drill and how
Shelley will show me how to hate.

There is a pause. Owen lights a cigarette; Thomas taps his pipe.
Then, reluctant to lose the opportunity, Owen starts to recite favourite
passages from Keats's poems, many of which he clearly knows by
heart. Thomas notes that it is the luxurious Keats that Owen prefers.
One extract, delivered with special feeling, is the description of the
sleeping Adonis in *Endymion*:

> Not hiding up an Apollonian curve
> Of neck and shoulder, nor the tenting swerve
> Of knee from knee, or ankles pointing light;
> But rather, giving them to the filled sight
> Officiously. Sideway his face repos'd
> On one white arm, and tenderly unclos'd,
> By tenderest pressure, a faint damask mouth
> To slumbery pout: just as the morning south
> Disparts a dew-lipp'd rose . . .

Yes, says Thomas politely, it is true no poem of the same length is so
crammed with loveliness and love of loveliness. But, he continues,
that passage about Adonis seems to me one of those frequent pauses
in *Endymion* which show us not a picture, but a painter at work. Think

of the conclusion of 'To Autumn': 'And gathering swallows twitter in
the skies'. There is something light, thin, cold, and vanishing in that
line which contrasts achingly – Owen nods at the Keatsian word –
with the mellowness and slowness of an earlier line like 'Thou watchest
the last oozings hours by hours' with its long 'oo' and 'ou' and 'aw'
and 'z' sounds.

Impressed despite himself, Owen suggests that Thomas ought to
write a book about Keats. Then – he is quick – but perhaps you have,
haven't you? You are Mr Edward Thomas, the well-known critic and
essayist. To which Thomas agrees that he is that Edward Thomas and
he has, in fact, written a short book about Keats which will be published
in a month or two. (Owen will buy the book later in the summer after
joining the 5th Manchesters.) But, Thomas continues, keen to deflect
Owen's attention from Keats, the book he had wanted to write was
about Shelley, whom he had similarly discovered at sixteen or seventeen. It was Shelley and Jefferies and a few others who first made me
want to become a writer, he says. He pauses. This is already further
than he wishes to go in a chance conversation.

But the mention of Shelley reminds Owen of Thomas's review of
Brooke's *1914 & other Poems* that he read in London the previous June.
There Thomas had virtually called Brooke a poor man's Shelley. Now
he is tapping his pipe again. His hands, Owen notices, are powerful
and bony. Thomas has them clasped under his chin, his attention is
plainly wandering. Owen makes a last effort. And do you really think
Brooke is like Shelley as you said in your review? Brooke's poetry is
very fine, I think. Beauty and Truth. I am thinking of writing an
imperial elegy myself. It might begin: 'Not one corner of a foreign
field / But a span as wide as Europe.' What was Brooke like as a
person? He had met him, hadn't he? Thomas decides that the last
thing he wants to do is talk about his friendship with Brooke and
explain his rather complicated reservations about the poetry. He stands
up. The conversation is over, and Owen is left reflecting that there is
rather more to Lance Corporal P E Thomas than meets the eye.

The conversation one would most like Thomas and Owen to have
had – and the least probable – is about their own poetry. This again
begins with Thomas encouraging Owen to talk about Shrewsbury,
and progresses via Hazlitt to Keats, but this time, after Owen has

admitted that he writes poems himself, Thomas kindly prompts him
to say more.

And do your own verses resemble Keats's? he asks. It is as though
he has released a pent-up dam. I like to think they do, says Owen. I
want – I think I will be with him 'among the English poets':

> a meteor, fast, eccentric, lone,
>   Lawless; in passage through all spheres,
> Warning the earth of wider ways unknown
>   And rousing men with heavenly fears . . .

Not Keats, thinks Thomas, more like Shelley, probably Owen's own.
Everything I have written during the last seven years, Owen continues
earnestly, has been done to dedicate myself to poetry. Teaching and
tutoring in Bordeaux, I began to know myself. My mother under-
stands this, I believe, although she once hoped I would enter the
Church. And now, he concludes, 'I have fears that I may cease to be /
Before my pen has glean'd my teeming brain.' Thomas smiles at the
quotation but reflects that it also fits his own case. Since he started
making poems fifteen months ago, he has produced a hundred, none
of which has been accepted for publication – unless you counted the
annual Bottomley was supposed to be bringing out and the two he
had put in his own anthology *This England: an Anthology from her
Writers* the previous year.

Owen tells him he is off to London on Wednesday for a lecture
course. He intends to visit Harold Monro at the Poetry Bookshop.
There is a slight thrill in his voice as he says Monro's name and the
words 'Poetry Bookshop'. Thomas recalls his own early encounters
in the book world: how when Nevinson at the *Daily Chronicle* asked
him what he could review, he said 'Nothing', but Nevinson gave him
a start all the same. Owen is saying he may even be able to stay at
the Poetry Bookshop itself. He hopes to show Monro some of his
work. Do you know Monro? he asks Thomas. Yes, I know Monro.
Indeed he does. Last year he sent Monro a selection of his poems,
hoping he might publish them, but Monro returned them, muttering
something about conception and execution – as if they were different
things. Monro had not liked his poems any more than Eddie Marsh
had. There had seemed a faint chance that he might get into Marsh's

second *Georgian Poetry* anthology. At least Bottomley had said he would show some poems to Marsh. But nothing had come of it. And when the anthology came out, the only poems he had really liked were de la Mare's, though Davies's were all right. The sole newcomer was Ledwidge. And he wasn't any good. He says nothing of this to Owen. No need to subject one's failures to a full-dress parade. The fact that Monro did not care for his poems does not mean he will dislike Owen's.

He must concentrate. Perhaps you can say some of your lines, Thomas says politely, as much to stop thinking about Monro as anything else. Owen thinks quickly. Probably better not to recite the lines about the navy boy with his head golden like the oranges that catch their brightness from Las Palmas sun. Or the one about taking antidotes, 'though what they be / Unless yourself be poisoned, do not ask.' Those might be too revealing. He has not shown those even to his mother and he sends her everything. He settles for a sonnet, written a couple of years earlier:

> When late I viewed the gardens of rich men,
> Where throve my darling blossoms plenteously,
> With others whose rare glories dazed my ken,
> I was not teased with envious misery.
> Enough for me to see and recognize;
> Then bear away sweet names upon my tongue,
> Scents in my breath, and colours in my eyes.
> Their owners watch them die: I keep them young.
>
> But when more spacious pleasances I trod,
> And saw their thousand buds, but might not kiss
> Though loving like a lover, sire, and God,
> Sad was the yearning of my avarice.
> The rich man gives his parting guest one bloom,
> But God hath vouchsafed my meek longing – whom?

A silence succeeds his recitation. I wrote that some years ago, says Owen. 'Spacious pleasances!' thinks Thomas. Rhyming 'avarice' with 'kiss' is good, he offers eventually. Rhymes should not be too predictable. 'God' is a hard rhyme, because only 'trod' and 'rod', or perhaps 'sod', can easily follow it. 'Love' is worse. He smiles. Owen

does not smile. His sense of humour did not extend to his own
poems. I am sorry, says Thomas, seeing his disappointment. I often
find it hard to get in track with other people's poems.

I have been reading Rupert Brooke's sonnets, says Owen, and thinking
of attempting something larger about the war, something less personal
– an imperial elegy perhaps: 'Not one corner of a foreign field / But
a span as wide as Europe.' Yes, it is hard to avoid Brooke, agrees Thomas,
however one might try to. So you write poems too, says Owen.
Thomas had not meant that, but, caught off guard, he admits he has
belatedly turned to poetry. How do you find the time and privacy? asks
Owen. The others think I am writing a letter or making notes for a
lecture, says Thomas. Keats is hard to avoid too; I found myself using
the word 'ken' recently. But not as hard as Brooke. He was eloquent, but
I don't think those sonnets are very personal, more a nervous attempt
to connect himself with the idea of self-sacrifice. Yet his phrases often
come back to me when I am thinking about something else entirely. I
sometimes feel I am carrying on an argument with him almost in spite
of myself. This is Owen's cue to ask Thomas to recite a poem of his.
He decides on 'Rain' since it has a few clear links to Brooke:

> Rain, midnight rain, nothing but the wild rain
> On this bleak hut, and solitude, and me
> Remembering again that I shall die
> And neither hear the rain nor give it thanks
> For washing me cleaner than I have been
> Since I was born into this solitude.
> Blessed are the dead that the rain rains upon:
> But here I pray that none whom once I loved
> Is dying tonight or lying still awake
> Solitary, listening to the rain,
> Either in pain or thus in sympathy
> Helpless among the living and the dead,
> Like a cold water among broken reeds,
> Myriads of broken reeds all still and stiff,
> Like me who have no love which this wild rain
> Has not dissolved except the love of death,
> If love it be towards what is perfect and
> Cannot, the tempest tells me, disappoint.

Blank verse, thinks Owen, rather rough. He can hear the Brooke echoes but lacking the patriotic uplift. He can hear the melancholy too, but finds something thin about the poem. He smiles. Thomas taps his pipe against his boot. The conversation is over, leaving both frustrated by the encounter.

Owen left Hare Hall on 19 May 1916 on leave pending gazetting to the Manchesters. That was the day before Edward Thomas and the artist Paul Nash attended a trio of short plays, including Rupert Brooke's *Lithuania*. (Eddie Marsh standing close to Thomas failed to recognise him in military uniform.) By September he was an officer-cadet himself with the Royal Artillery and busily arranging manuscripts of his poems. In October he was still trying to work out what he thought of Brooke. He told Frost that Brooke 'could only think about his feeling' and 'was a rhetorician, dressing things up better than they needed'. In December he volunteered to serve overseas. Owen, after further training, was posted to Étaples in late December and in the new year joined the 2nd Manchester Regiment near Beaumont Hamel.

By Easter Day, 8 April 1917, Owen's battalion was advancing on Saint-Quentin. He 'kept alive', he told his mother, 'on brandy, the fear of death, and the glorious prospect of the cathedral Town just below us'. That afternoon he watched a German plane, hit by machine-gun fire, 'shuddering down the sky'. He ran across the fields and collected two souvenirs: a bit of wood from the body of the plane and the pilot's handkerchief with a 'spatter of blood in the corner'.

Thirty miles away, just south of Arras, Edward Thomas of the 244 Siege Battery wrote in his 'Walker's Back-Loop pocket book (bound in pigskin, price 2*s*.)':

A bright warm Easter day but Achicourt shelled at 12.39 and then at 2.15 so that we all retired to cellar. I had to go over to battery at 3 for a practice barrage, skirting the danger zone, but we were twice interrupted. A 5.9 fell 2 yards from me as I stood by the f/c post. One burst down the back of the office and a piece of dust scratched my neck. No firing from 2–4. Rubin left for a course.

In the mess that evening, the other officers ribbed him about his lucky escape. The next morning at 7.36 a.m. precisely, his luck ran out. He was standing at the Beaurains Observation Post directing fire when he was killed instantaneously by the blast from a shell.

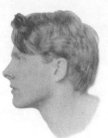

6

A Good Man, Sir, but He's a Musician

Ivor Gurney and Rupert Brooke,
7 and 14 February 1917

On the evening of 7 February 1917, Private Ivor Gurney of the 2nd/5th Glosters wrote to his friend Marion Scott at the Royal College of Music in London. He wrote by candlelight from a cold billet not far from Amiens. He hoped her influenza was better. He thanked her for 'the pretty and stern things' she had said about recent poems he had sent her. He hoped for leave, hated army life. After two years of service – the last nine months or so out in France – he felt he had earned the right to 'a soft job'. None of his comrades would blame him if he secured one; they would simply envy him. He enclosed a new sonnet, 'Pain':

> Pain, pain continual, pain unending;
> Hard even to the roughest, but to those
> Hungry for beauty . . . Not the wisest knows,
> Nor most pitiful hearted, what the wending
> Of one hour's way meant. Gray monotony lending
> Weight to the gray skies, gray mud where goes
> An army of grey bedrenched scarecrows in rows
> Careless at last of cruellest Fate-sending,
> Seeing the pitiful eyes of men foredone,
> Or horses shot, too tired merely to stir

Left: Ivor Gurney, 1915
Right: Rupert Brooke: the frontispiece to *1914 & other Poems*

> Dying in shellholes both, slain by the mud.
> Men broken, shrieking even to hear a gun . . .
> Till Pain grinds down, or lethargy numbs her,
> The amazed heart cries angrily out on God.

The poem, Gurney added sarcastically, was intended 'for admirers of Rupert Brooke'. It was to be the first of five 'Sonnetts 1917', of which 'Pain', Gurney told Marion Scott, would be 'the blackest' of them.

On 13 February, Gurney dispatched another sonnet, followed the next day by two more. He explained more fully to Marion Scott what he had in mind. His four sonnets – now ordered 'For England', 'Pain', 'Home Sickness' and 'Servitude' – plus one still to be written, were to act as 'a sort of counterblast' against Brooke's 1914 sonnets. Gurney spelt out the contrast. Brooke had been writing 'before the grind of war' set in, and from the point of view of 'an officer (or one who would have been an officer)'. Against his 'exalted spiritual' version of the war, Gurney now offered 'the protest of the physical'. Against Brooke's 'one large' fact, he offered 'the cumulative weight of small facts'. Brooke's version had necessarily been 'uninformed (to put it coarsely and unfairly)'; his version was informed. His own sonnets filled a gap. While they would not please old ladies, they might please soldiers. And it was soldiers and knowledgeable civilians he was writing for. What had brought Gurney to this pitch of indignation and outrage? Was he really as antagonistic towards Brooke and his sonnets as he claimed?

Gurney had not always hated life in the army. He had tried to enlist as soon as war broke out but been turned down because of his eyesight – he wore glasses. When he was eventually accepted in February 1915, he was not just relieved at being able to do his duty, although he was supremely patriotic about his own corner of England, in and around Gloucester. He hoped that joining up would help to restore his physical and mental equilibrium, which had been decidedly shaky since a nervous breakdown in 1913. And so it proved. 'I think there is no danger of my breaking down,' he told his friends the Chapman family that February, 'and a large prospect of my becoming much better, thank the Lord, and paid a bob a day for it, too!' Life in the army was tough, and he was always tired, he told Gloucester friend and fellow Royal College of Music student Herbert Howells, but he kept going 'in a very much happier frame of mind' than he had been for years. Even seventeen months later in June 1916 after heavy strafing in the Fauquissart–Laventie sector, he could assure Marion Scott that 'It was a great time; full of fear of course, but not so bad as neurasthenia', and that the whole experience had given him 'still further confidence that once I get back to work my mind will take proper paths and let me be happy'.

The nervous breakdown had occurred during his second year at the Royal College of Music. He had arrived there in 1911 – a twenty-one-year-old tailor's son from Gloucester – hailed by Sir Hubert Parry and Sir Charles Stanford as a Schubertian prodigy. With his striking features, 'profusion of light brown hair (not too well brushed!)' and 'thick, dark blue Severn pilot's coat', he certainly looked the part. In late 1913 or early 1914, his settings of five Elizabethan songs by Shakespeare, Nashe and Fletcher – the five Elizas as Gurney called them – confirmed his promise. He had also sporadically begun writing poems. But in between had come the breakdown.

A combination of factors seems to have caused it. These included separation from his beloved Gloucestershire, a dislike for London and the pressures of being a star pupil at the RCM. Gurney might jokingly refer to himself in letters to Marion Scott as the Young Genius – as he undoubtedly believed himself to be – but the label came with a high price tag. His particular talent was for setting poems and songs to music, but, like many other natural miniaturists, he considered real achievement lay in tackling the grander forms, such as the symphony and concerto. There were other disquieting indicators too. Gurney clearly had some kind of eating disorder, often skipping regular meals and gobbling bags of apples or platefuls of cake. No wonder he used to complain that 'The trail of the dyspeptic serpent is over me still'. From his late teens he was a wanderer, rarely staying at home for long, going off for days on end, a stray who preferred sleeping in barns or at the houses of friends whom, cuckoolike, he would adopt as substitute families. While some of this could be attributed to conscious eccentricity, playing out the role of an Arnoldian scholar gypsy, part of it was a product of a profound inner restlessness – an attempt, too, to keep at bay a tendency to intense introspection. In

spring 1913 he broke down and retreated to Gloucestershire where he
recuperated for the whole of the summer.

He came to relate his collapse to his 'all too subtle observation
off [*sic*] myself', and letters to Howler (Howells) often mention
'the danger of introspection and self analysis'. When in August 1916
he thought, wrongly as it turned out, that his dearest friend, the
Gloucestershire poet F W Harvey, had been killed, he told Howells
that Harvey's sole flaw was 'that cursed one of introspection'. It was,
Gurney observed, 'Not a bad flaw as regards other people, but a great
misery to ones-self [*sic*]'. Occasionally he could be mock-Blakeian on
the subject:

> Who peers in his own anatomy
> Will dread the smallest shade, and flee.
> But he who keeps his eyes turned *out*
> 'S a blooming nut or thereabout.

But earnest or flippant, when it came to depression, Gurney, like
Edward Thomas, knew exactly what he was talking about. Again, as
with Thomas, life in the army seems to have suited him, at least up
to a point. Physically, it kept him fit. The diet was regular if dull. The
daily tasks were often boring, but these and the companionship of
the other soldiers precluded solitary brooding. And once he was out
in France he usually had more than enough to keep his mind on. The
army became, in effect, the largest of his substitute families.

Friends like Marion Scott, Howells and Harvey loved Gurney for
his honesty, his lack of pretence, even for his extreme self-absorption.
Howells called him 'a most lovable egotist'; Stanford later described
him as his 'least teachable' pupil. And then there was his zany humour.
His letters suggest what good company he must have been when
free from brooding. With young Arthur Chapman, he would play
J M Barrie:

> To the paleface Arthur
> Glass-eyes, the player on instruments, sends thee greetings.

With 'Howler', he would send up a notion of genteelspeak: 'Today
. . . there was no *Times*, no *Daily News*, my usual matutinal mental

pabulum, as a really educated person would say.' The novelist and composer Mrs Voynich would be treated to trench witticisms ('Apres le gore, our men say, as a joke, and not a bad one') or snippets of the Gloucesters' slang like 'Twallet', meaning 'One of small intellectual powers'.

Marion Scott, who played Marsh to Gurney's Brooke – being champion, confidante, self-appointed literary agent and unrequited lover – was offered the widest range of his humour. There were high-spirited Young Genius jokes (a circled fingerprint inscribed 'Please keep this for posteries [sic] sake') and Brookelike gags about how their correspondence would one day be 'the joy and wonder of my biographers'. There were suggested cures for insomnia: 'Read Doctor Johnson's works, or Addison's, which are nearly as bad. If these are inutile then parts of the *Excursion* might meet the needs of the case.' Best of all were the vivid vignettes of army life, including a gleeful description of the incorrigibly unmilitary Gurney being inspected:

> Today there was an inspection by the Colonel. I waited trembling, knowing that there was six weeks of hospital and soft-job dirt and rust not yet all off; no, not by a long way. I stood there, a sheep among the goats (no, vice versa) and waited the bolt and thunder. Round came He-Who-Must-Be-Obeyed. Looked at me, hesitated, looked again, hesitated, and was called off by the R.S.M. who was afterwards heard telling the Colonel (a few paces away from me), 'A Good man, sir, quite all right. Quite a good man, sir, but he's a musician, and doesn't seem able to get himself clean.' When the aforesaid RSM came round for a back view, he chuckled, and said 'Ah Gurney, I'm afraid we shall never make a soldier of you.'

Even the censor – who had told Gurney to shorten his letters – was treated to a comic disclaimer at the head of another lengthy effort: 'Pas de contraband / lectures pour tous / De la musique De la litterature etc etc'. But, despite his ability to see and capture the lighter side of army life, Gurney struggled to survive the 'Mud and Monotony . . . Minnies and Majors'. He knew what it was like 'when the bottom of one's mind seems to fall out suddenly at the horror of it all'. He was one of 'those / Hungry for beauty', and being a member of 'An army

of grey bedrenched scarecrows in rows' eventually ground him down.
By early 1917, he wanted to register his own front-line protest against
the war and the image of war enshrined in Brooke's sonnets. To
dedicate his own sonnet sequence to 'the Memory of Rupert Brooke'
was an additional way to register his protest and likely to get it
noticed.

For all that, the development of Gurney's response to Brooke did
not follow a simple trajectory. On 9 May 1915, a fortnight after
Brooke's much-publicised death, Gurney was rhapsodising about
'The Dead' ('These hearts were woven of human joys and cares')
and 'The Soldier' ('If I should die, think only this of me'). At that
stage these were the only two of Brooke's war sonnets he had come
across. They 'outshine by far anything yet written on this upheaval',
he told Marion Scott. 'They are so beautiful that at last one forgets
that the words are there and is taken up into ecstasy just as in music.'
He included a four-line extract from 'The Dead' and urged her to
hunt up a recent issue of the *Times Literary Supplement* which had
quoted both sonnets in full.

Gurney was still equally enthusiastic in late June 1915 after reading
Edward Thomas's review of Brooke's *1914 & other Poems* in the *Daily
Chronicle*. 'I got another sonnet out of that,' he told Marion Scott
triumphantly, slightly misquoting the opening line of 'Peace'. Musing
on a point Thomas had made, he reflected: 'It *is* curious how little
great youthful-seeming poetry has been written; and sonnets seem
fated to be the work of "solemn whiskered men, pillars of the state".'
A month later, however, he had changed his tune. 'The Sonnet of R.B.
you sent me, I do not like', Marion Scott was tersely informed. It
suggested that Brooke 'would not have improved with age, would not
have broadened'. Brooke's manner, as Gurney neatly put it, had turned
into a mannerism. Whereas great poets only very slowly absorbed
what was going on around them, Brooke 'soaked it in quickly and gave
it out with as great ease'.

So much for being 'taken up into ecstasy just as in music'. Except
that for all his lofty dismissal of Brooke, Gurney had been bitten by
the sonnet bug – and bitten too by something of Brooke's manner or
mannerism. Later in the very same letter, he offered Marion Scott his
own first attempt, 'To the Poet before Battle':

Now, Youth, the hour of thy dread passion comes;
Thy lovely things must all be laid away,
And thou, as others, must face the riven day
Unstirred by the tattle and rattle of rolling drums
Or bugles strident cry. When mere noise numbs
The sense of being, the fearsick soul doth sway,
Remember thy great crafts honour, that they may say
Nothing in shame of Poets. Then the crumbs
Of praise the little versemen joyed to take
Shall be forgotten; then they must know we are,
For all our skill in words, equal in might
And strong in mettle, as those we honoured. Make
The name of Poet terrible in just War;
And like a crown of honour upon the fight.

He encouraged Marion Scott to comment on this effort without holding back, but also not to compare it with any of Wordsworth's great sonnets: 'It is not meant to compete', he warned her. But of course it was. By following Wordsworth in using the strictest of the sonnet forms, the Petrarchan, Gurney was asserting his poetic credentials. And even if he was not directly competing with Wordsworth, he was certainly competing with Brooke, whose phrasing and cadences he half-echoed in various places, and who was presumably being ticked off here as one of 'the little versemen'. But then, as Sassoon, Graves and even Sorley were discovering around this time, it was hard to write poems about the war and not sound like a follower of Brooke.

In fact, Gurney's seesaw reaction to Brooke was characteristic of him. He greatly admired Hardy but dismissed *Jude the Obscure* as 'grimy nonsense'. He thought the opening lines of *Paradise Lost* Bachlike and beyond praise, and learnt and recited them along with Wordsworth's sonnets during route marches; yet he was soon berating Milton for being insufficiently national and writing 'most dastardly half-English'. Keats was one of the few writers not to arouse these yo-yoing feelings, and before leaving for France as a signaller in late May 1916 Gurney sent Marion Scott a copy of Thomas's newly published book on the poet. In France even Shakespeare's sonnets came to seem distant and a strain to read, while out there he found

Shelley was simply 'a wash out' and Marcus Aurelius 'a pious swanker'.

So Gurney's reservations about Brooke, though perfectly genuine, were only part of the story. Sometimes he was disparaging, sometimes appreciative. In March 1916 he read with interest a review of Brooke's posthumously published *Letters from America* with its fulsome introduction by Henry James. In May, shortly before going to France, he pointedly slipped an 'If I must die think only this of me' into a letter to Howells, while bequeathing him his 'rag of a [musical] mantle'. Yet come Christmas 1916, by which time Gurney was seriously working on a collection of his own poems, Brooke was among the writers he wished he were able to read. And in the New Year, Brooke was in his list of poets who had written well about the war, together with Harvey, Laurence Binyon, Wilfrid Gibson, Julian Grenfell and Hardy.

Furthermore, for all Gurney's anti-Brooke protestations in February 1917, his own 'Sonnetts 1917' were not as different from Brooke in sentiment, and even in rhythm and phrasing, as he might have liked to think. 'For England' claimed that no one would 'willingly let slip . . . Earth's loveliness', but that if one had to, then there was no 'better passing than to go out like men / For England'. 'Servitude' railed against the harrying 'brass-cleaning' tyranny of army life and the 'bluster and noise' of the sergeant-majors who enforced it. Yet there was a definite flicker of Brooke in the unquenchable 'laughing spirit' of the comrades who helped one to survive. 'Home Sickness' achingly evoked the longed-for minutiae of 'Home' – 'violet, and wren, / Blackbird, bluebell, hedgesparrow, tiny daisies' – but the list recalled nothing so much as Brooke's equivalent list in 'The Great Lover'. Only 'Pain' – with its anguished images of men and animals 'Dying in shellholes both, slain by the mud' – really delivered the promised counterblast to Brooke.

The first four sonnets had come quickly. The fifth, 'England the Mother', did not emerge until late May, and when it did, it was a failure. The opening sounded like bad Kipling: 'We have done our utmost England, terrible / And dear taskmistress, darling Mother and stern.' The sestet was less a counter to Brooke than a feeble and strained expression of Gurney's own brand of pastoral patriotism and his ongoing anxieties about his mental health:

Thy Love, Thy Love shall cherish, make us whole,
Where to the power of Death's destruction is weak,
Death impotent by boys bemocked at, who
Will leave unblotted in the soldier-soul
Gold of the daffodil, the sunset streak,
The innocence and joy of England's blue.

In fact, the vacuous final line of the poem (and the sequence) – 'The innocence and joy of England's blue' – was not that different from the concluding line of Brooke's 'The Soldier': 'In hearts at peace, under an English heaven'. This was not inappropriate. A year in France had shown Gurney a war very different from the cleansing, chivalric adventure Brooke had envisaged. Personal outrage and altruism made him want to challenge the Brooke version. Personal ambition made him want to challenge Brooke's continuing status as The War Poet. Yet another part of him knew that poetry, like music, was an accretion rather than a competition.

Soon after receiving Marion Scott's telegram in mid-July 1917 informing him that Sidgwick & Jackson, also Harvey's publisher, wanted to produce his poems, Gurney returned to the subject of Brooke. By then he had been wounded in the arm, retrained, emerged as the platoon crack shot and been attached to 184 Machine Gun Corps in the course of general preparations for the third battle of Ypres. Mulling over the strengths and weaknesses of his forthcoming collection, he felt readers would miss 'the devotion of self sacrifice, the splendid readiness for death that one finds in Grenfell, Brooke, Nichols, etc.'. The absence of that self-sacrificing element he attributed in part to his continuing health problems but also to his own particular notion of patriotism which rejected the 'hard and fast system which has sent so much of the flower of England's artists to risk death'. And in that frame of mind, how was he going to write poems like 'The Soldier'? Nor was he persuaded that 'poets believe what they write always'. But, having gone that far, he checked himself, unwilling to include Brooke in his gathering scepticism. 'Brooke was a sincere exception,' he admitted, adding 'but then, he was lucky; he died early in the war.' From then on, equivocal admiration seems to have settled as his position on Brooke. As he told Edward Thomas's friend John Haines in December 1917, he agreed that '*save* "The Great Lover" and the 5 Sonnets there is not much; and I doubt whether [Brooke] would have gone much further. But that is a great *"save".'*

Severn & Somme came out in mid-November 1917 with a red cover, price 2s. 6d. 'Sonnets 1917' concluded the volume (losing the second 't' on publication). Their dedication 'To the Memory of Rupert Brooke', on which Gurney insisted, had become a complicated mixture of tribute and riposte rather than the ironic counterblast he had originally intended. By then Gurney was back in England, after being gassed at St Julien in September, and had spent a spell in Edinburgh War Hospital, Bangour. He read the generally enthusiastic reviews while on a signalling course in Northumberland. The *Daily Telegraph* gratifyingly claimed that he possessed 'the authentic voice of the true poet'.

One of the most distinctive poems in the volume was 'Ballad of the Three Spectres', sent to Marion Scott in February 1917, the same month as the first four of his 'Sonnetts 1917'. The ballad described a route march to Ovillers 'In mud and water cold to the knee' during the Somme offensive in late 1916. The soldier protagonist, a descendant of Coleridge's Ancient Mariner, finds himself accompanied by 'three jeering, fleering spectres'. The first spectre predicts that the soldier will soon be returning 'on a fine stretcher', laughing because he has 'a nice Blighty' which will send him back to England. The second spectre disagrees, predicting that one day the soldier will 'freeze in mud to the marrow, / Then look his last on Picardie'. The third spectre trumps the other two. His prediction is that the soldier will 'stay untouched till the war's last dawning / Then live one hour of agony'. The ballad ended ominously:

> Liars the first two were. Behold me
>   At sloping arms by one–two–three;
> Waiting the time I shall discover
>   Whether the third spake verity.

By March 1918 the third spectre's prophecy was starting to come true. On the 28th Gurney wrote Marion Scott from the convalescent depot at Brancepeth Castle that he had 'felt and talked to (I am serious) the spirit of Beethoven'. The visitation heralded some kind of breakdown. On 19 June he sent Marion Scott a farewell letter from Lord Derby's War Hospital in Warrington:

My Dear Friend

    This is a good-bye letter, and written because I am afraid of slipping down and becoming a mere wreck – and I know you would rather know me dead than mad, and my only regret is that my Father will lose my allotment.

    Thank you most gratefully for all your kindness, dear Miss Scott. Your book is in my kit bag which will be sent home, and thank you so much for it – at Brancepeth I read it a lot.

    Goodbye with best wishes from one who owes you a lot.

    May God reward you and forgive me.

    Ivor Gurney

It was not the end. Gurney did not take his own life. In fact, his long 'hour of agony' had only just begun.

7

Dottyville

Siegfried Sassoon and Wilfred Owen, 18 August 1917

Craiglockhart War Hospital, Edinburgh. Saturday 18 August 1917. A sunny morning. Wilfred Owen stands outside the room occupied by Siegfried Sassoon. He is holding several copies of Sassoon's *The Old Huntsman and Other Poems*. He feels extremely nervous. He has told his mother (to whom he tells almost everything) that nothing like Sassoon's 'trench life sketches has ever been written or ever will be written'. Sassoon, he knows, is at Craiglockhart because of 'a letter to the Higher Command which was too plain-spoken'. He has already been there nearly a month, and Owen has finally got up the nerve to introduce himself.

He knocks softly. A voice tells him to enter. On the bed by the window sits Sassoon in a 'purple dressing suit', cleaning his golf clubs. He looks up briefly, not actually at Owen but at a spot somewhere above his head. For a moment Owen says nothing. He cannot take his eyes off the dressing suit. Purple is his favourite colour. He has a pair of purple slippers. He has even written a sonnet on the colour, and the way the sun lights up the fabric makes him think of one of his own phrases, 'bright darkling glows'. Even sitting down, Sassoon looks extremely tall. Also 'stately, with a fine firm chisel'd . . . head'. How old? Twenty-five? Owen is already storing up details to tell his

Left: Siegfried Sassoon by Glyn Philpot, 1917
Right: Wilfred Owen at Leith, July 1917

mother and his cousin and fellow aspiring poet, Leslie Gunston. Leslie is about to publish his first collection, *The Nymph and Other Poems*. He will particularly appreciate 'chisel'd', since he used the word in one of his own poems.

All this only takes an instant to flash through Owen's mind, but all the same he must say something. Which is a slight problem, because, in addition to his almost swooning excitement at actually being in Sassoon's presence, Owen has a slight stammer, a consequence of his shell shock. Advancing to the window, he shyly stammers out his request. Will Sassoon sign these copies of *The Old Huntsman*? Sassoon agrees, looking and sounding rather bored by the interruption. On the flyleaf of Owen's copy, he writes: 'To W.E.S. Owen, from Siegfried Sassoon. Craiglockhart. August 1917.'

If Owen stammers, Sassoon slurs and blurts. Sometimes he sounds positively incoherent so that it is hard to catch what he is saying. Disconcertingly, he never really meets your eye. But while he may look bored, the impression is misleading. He takes in much more than he lets on and is quietly registering certain details about his unexpected visitor. There is the stammer, of course; but that is common enough at Craiglockhart, or Dottyville as he calls it. Many of the 150 or so officers there have a stammer or a stutter; it seems to go with the authority role. Other ranks, conversely, tend to suffer from mutism. Owen, he notices, is on the short side, almost dapper with his neat moustache and centre parting. Just at the temples, his dark hair is already speckled with white. As Sassoon takes his time autographing the copies, he is aware of Owen standing deferentially at his side: rather like a subaltern conferring with a senior officer, he thinks to himself. Sassoon is struck by Owen's occasional 'charming honest smile'. Also by his voice. It has an unusual velvety quality rather at odds with his accent which, Sassoon cannot help noticing with an inner wince, is 'perceptively provincial'. All the same, man cannot live on golf alone, and Owen's palpable admiration for his poetry is undeniably gratifying, and he asks him to drop in again.

He does so three days later on the evening of 21 August. Sassoon is trying to decipher a letter from H G Wells. The letter, not to mention the 'dim pink ink' in which it is written, reminds Owen of Sassoon's literary connections. He has of course read some of Wells's

novels, but Sassoon actually knows Wells, receives letters from him.
Wells, as far as the two of them can make out, is even suggesting a
visit to Craiglockhart to see Sassoon and his doctor and mentor,
W H R Rivers. Not, it seems, because he is concerned about Sassoon
himself, but because Wells wants to talk about his latest book. It
occurs to Owen that Wells's handwriting is an almost exact analogy
to Sassoon's speech: both 'accord a slurred *suggestion* of words only'.
He is pleased with the thought. He will put that in his next letter
to his mother. On leaving, he mentions not very casually that he
writes poems himself. Sassoon suggests he bring some along the
next day.

Owen's poetry is much what Sassoon expected. Naturally there are
sonnets. Old-fashioned, over-literary. Used to Eddie Marsh's tough
criticism and his cut-and-thrust sessions with Graves, Sassoon does
not mince his words. No point in being polite. (Old work, Owen
quickly assures him.) But this piece of blank verse about Herakles and
Antaeus (misspelt, he cannot help noticing, as Antaeas) is really quite
good. Set apparently as an exercise by Owen's doctor, Brock. Sassoon
can imagine his Half Moon Street friends like Robbie Ross enjoying
some of the physical detail:

> those huge hands which small had strangled snakes
> Let slip the writhing of Antaeas' wrists;
> Those clubs of hands that wrenched the necks of bulls
> Now fumbled round the slim Antaeas' limbs
> Baffled.

Perhaps if they get to know each other better, they may turn out
to have more in common than Dottyville and poetry. He starts to
praise the piece, conscious that Owen is drinking in every word. And
this short lyric is rather lovely, too, in its way. Also written here. Called
'Song of Songs'. Begins 'Sing me at morn but only with thy laugh'.
In triplets. Not blank verse but some sort of near-rhyme: laugh / leaf
/ Life. Rather ingenious. French? Robert would be bound to know.
'Perfect,' he says, 'absolutely charming.' He asks for a copy. He could
send it to Ottoline Morrell.

Finally, Owen with a suppressed eagerness produces something
called 'The Dead-Beat'. It opens:

He dropped, more sullenly, than wearily,
  Became a lump of stench, a clot of meat,
  And none of us could kick him to his feet.
He blinked at my revolver, blearily.

Interesting, the same stanza as Tennyson used for 'In Memoriam'. This is certainly different – or is it? He reads on:

He didn't seem to know a war was on,
  Or see or smell the bloody trench at all . . .
  Perhaps he saw the crowd at Caxton Hall,
And that is why the fellow's pluck's all gone –

Now he has it. This is Owen's attempt to write like him. And not bad either. He remembers his Masefield take-off which Gosse had liked and passed on to Eddie. Which was what really started things off. That had begun as a parody and ended up as rather good pastiche. He reads on:

Not that the Kaiser frowns imperially.
  He sees his wife, how cosily she chats;
  Not his blue pal there, feeding fifty rats.
Hotels he sees, improved materially:

Where ministers smile ministerially.
  Sees Punch still grinning at the Belcher bloke;
  Bairnsfather, enlarging on his little joke,
While Belloc prophecies of last year, serially.

Not so good. In fact, pretty lame. But it picks up again in the last verse:

We sent him down at last, he seemed so bad,
  Although a strongish chap and quite unhurt.
  Next day I heard the Doc's fat laugh: 'That dirt
You sent me down last night's just died. So glad!'

For once he can see exactly what is wrong and explains it to Owen. The 'facetious bit' in the middle (stanzas three to four) is entirely out of key with the opening and the ending. This ruins the poem as a whole, but in themselves stanzas one, two and five are rather effective.

Owen takes the point. He admits he wrote 'The Dead-Beat' the previous evening after seeing Sassoon and that the poem is an attempt to do a 'trench life sketch' à la Sassoon. He switches the conversation to *The Old Huntsman*. His favourite is 'The Death-Bed', which describes the last thoughts of a dying officer in a military hospital. This is not, in fact, in Sassoon's colloquial, hard-hitting style, but forty-odd lines of blank verse in his lyrical, elegiac vein:

> He drowsed and was aware of silence heaped
> Round him, unshaken as the steadfast walls;
> Aqueous like floating rays of amber light,
> Soaring and quivering in the wings of sleep.
> Silence and safety; and his mortal shore
> Lipped by the inward, moonless waves of death.

Sassoon says it is his own favourite. Eddie Marsh is going to include it with some other poems of his in the next *Georgian Poetry* anthology which will be coming out before the end of the year. Perhaps, suggests Sassoon (repeating what he did not manage to say to Graves), Owen himself should not be too eager to rush into print. When Owen at last reluctantly takes his leave, Sassoon gives him one final piece of encouragement: 'Sweat your guts out writing poetry.'

What had brought Owen and Sassoon to Craiglockhart? Owen was there as an out-and-out shell shocker. After training with the 5th (Reserve) Manchesters, he had gone out to France in late December 1916, tingling with 'fine heroic feeling', and joined the 2nd Manchesters as a platoon commander. By 16 January, he could tell his mother that he had already 'suffered seventh hell': 'I have not been at the front. I have been in front of it.'

He had indeed. He and his platoon had held a dug-out for fifty hours in no man's land in the Serre–Beaumont Hamel section of the line. There, under constant bombardment, twenty-five of them stood squashed together underground in a foot or two of water with about four feet of air between them and the roof. Being an old German dug-out, it was deep and well-made but naturally had the disadvantage that the two entrances faced the German guns. One of these had been 'blown in & blocked'; a sentry was posted in the other, Owen ordering him to come halfway down the steps when the shelling was worst. Owen's other responsibilities included another dug-out even further ahead to which he had led eighteen bombers. It was only a matter of 150 yards, but, when he checked on them at 6 p.m. on the Sunday evening, it took him half an hour to cover the distance. 'I was chiefly annoyed by our own machine guns from behind,' he noted laconically. 'The seeng-seeng-seeng of the bullets reminded me of Mary's canary. On the whole I can support the canary better.'

During that lost weekend in the waterlogged, claustrophobic dugout, time seemed to stop. Owen admitted to his mother that his nerve almost cracked and he was close to letting go and drowning in the slowly rising water. Somewhat miraculously, he only had one casualty, one of the sentries, who, despite Owen's precautions, was blown down the steps and blinded by the blast of a nearby shell.

This first experience of the front seared itself into Owen's imagination. No man's land came to embody the horror. 'It is pock-marked like a body of foulest disease and its odour is the breath of cancer,' he wrote his mother, adding that, covered with snow, it resembled 'the face of the moon chaotic, crater-ridden, uninhabitable, awful, the abode of madness'. No one in England, he insisted, had any idea what conditions were like, what the troops suffered: 'Coal, water, candles, accommodation, everything is scarce.' But while he was storing up images of the terrors of war, he was also, inevitably and necessarily, adopting the mind-set of the serving officer. Elated at having survived and 'already done "a Bit"', he was starting to feel the traditional military contempt for civilian ignorance and smugness. 'Those "Somme Pictures,"' he told his mother, referring to a popular propaganda film made about the Somme, 'are the laughing stock of the army – like the trenches on exhibition in Kensington.'

That first stint was succeeded by another in the same sector only days later. For two days and nights Owen and his men lay 'marooned on a frozen desert' up on Redan Ridge, looking across to Serre and vulnerable to fire from the east and north. This time they were 'almost wusser' off than in the dug-out, having 'to lie in the snow under the deadly wind'. The position was so exposed that it was too dangerous to stand up or move about and so cold that their army cookers were useless for melting ice for water. They lay there until relieved, tormented by thirst and aching feet, rained on by showers of earth from the hourly barrage of whizz-bangs which landed only yards away, but never quite found their mark. Occasionally a hawk would circle overhead.

All that was terrible enough. But, he told his mother, it was not so much the weather, tiredness and the proximity of death that really got him down. It was, as Gurney had told Marion Scott, the 'Ugliness':

> Hideous landscapes, vile noises, foul language and nothing but foul, even from one's own mouth (for all are devil ridden), everything un-natural, broken, blasted; the distortion of the dead, whose unburiable bodies sit outside the dug-outs all day, all night, the most execrable sights on earth . . . and a week later to come back and find them still sitting there . . .

Although he spent February safe in Abbeville doing a transport officer course, those two initial experiences had affected Owen more than he or anyone else realised. One dark night in early March, he tumbled fifteen feet into a wrecked cellar, hitting his head. He seems to have lain there concussed and semi-conscious for a considerable time before being discovered. A spell in a casualty clearing station was followed by a further spell at the front in April as part of the attack on Saint-Quentin. Here Owen and the rest of his battalion went over the top in a Somme-like advance in waves, completely exposed to the German guns. This act of 'slowly walking forward, showing ourselves openly' produced in Owen, he said, a feeling of 'extraordinary exul-tation', almost it seems a kind of sexual thrill. He kept himself and his men going by chanting:

> Keep the Line straight!
> Not so fast on the left!
> Steady on the Left!
> Not so fast!

At that point they were hit by a 'Tornado of Shells', which smashed the wave formation. Looking back, Owen saw 'the ground all crawling and wormy with wounded bodies'. He remembered no sense of horror, just 'an immense exultation at having got through the Barrage'. He spent the afternoon under fire in a shallow, captured trench, eating food left by the German troops and looking at their letters, abandoned mid-word. He and the others stayed in the line for another eight days, possibly longer, unable to wash or even take their boots off, lying 'in holes, where at any moment a shell might put us out'. One night he was literally blown up into the air by the impact of a large shell close by.

The culmination of all this led to some kind of breakdown. On 1 May, Owen was 'observed to be shaky and tremulous, and his conduct and manner were peculiar, and his memory was confused.' There seems also to have been an imputation of cowardice from his temporary commanding officer. On 2 May he was back at the casualty clearing station he had been in for concussion in March. From there, via another hospital near Le Havre, he was evacuated to Welsh Hospital, Netley in Hampshire and so on 26 June to Craiglockhart.

Sassoon's road to Craiglockhart was both less and more eventful. In 1916, after the death of his beloved friend David Thomas, he had been awarded the MC for his Mad Jack exploits. Trench fever then sent him back to England. There, through his friend the aesthete Robbie Ross, he was taken up by Lady Ottoline Morrell. (At their manor-house in Garsington outside Oxford, Lady Ottoline and her husband Philip had gathered round them a largely pacifist circle of writers, artists, intellectuals and conscientious objectors, including D H Lawrence, Bertrand Russell and Lytton Strachey.) After a lengthy convalescence, Sassoon was passed fit to go back to France in late January 1917, mostly glad that he had 'got another chance given me to die a decent death. And a damned uncomfortable one, probably.' A fortnight later, on the Waterloo–Southampton train, he was struck by how 'People seem to become happy in a bovine way as soon as they are relieved of all responsibility for the future. Soldiers going to the War are beasts of burden, probably condemned to death.'

This time Sassoon's reading matter for the front included Shakespeare's tragedies, Hardy's *The Dynasts*, Conrad's *A Set of Six*, Charles

Lamb's essays and Chaucer's *Canterbury Tales*. He was soon glad of
his little library in hospital in Rouen with German measles. His fellow-
patients played cards and talked 'the dullest obscenity'. He jotted down
one endlessly repeated witticism: "'I will arise and will go to my Father
and will say unto Him; 'Father, *Stand-at—ease!*'" So much for God.'
He lay awake at night, desperate at what he knew awaited him. Also,
and entirely characteristically, he knew that he would hate it if he had
to return to England 'without having been scarred and tortured once
more'.

He watched the older staff officers in Rouen, wining and dining
themselves. His disgust produced 'Base Details', a curtal or shortened
sonnet with, as it were, the legs (lines nine to twelve) cut away and
the torso of the poem jammed onto the feet:

> If I were fierce, and bald, and short of breath,
>   I'd live with scarlet Majors at the Base,
> And speed glum heroes up the line to death.
>   You'd see me with my puffy petulant face,
> Guzzling and gulping in the best hotel,
>   Reading the Roll of Honour. 'Poor young chap,'
> I'd say – 'I used to know his father well;
>   Yes, we've lost heavily in this last scrap.'
> And when the war is done and youth stone dead,
> I'd toddle safely home and die – in bed.

Typically, much of the poem's tight-lipped anger was expressed through
parody (both literary and social). The opening line parodied Yeats's
'When you are old and grey and full of sleep'; later phrases parodied
the euphemisms of upper-middle-class speech: scrap, toddle. The
parody set up the elegiac irony of the most telling lines: 'And speed
glum heroes up the line to death' and 'And when the war is done and
youth stone dead'. Sassoon longed to be a lyric poet but his real gifts
were for parody, irony and satire which the war caused to flower. For
him, there was also the secret thrill in playing the literary and class
renegade.

While Owen had sped up the line almost immediately, it took the
glumly heroic Sassoon nearly two months to see any action. He
communed with trees in the rain, thought of his and Graves's poetic

discovery Charles Sorley, who had loved the rain. He went to rest camp at Chipilly to join the 2nd Royal Welch Fusiliers. Had two outings to Amiens. Good dinners, bath, clean bed. Felt one night after drinking a good wine that he 'would gladly die to guard Amiens Cathedral from destruction'. Realised the next morning such feelings were not possible. Daydreamed of old point-to-point victories on Cockbird. Wondered whether he would live to see copies of *The Old Huntsman* from William Heinemann, his first collection of poems to be commercially published.

On Easter Monday, 9 April, he was closer, close enough at Basseux to hear the guns at Arras (where Edward Thomas was killed that morning by the blast from a shell). To escape the 'restlessness and forced gaiety', Sassoon retreated into *Far from the Madding Crowd*. The following Sunday night, 15 April, he was sitting in an underground tunnel on the Hindenburg Line, having seen dead bodies 'beyond description' – dismembered Tommies and Germans – and expecting to die the next morning.

He did not die. Instead he received a shoulder wound, a Blighty, and in four days was back in a London hospital at Denmark Hill. At some level it had all been an enormous anticlimax. He had failed to live up to his own heroic expectations. He was haunted by what he had seen, by what he knew was still going on. At night in the half-dark of the ward, 'horrors [came] creeping across the floor . . . a livid grinning face with bristly moustache [peered] at me over the edge of my bed, the hands clutching my sheets'. Compounding the trauma was survivor guilt. He had expected to die. He had gone to be a dead hero, a martyr. But here he was again safely back in England. Once his shoulder began to heal, he was sent to convalesce. *The Old Huntsman* appeared and was much praised. Gosse, Hardy and Arnold Bennett sent enthusiastic letters. The poet laureate Robert Bridges passed on his commendations. But it was E B Osborn in the *Morning Post* who wrote the words that Sassoon had longed to see in print: 'If this is not a great poet, true as well as new, then I have wasted a lifetime on trying to find what is, and what is not, the sovereign stuff.' He would have been less pleased to hear Gurney's reaction. He thought 'the Sassoons not as good as a whole as they might be'; but added percep- tively: 'They are charms to magic himself out of the present.'

The success was gratifying, but it made no difference. He talked to

Bertrand Russell and read his book *Justice in War-time*. He talked to other Garsington pacifists like Middleton Murry. He wrote bitterly facetious poems like 'The General': '"Good-morning, good-morning!" the General said'. He wrote valedictions to dead friends like 'To Any Dead Officer': 'I'm blind with tears, / Staring into the dark. Cheero! / I wish they'd killed you in a decent show.' He wrote the disturbed and disturbing 'The Rear-Guard' in which a dead body is mistaken for a sleeping soldier. He began to feel that he must make some larger, more decisive, more public protest against the war. On 15 June 1917, after much heart- and conscience-searching, and with Russell's and Murry's help, he wrote a terse statement of his views, initially for private distribution but with a much wider audience ultimately in mind:

> I am making this statement as an act of wilful defiance of military authority, because I believe that the War is being deliberately prolonged by those who have the power to end it. I am a soldier, convinced that I am acting on behalf of soldiers. I believe that this War, upon which I entered as a war of defence and liberation, has now become a war of aggression and conquest. I believe that the purposes for which I and my fellow-soldiers entered upon this War should have been so clearly stated as to have made it impossible for them to be changed without our knowledge, and that, had this been done, the objects which actuated us would now be attainable by negotiation.
>
> I have seen and endured the sufferings of the troops, and I can no longer be a party to prolonging those sufferings for ends which I believe to be evil and unjust.
>
> I am not protesting against the military conduct of the War, but against the political errors and insincerities for which the fighting men are being sacrificed.
>
> On behalf of those who are suffering now, I make this protest against the deception which is being practised on them. Also I believe that it may help to destroy the callous complacence with which the majority of those at home regard the continuance of the agonies which they do not share, and which they have not sufficient imagination to realise.

As a statement, it was naive, intellectually muddled and never going to make any difference to the progress of the war. As an act, it was conspicuously courageous in addition to being martyrous and, probably, as a not unsympathetic Arnold Bennett told Sassoon, a product of spiritual pride. Sassoon was prepared for a furore, even welcomed it. Most of his friends were thrown into a state of serious agitation and trepidation on his account. What Sassoon planned was to have his statement read out in the House of Commons and subsequently printed in *The Times*.

It was clear that once the army knew of his views a court martial was likely, possibly further action. But, as in April when he expected to die, things turned out very differently. On being ordered to report back for duty in early July, Sassoon sent a copy of his statement to his commanding officer. In an accompanying note, he apologised for the unpleasantness he knew he was causing, reaffirmed his determination not to undertake further military duties and ended by saying that he was 'fully aware of what he was letting himself in for'. What happened next was something nobody had counted on. Partly as a result of earnest representations from Robert Graves, now an instructor in England, the army played it remarkably cool. There was no court martial. Instead Sassoon was put in front of a second medical board – he cut the first – which diagnosed a nervous breakdown and recommended he be sent to Craiglockhart. On 23 July he arrived at Dottyville. Graves had been supposed to escort him, but missed the train. When his protest was read out in the House of Commons a few days later, the Under-Secretary for War 'was able to reassure the House that the 'extremely gallant officer' was ill and that members should not exploit 'a young man in such a state of mind'.

After the first three meetings had broken the ice, Owen began going to Sassoon's room most evenings to talk poetry. They talked about contemporary poets and showed each other work in progress. Since Sassoon had already hit on his own method, what Owen initially had to offer was ardent – even embarrassingly ardent – hero-worship. This was not the kind of response Sassoon was used to, and, though gratifying, it made him uncomfortable. It is true that he had at last broken into the Georgian fold, and Marsh wanted no fewer than eight pieces from *The Old Huntsman* for his forthcoming third anthology, *Georgian Poetry 1916–1917*. But Marsh remained, as D H Lawrence had said, 'a bit of a policeman in poetry'. So in his way did Graves, who could be very blunt in his criticism as well as affectionate in his friendly concern. What Owen was offering was something different. He was offering to play the faithful squire to Sassoon's quixotic knight. And Sassoon felt flattered.

Not that Owen was entirely acquiescent. As he gained confidence, he too began to suggest improvements to the poems Sassoon was showing him. On 7 September, he was agog to tell his mother that, on his prompting, Sassoon was going to change some lines he had read Owen that very evening. But in the main Owen saw himself as disciple to Sassoon's teacher. As a teacher, what Sassoon principally had to offer was encouragement, permission really, to write directly about the war. Also to adopt a more inclusive – a tougher – version of Keats's aesthetic mantra 'Beauty is truth, truth Beauty'. Owen had asked his mother and cousin Leslie to send him any old manuscripts they had, and Sassoon seems to have gone through these. In contrast to the emotional understatement he himself was now aiming for, what he detected in much of Owen's poetry, despite its 'skill in rich and melodious combinations of words', was an over-ripe quality, 'an almost embarrassing sweetness in the sentiment'. One example he later claimed to have pointed out was the line 'She dreams of golden gardens and sweet glooms' – rather the sort of line that Marsh had blue-pencilled in Sassoon's own poems back in 1913. As helpful as anything in rescuing Owen from the thrall of his own juvenilia was Sassoon's summary debunking of Leslie Gunston's old-fashioned poetry. 'Sassoon considers E L Gunston not only flatulent, but hopeless', Owen told his mother. He would have to have been extremely saintly not to feel a certain *Schadenfreude* at this dismissal. But Owen also – mostly – saw that poetry, as he had previously conceived it, was not the point.

Sassoon endorsed the lesson with the firm but sympathetic reading he gave the new poems Owen immediately started to produce. One instance was 'Anthem for Doomed Youth'. The first draft opened 'What minute bells for these who die so fast?' with 'minute' crossed out and 'passing' substituted; it was mostly unrhymed. Very much a rough sketch though clearly a sonnet in embryo, it did, however, already contain the poignant final line with its extra restraining beat: 'And each slow Dusk, a drawing-down of blinds'. Sassoon pencilled in various changes, including 'the guns' in the second line, which had originally read: 'Only the monstrous anger of our guns'. There were several

subsequent versions, now rhymed, in which the opening line became
'What passing bells for you who die in herds' – rhyming with 'Only
the stuttering rifles' rattled words' – and the title flickered between
'Anthem to' and 'Anthem for Dead Youth'. Eventually with additional
emendations from Sassoon, Owen achieved the form of the poem
that has become famous:

> What passing-bells for these who die as cattle?
>   – Only the monstrous anger of the guns.
>   Only the stuttering rifles' rapid rattle
> Can patter out their hasty orisons.
> No mockeries now for them; no prayers nor bells;
>   Nor any voice of mourning save the choirs, –
> The shrill, demented choirs of wailing shells;
>   And bugles calling for them from sad shires.
>
> What candles may be held to speed them all?
>   Not in the hands of boys but in their eyes
> Shall shine the holy glimmers of goodbyes.
>   The pallor of girls' brows shall be their pall;
> Their flowers the tenderness of patient minds,
> And each slow dusk a drawing-down of blinds.

One of Sassoon's principal contributions was to line thirteen, where
the minds had originally been 'sweet white' and then 'silent' before
Sassoon's more sympathetic 'patient'. He also changed the title to the
more ominous 'Anthem for Doomed Youth' and suggested Owen try
it on the *Nation*.

This was the poem that apparently convinced Sassoon that little
Wilfred, as he sometimes thought of his friend, was a poet to be taken
seriously and not merely the talented amateur he had previously
assumed. Owen was soon providing plenty of evidence of what he
could do, now that Sassoon had helped to unlock the floodgates. The
results included 'The Next War', early drafts of 'Dulce et Decorum Est'
and 'Disabled', probably also 'The Chances', 'Conscious', 'Inspection',
'The Letter' and 'At a Calvary near the Ancre'.

'Dulce et Decorum Est' was a visceral description of a gas attack:
'Gas! GAS! Quick, boys! – An ecstasy of fumbling'. One exhausted

soldier fails to put on 'the clumsy helmet' in time, and his terrible fate continues to haunt the speaker. Owen's poem, a kind of irregular double-sonnet, offered a verse complement to the concluding section of Sassoon's public letter of protest. It too was aimed at 'the callous complacence with which the majority of those at home regard the continuance of the agonies which they do not share, and which they have not sufficient imagination to realise'. The ending of the poem spelled out the message in terms more graphic than anything in Sassoon's own war poems:

> If in some smothering dreams you too could pace
> Behind the wagon that we flung him in,
> And watch the white eyes writhing in his face,
> His hanging face, like a devil's sick of sin;
> If you could hear, at every jolt, the blood
> Come gargling from the froth-corrupted lungs,
> Obscene as cancer, bitter as the cud
> Of vile, incurable sores on innocent tongues, –
> My friend, you would not tell with such high zest
> To children ardent for some desperate glory,
> The old Lie: Dulce et decorum est
> Pro patria mori.

'Dulce et Decorum Est' was originally dedicated to the popular children's writer and author of patriotic verses, Jessie Pope. The intended irony was similar to that of Gurney's dedication of his five sonnets to Brooke, and, by an odd coincidence, Gurney himself was not far away in Ward 24, Edinburgh War Hospital, Bangour. Unlike Gurney, however, Owen soon dropped the ironic dedication. Perhaps, following Sassoon, he came to feel that it was more a class – upper-middle, public school – he wanted to excoriate rather than an individual. He translated the Latin tag to his mother as *It is sweet and meet to die for one's country*, adding scornfully: *'Sweet and decorous!'*

'Disabled' brought Owen to the attention of Graves. On 13 October Graves visited Craiglockhart to see Sassoon and briefly met Owen. Sassoon showed the recently written 'Disabled' to Graves, who wrote Owen a letter in which enthusiasm was liberally laced with technical instruction. While Graves called it 'a damn fine poem', he definitely wanted to put Owen in his poetic place and listed a series of howlers which Owen had perpetrated. Graves ended with a nice compliment about having 'no doubt that if you turned seriously to writing, you could obtain Parnassus in no time while I'm still struggling on the knees of that stubborn peak', but Owen had already detected a note of condescension in Graves's manner towards him during his visit. He told his mother: 'It seems Graves was mightily impressed, and considers me a kind of *Find*!!' It was a boast, of course, to his proudest supporter, and he was obviously chuffed by Graves's interest – he may have known by this time that Graves would also be substantially represented in *Georgian Poetry 1916–1917*. But the pointed addition of the latter's rank in the follow-up remark shows that Owen knew he had been patronised: 'No thanks, Captain Graves! I'll find myself in due time.' In fact, Graves was probably impressed despite himself as well as a bit jealous too of his old friend Sassons's protégé.

Sassoon kept his own feelings of superiority towards Owen well hidden as the two became closer friends. Or else Owen was so besotted that he did not notice it or mind. They seem to have traded more than literary confidences. Sassoon might not have been as hot as Graves at guessing who was 'so', but he could spot homo-erotic poetry when he saw it. If the physicality of the lines about Herakles and Antaeus wrestling did not give away Owen's sexual preferences, any number of other poems he was shown would have done so: 'It was a navy boy', for instance, or 'Maundy Thursday' in which, instead of kissing the proffered cross, the speaker kisses 'the warm live hand that held the thing'. Sassoon himself could easily have responded by showing Owen 'A Subaltern' about David Thomas, or *Hyacinth*. A meaningful look would then have been enough. However, Sassoon later said that he received Owen's 'fullest confidences', so there may well have been some mutual confessions – at least on Owen's side; Sassoon at thirty-one seems still to have been a virgin.

A more obvious way in which Sassoon was able to help Owen was by agreeing, or offering, to give him poems for the *Hydra*, the fortnightly Craiglockhart magazine which Owen was editing. The 1 September issue contained both Sassoon's 'Dreamers' and Owen's 'Song of Songs'. 'Dreamers', another sonnet, contrasted the extra-ordinary conditions of trench life – 'Soldiers are citizens of death's grey land / Drawing no dividend from time's to-morrows' – with the

ordinary peacetime pursuits and routines which both distract and
sustain the soldiers:

> I see them in foul dug-outs, gnawed by rats,
>   And in the ruined trenches, lashed with rain,
> Dreaming of things they did with balls and bats,
>   And mocked by hopeless longing to regain
> Bank-holidays, and picture shows, and spats,
>   And going to the office in the train.

Either the editor or his new friend had the happy thought of placing
'Dreamers' on the same page as 'News' items about bowls, golf and
tennis – not quite cricket, but close enough to 'things they did with
balls and bats'. The 15 September issue of the *Hydra* carried 'The
Rear-Guard', while 29 September had 'Wirers' as well as Owen's 'The
Next War' with an epigraph from Sassoon. 'The Next War' shows
how, chameleonlike, Owen was able to pick up and use Sassoon's
colloquial tone – 'Out there, we've walked quite friendly up to Death /
Sat down and eaten with him, cool and bland' – while preserving his
own more ornate vocabulary. Sassoon could easily have written 'Out
there . . . eaten with him', but not the more Keatsian 'cool and bland' –
he would have put something mock-jaunty like 'shook his hand'. Owen
was starting to see how he could play one tone off against the other.

All in all, Owen and Sassoon had eleven weeks together at Craiglockhart before Owen was passed fit and left for leave followed by a return
to light military duties. Two final evenings in Edinburgh at the Conser-
vative Club on 26 October and 3 November allowed the teacher to
give his departing disciple one final lesson plus a parting gift. On the
first evening, after dinner, Sassoon read some new verse to Owen. Not
his own this time but lines from *A Human Voice*, a book he had been
sent by its author Aylmer Strong:

> O is it true I have become
> This gourd, this gothic vacuum? . . .
>
> What cassock'd misanthrope,
> Hawking peace-canticles for glory-gain,
> Hymns from his rostrum'd height th'epopt of Hate?

The word that apparently really set them off was 'epopt' – meaning epic song – though the first couplet had 'already scored heavily'. Soon the two were paralytic with laughter. The lesson – which the over-earnest Owen certainly needed to learn and apply – was that some poetry is so splendidly bad that it is funny. On the second evening, Owen's last day in Edinburgh, Sassoon gave him an envelope to be opened later when he was on his own. The contents were a kind of graduation certificate.

8

Cool Madness and Dead Man's Dump

Robert Nichols and Isaac Rosenberg,
November 1917

Isaac Rosenberg and Robert Nichols never met in person, yet in September 1917 they had an unlikely meeting of a kind.

They were born at opposite ends of the social scale: Rosenberg in Bristol in 1890, Nichols on the Isle of Wight three years later. Rosenberg was the eldest son of Lithuanian Jewish immigrants who moved to Stepney in East London when he was seven. The Nichols family London address was off Portman Square, W1; they also had a place in Essex. Rosenberg left Baker Street Board School at fourteen and worked for an art publisher. Nichols left Winchester College under a cloud at sixteen and spent the next three years being crammed for Trinity College, Oxford. Both from an early age saw themselves as poets.

Rosenberg also saw himself as a painter, and his first big break came when he was discovered by a wealthy art-lover who sponsored him to go to the Slade. There, before dropping out in March 1913, he studied with fellow-students Stanley Spencer, Dora Carrington, Mark Gertler and David Bomberg, and learnt that 'Art is not a plaything, it is blood and tears'. At the same time he kept plugging away at the poetry and in 1912 had a small pamphlet *Night and Day* privately printed: fifty copies at a cost of £2.

Left: Robert Nichols, c.1915
Right: Isaac Rosenberg, 1917

Rosenberg's next break came in November 1913 when he met Eddie Marsh through Mark Gertler. Marsh at once took Rosenberg up, invited him to breakfast at Gray's Inn and earmarked him as a potential contributor to *Georgian Drawings*, a companion project to *Georgian Poetry* which never in the end got off the ground. Marsh's support included buying Rosenberg's *Sacred Love*, probably in May 1914. This study of semi-clothed young men and women was foregrounded by a young man, supplicating, naked. Marsh hung the painting at the foot of the bed in his spare room, where Brooke presumably woke up to it a couple of months later before breakfasting with Sassoon. Marsh also gave Rosenberg detailed criticism of his knottily impressive but obscure poems, of which the opening lines of 'Midsummer Frost' are characteristic:

> A July ghost, aghast at the strange winter,
> Wonders, at burning noon, (all summer seeming),
> How, like a sad thought buried in light woven words,
> Winter, an alien presence, is ambushed here.

The same poem contained the arrestingly mysterious image of the heart as 'A frozen pool whereon mirth dances; / Where the shining boys would fish'. For Rosenberg, it was mostly Marsh's attention that mattered, although he did make changes at Marsh's suggestion, cutting 'woven' from the third line of 'Midsummer Frost'.

The crammers duly did their stuff for Nichols, and he went up to Trinity College in October 1913. *His* big break was meeting the eccentric, musical undergraduate Philip Heseltine (later known as Peter Warlock). Grieg, poetry, D H Lawrence, lovelorn stories and *Crème Napoléon* sealed the friendship. Like Rosenberg, Nichols was producing poetry at a prodigious rate: pastoral poems with fauns, fragments of poetic drama, lyric sequences. 'The Hill', the first section of a sequence entitled 'A Triptych', showed Mary singing a prophetic song to baby Jesus; the second section, 'The Tower', described Judas slipping away from the Last Supper ('night went out to the night'); the third, 'The Tree', portrayed Judas hanging himself ('The thing that stared up at the giddy day').

While Rosenberg, after giving up the Slade, was trying to gain a precarious foothold in the London cultural world, Nichols was getting

into scrapes – something for which he had a particular talent. On
21 November 1913, the Chancellor of the Exchequer, Lloyd George,
spoke at the Oxford Union to promote the Liberal Government's Land
Reform programme. Speaking at Bedford the previous month, he had
caused a stir with his remarks on crop damage: 'Here is one farmer
who was sowing his crop – it was a field of mangolds. The man assured
me that there was not one mangold out [of] a dozen which was not
pecked and destroyed by pheasants . . .' The idea of the gentry's
pheasants eating the hard-working farmer's mangel-wurzels caught
the public imagination, and there was a lively debate in the press
about whether mangel-wurzels did or did not form part of a
pheasant's ordinary diet. As the Chancellor of the Exchequer
processed with other dignitaries into the Oxford Union, Nichols and
other undergraduates bombarded him with pheasants and mangel-
wurzels. Nichols may even have been the one to score a direct hit
on Lloyd George with a large pheasant, though he later claimed only
to have knocked off His Grace of Winchester's 'episcopal top-hat' with
a mangel-wurzel.

Harmless as the jape was, it was noticed and cannot have helped
when Nichols failed his exams in his second term, was rusticated and
then failed his re-sits. That ended his Oxford career, and when war
broke out at the beginning of August, his future was very much up
in the air. Towards the end of September, aged twenty-one, he applied
for a commission, and on 13 October, after some uncertainty as to
whether he was up to the marching, he was accepted as a second
lieutenant in the 104th Brigade, Royal Field Artillery.

By this time Rosenberg was a couple of continents away. His never
robust health had collapsed and, with Marsh's help, he had joined
his married sister in Cape Town. He thought Cape Town 'an infernal
city', full of money-grubbing Philistines, but he was soon making
his mark. He lectured on art, published poems, did commissions,
and met and stayed with people of wealth and influence. Even his
health improved. Two self-portraits – a right and a left semi-profile
in which he wore the same green felt hat – suggested contrasting
takes on this new world. The more full-face right profile he described
to Marsh as 'very gay and cocky', although quizzical and self-
contained might have fitted just as well. The left profile, with a
pronounced five o'clock shadow, was distinctly sardonic, wary, even

supercilious. In a different key again, he had written his first war poem, 'On Receiving News of the War'. It had a hauntingly chilly opening line – 'Snow is a strange white word' – and an apocalyptic, Blakeian conclusion:

> O! ancient crimson curse!
> Corrode, consume.
> Give back this universe
> Its pristine bloom.

But even while enjoying his successes, Rosenberg was thinking of returning to England and left Cape Town in February 1915. Apparently when boarding the ship, he failed to secure his paintings properly and lost many of them in the harbour.

March saw Rosenberg back with his parents in Stepney and in April – thanks to Marsh buying three paintings – he had another pamphlet of poems published: *Youth* (a hundred copies at a cost of £2 10*s*.). When news of Rupert Brooke's death reached England in late April, Rosenberg at once wrote to Marsh:

> I am so sorry – what else can I say?
>   But he himself has said 'What is more safe than death?' For us is the hurt who feel about English literature, and for you who knew him and feel his irreparable loss.

Such praise was not just flannel for his main patron. Rosenberg did admire Brooke's more metaphysical poems like 'Town and Country' and 'Clouds', though he never took to the 'begloried sonnets', as he called them, and never, like Sassoon, Nichols and others, felt remotely drawn to imitate Brooke. He was, however, like Edward Thomas, soon seriously thinking of enlisting. This was a direct consequence of poverty and lack of available work; it had nothing to do with a Brookeian or Thomasian patriotism. Quite the contrary: by enlisting, as he told a new patron Sydney Schiff, 'I would be doing the most criminal thing a man can do'.

By this point Nichols was six months into his training as a horse gunner. A photograph that April of 1915 shows him in uniform, legs crossed, fingers laced, looking full-faced and composed. Inside, however, he was starting to prepare himself for the front and, like Sassoon, trying to write himself into an appropriate frame of mind. Following Brooke, Nichols produced his own 'Five Sonnets upon Imminent Departure'. The final sonnet mixed Brooke and Hamlet:

> If it should hap, I being summoned hence
>   To an unknown and all too hazardous bourne,
> One should bring news charged with this heavy sense: –
> *He has gone further and cannot return* . . .

Brooke's was not the only voice he was trying out. The conclusion of 'Invocation' sounded plausibly Kiplingesque in its calculated archaisms and syntactical compressions:

> Therefore possess me and so dower
>   The sword's weak spot that the true blade
> May not in least nor direst hour
>   Betray the spirit unafraid.

This appeared in *The Times* on 15 May and was reprinted in early August in a sixteen-page *Times* supplement of war poems by Hardy, Kipling, Bridges, de la Mare and others. Nichols was beginning to find his poetic feet.

Soon afterwards, he was off. On 27 August he and D Battery, 104th Brigade Royal Field Artillery reached Calais. Over the next few days the battery marched via St Omer and Hazebrouck to Armentières. En route, they passed Ploegsteert where Charles Sorley was stationed, and Nichols later claimed to have caught a glimpse of him, 'asleep in a dugout'. On 31 August he heard that Elkin Matthews had agreed to bring out his first collection, *Invocation*. September 6th, his twenty-second birthday, was, according to the last entry in his brief diary, 'all gold and blue' as they trekked in the heat past harvested corn. 'Men and teams going a little better', he noted; he felt perfectly content.

Then they were at the front itself: 'an ignominious rabbit-warren to the eye and sewage-farm to the nose', as he much later remembered it. Over the next two to three weeks, he and his battery took part in the bombardment which preceded the Artois–Loos Offensive. He visited his younger brother Phil in a neighbouring battalion. 'Brother meets brother in the face of the enemy', he greeted him heroically. He sent his sister Anne a jaunty description of having his hair cut in a field before beating a hasty retreat when the German shells got too close. A letter on 22 September informed his father: 'the past is cut off, or rather connected only by the slender thread of letters etc.'

His next letter, on 25 September, came from hospital, and the following day he left the front. 'They found me done up utterly,' he told his father, '. . . having been knocked down twice, once by the blast of a gun and once by a spent bullet.' But he was eager to assure his father, and himself, that though 'my nerves have played me false, do not think that I disgraced myself', adding ' – as a matter of fact I think I did all right in that way.' All the same his anxiety in 'Invocation' had proved prophetic: 'The sword's weak spot' had let him down in the 'direst hour'. Or, as he more prosaically explained to his father, 'the strain tells on you and saps your strength'.

By early October 1915, Nichols was in a military hospital in Lincoln. The medical board that assessed him on 12 October entered his disability as neurasthenia, exacerbated by serving at the front. The board noted, however, that he had been under treatment for neurasthenia before joining the army. Nichols was described as in an excitable nervous condition and complaining of headaches and sleeplessness. The board thought him unlikely ever to return to General Service. He was sent to another hospital, this time in Palace Green, Kensington, London and ordered to present himself to a further board in two months' time.

It was at Palace Green that he received news of the death of an Oxford friend, started to have hallucinations and his 'heart began to go'. He was put under the care of the neurologist Henry Head, 'a plump, bland, slightly Mephistophilean figure', whose first question to Nichols was whether he liked Conrad's work. The two immediately clicked, and Head quickly became Nichols's equivalent to Sassoon's Rivers: a combination of mentor, friend, confidant and recipient of many letters. When his old Oxford friend Philip Heseltine visited Nichols in hospital, he brought D H Lawrence with him. The meeting initiated a convoluted, sometimes comic relationship between Nichols, Lawrence and Frieda, his 'hard-soft great female egg of a wife', as Nichols described her. In addition to the hallucinations and neurasthenia, Nichols would by now have been well aware that he had syphilis. According to one later version, he picked it up from a prostitute at a party before embarking for France. Robert Graves, writing much nearer the time, claimed that Nichols contracted syphilis after his return to England: 'It was the usual story – shellshock, friends all killed, too much champagne, sex, desperate fornication, syphilis.'

As Nichols was leaving the front, Rosenberg was inching his way towards it. In September and early October 1915, he took evening classes in block-making, hoping this would lead to work in the printing trade. It didn't. His patrons Marsh and Sydney Schiff helped out where they could with small purchases and loans; but it was not enough. Rosenberg had not changed his attitude towards enlisting. He was fully aware of 'the immorality of joining with no patriotic convictions', of the prospect of getting killed 'in the prime and vigour' of his powers, and of the shock to his mother. But, by late October 1915, he had run out of options. He had hoped to join the Royal Army Medical Corps, but found himself instead at Bury St Edmunds in the 12th Suffolk Regiment, 40th Division. Less than five foot three inches in height, he was placed in the Bantam Battalion. The other bantams were 'a horrible rabble,' he informed Marsh, before dropping in the kind of literary allusion he knew his patron would appreciate: 'Falstaff's scarecrows were nothing to these.' To Schiff, a fellow-Jew, he could be, and was, more direct:

> I have to eat out of a basin together with some horribly smelling scavenger who spits and sneezes into it . . . I don't mind the hard sleeping the stiff marches etc but this is unbearable. Besides my being a Jew makes it bad amongst these wretches.

Within weeks he too was in hospital, having tripped up 'running before the colonel' and cut his hands.

In early January 1916, Rosenberg was transferred to the 12th South Lancashires at Blackdown Camp, Farnborough. He wrote to Marsh to inform him of the move and to thank him for sorting out the

16s. 6d. separation allowance which had not reached his mother as arranged. The food was skimpy; he had had a bad cold and been 'coal fatiguing all day (a most inhuman job)'. He bemoaned the introduction of conscription that month: both in itself and because of 'the hope it will give to the enemy to have brought England to that step'.

For Nichols, the first half of 1916 revolved around more medical boards. Each one recorded slightly different versions of his condition and circumstances. The first on 12 January described him as having gone into the firing line on 16 September 1915 and from the first showing signs of sleeplessness and lack of concentration. It added that he was engaged in the preparation for the offensive of 25–6 September but had not actually been under fire, that he had collapsed on the 26th and been invalided home with nervous lack of control and emotional instability. The board considered him much improved though still unfit for General Service for a further four months and from any service for three. The major difference from his initial board was whether or not his disability had been caused by his military service. This time the answer was a simple Yes.

The board in April sent Nichols back to his depot for light duties but within a couple of days he broke down again and was back on sick leave. According to a Red Cross report, hospitality was arranged for him at a Mrs Denny's at Staplefield Place in Sussex, but his condition showed no improvement. While confirming the general diagnosis of a nervous breakdown, the report added – with a certain note of impatience – that Nichols was 'very highly strung, and full of himself and of his ailments' and seemed to have no friends. Also that he had 'very pronounced literary tastes, and will sit indoors all day writing poetry, while the following day he will be rushing about all over the country'. By 8 August, the date of his final board, the army had had enough of him and his subjective symptoms. The board reaffirmed the earlier finding that his disability had in no way been caused by his military service and concluded that, while apparently organically sound, temperamentally he was in no condition to continue as an officer. It was, no doubt, a relief to both sides when on 9 September he was gazetted as 'relinquishing his commission on account of ill health' and declared permanently unfit for General or Home Service. Sometimes at Mrs Denny's in Sussex, sometimes with his grandfather

in Torquay, sometimes in London or in Essex, Nichols yo-yoed around
the country, writing furiously.

Rosenberg was no more cut out to be a private than Nichols an
officer. He was, like Ivor Gurney, a completely hopeless soldier:
clumsy, untidy and absent-minded. Also, like Gurney, Rosenberg was
ironically much healthier in the army than in civilian life due to the
regular exercise and diet. But whereas Gurney was able – up to a
point – to mitigate his situation by playing the fool, Rosenberg could
not. He felt a sense of difference between himself and those he
served with – as a writer, a painter and a Jew – and he showed it.
One thing which kept him going was the interest of Lascelles
Abercrombie, whose 'Hymn to Love' he had long admired and to
whom he had sent some poems in 1915. Abercrombie was encouraging: 'what I like most in your songs is your ability to make the
concealed poetic power in words come flashing out. Some of your
phrases are remarkable; no one who tries to write poetry would help
envying some of them.' Rosenberg was soon quoting Abercrombie's
praise to Marsh and Schiff. It was not long before he was receiving
similar plaudits from another Georgian, Gordon Bottomley, to
whom he also sent his work.

In March 1916, Rosenberg was transferred to the 11th Battalion of
the King's Own Lancasters and expected to be sent to France. The order
came in May, and the troops were given six days' pre-embarkation
leave. Rosenberg spent his in London, getting another small pamphlet
printed. This contained a two-scene play *Moses* and nine shortish
poems, several recycled from *Youth*.

Moses imagined a lost episode from the life of the Old Testament
prophet and leader. The 'droll' plot, as Rosenberg outlined it to
Marsh, went like this: 'There is a famine in Egypt caused by the super-
abundance of slaves who eat up all the food meant for the masters.
To prevent this, all the back molars of the slaves are drawn, so they
eat less. The plot works around this.' Wisely, the odontological aspects
of the drama were kept to a minimum.

Moses, as a figure, deeply appealed to Rosenberg. He was Jewish, a
chosen one, an outsider forced to live among an alien and oppressive
people. The months of military training had sharpened Rosenberg's
sense of English anti-Semitism, and he certainly considered army life
a form of slavery. Even more sympathetically, Moses was a double

Recruiting Office, 1914.

German soldiers go to the Front, August 1914.

Russian transport travelling to Przemsyl, September 1914.

British soldiers wait before moving up at the Somme, 1916.

The road near Soissons, after the Battle of the Aisne, May 1917.

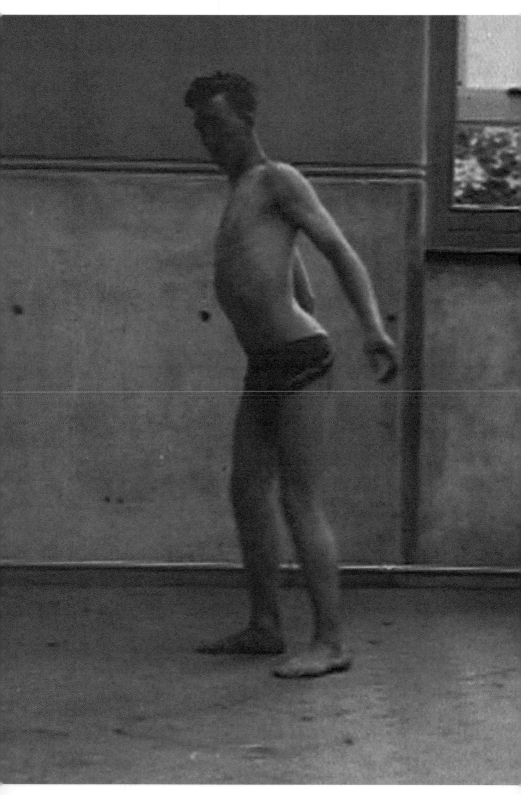

A shell-shocked soldier at Netley Hospital, Southampton, 1917.

Two French soldiers, an American sailor and an American Red Cross nurse celebrate
the signing of the Armistice, Vincennes, 11 November 1918.

merican soldiers on the Western Front celebrate the end of the war, 11a.m., 11 November 1918.

Ivor Gurney's gravestone, Twigworth, Gloucestershire, June 2000.

The Mametz Wood area, July 2002.

outsider: his special status among the Egyptians meant that, like Rosenberg among the London literati, he no longer really belonged with his own people.

One speech in particular made a lasting impression on Marsh. This was where Moses poured out in unequivocally sexual terms his undying passion for his lost love Koelue together with his (literally unbridled) lust for power and desire to do things his way:

> Ah, Koelue!
> Had you embalmed your beauty, so
> It could not backward go,
> Or change in any way,
> What were the use, if on my eyes
> The embalming spices were not laid
> To keep us fixed,
> Two amorous sculptures passioned endlessly?
> What were the use, if my sight grew,
> And its far branches were cloud-hung,
> You small at the roots, like grass,
> While the new lips my spirit would kiss
> Were not red lips of flesh,
> But the huge kiss of power?
> Where yesterday soft hair through my fingers fell,
> A shaggy mane would entwine,
> And no slim form work fire to my thighs,
> But human Life's inarticulate mass
> Throb the pulse of a thing
> Whose mountain flanks awry
> Beg my mastery – mine!
> Ah! I will ride the dizzy beast of the world
> My road – my way!

The play's final stage directions briefly but precisely described Moses's murder of the bullying overseer Abinoah, and then concluded: '*In the darkness ahead is seen the glimmer of javelins and spears. It is Prince Imra's cohorts come to arrest MOSES.*' Facing the dark and menaced by armed conflict, apparently trapped and unable to fulfil his destiny: Rosenberg could hardly have encapsulated his own predicament more exactly. In early June 1916 his contingent reached Le Havre and headed off for the Somme.

Nichols too was busy composing. Most of a new sequence loosely based on his brief stint in France was in draft form by November 1916. The thirty poems in 'Ardours and Endurances' told the exemplary story of a volunteer officer. The young man responded to Honour's call, leaving behind human love and 'the bondage of the past'. In France, he faced death and survived to mourn those he had 'friended with a care like love' in a suitably Brookeian sonnet:

> In every rainbow's glittering drop they burn;
> They dazzle in the massed clouds' architrave;
> They chant on every wind, and they return
> In the long roll of any deep blue wave.

The young man was left at the end free and ennobled, having learnt the meaning of life: 'I count mere life-breath nothing now I know/ Life's worth/Lies all in spending! that known, love Life and Earth.'

The conception was ambitious, the poetic achievement variable. 'The Day's March' began impressively:

> The battery grides and jingles,
> Mile succeeds to mile;
> Shaking the noonday sunshine,
> The guns lunge out awhile,
> And then are still awhile.

The unusual word 'grides' (meaning, clashes or grates against), the double stress and mimetic internal rhyme in line four, the odd muffled effect of the self-rhyme in the fifth line: these all effectively suggested the inexorable progression towards the Front.

'The Day's March' clearly derived from personal experience. So did 'Battery Moving Up to a New Position from Rest Camp: Dawn' although in the poem Nichols gave it a Sunday winter setting: 'Horse-breath goes dimly up like smoke' in 'The dark, snow-slushy, empty street'. The battery moved towards Golgotha where it 'Must soon be torn, pierced, crucified' – the same soldier-as-Christ image that Sassoon had been using quite independently in poems like 'The Redeemer' and 'The Prince of Wounds'.

'Battery Moving Up' dispatched the troops with a brisk couplet: 'Toward where in the sunrise gate / Death, honour, and fierce battle wait' – like some nobleman's exit line in a Shakespearean history play. 'Comrades: An Episode' and 'The Assault' took the reader into battle. The highly sentimentalised 'Comrades' portrayed the slow death of a subaltern hanging on the wire in no man's land. 'The Assault' tried to catch in expressionistic rhymed free verse an officer's experience of the long wait for zero hour and then going over the top:

> Bullets. Mud. Stumbling and skating.
> My voice's strangled shout:
> *'Steady pace, boys!'*
> The still light: gladness.
> *'Look, sir. Look out!'*
> Ha! ha! Bunched figures waiting.
> Revolver levelled quick!
> Flick! Flick!
> Red as blood.
> Germans. Germans.
> Good! O good!
> Cool madness.

Nichols sent the poem to Henry Head in November 1916. His excited postscript read: 'Is "Assault" poetry? if not what is it? It's something I'm sure.'

Rosenberg did not fight at the Somme, after all. However, he was soon experiencing the equally cool madness of the trenches: wet through, aching feet, lice, shells exploding close by and bullets zinging everywhere. Marsh wrote every week and kept him supplied with comforts. There were also letters from Bottomley – 'my great god of poetry' – and another Georgian, R C Trevelyan, praising the *Moses* pamphlet. On 4 August Rosenberg sent Marsh what with a bit of subsequent tinkering would become his first entirely successful poem. This was 'Break of Day in the Trenches'. It was quite unlike any poem previously written about the war. The lines had stillness, a coolly compelling voice, a sense of immensity, absurdity and suspended threat, a rat and a poppy, even Rosenberg's favourite word, droll:

The darkness crumbles away.
It is the same old druid Time as ever,
Only a live thing leaps my hand,
A queer sardonic rat,
As I pull the parapet's poppy
To stick behind my ear.
Droll rat, they would shoot you if they knew
Your cosmopolitan sympathies.
Now you have touched this English hand
You will do the same to a German
Soon, no doubt, if it be your pleasure
To cross the sleeping green between.
It seems you inwardly grin as you pass
Strong eyes, fine limbs, haughty athletes,
Less chanced than you for life,
Bonds to the whims of murder,
Sprawled in the bowels of the earth,
The torn fields of France.
What do you see in our eyes
At the shrieking iron and flame
Hurled through still heavens?
What quaver – what heart aghast?
Poppies whose roots are in man's veins
Drop, and are ever dropping;
But mine in my ear is safe –
Just a little white with the dust.

Rosenberg also sent the poem to Harriet Monroe, editor of the avant-garde literary magazine *Poetry* in Chicago, who published it along with 'Marching (as seen from the left file)' in the December 1916 issue. That month Nichols too was in correspondence with Marsh. So by the end of 1916 both poets were on their way.

Nichols held a card guaranteed to secure Marsh's attention: a 1912 letter by Brooke, mentioning a breakdown and a tortured love affair – presumably with Ka Cox. The gambit worked. Marsh replied warmly, having already noticed some of Nichols's poems in *Oxford Poetry 1915*. He did not want the Brooke letter, but offered to show Nichols his as yet unpublished memoir of Brooke when Nichols was next in London, and, the real point of the approach, he showed a gratifying interest in Nichols's own publishing plans.

Ardours and Endurances, published by Chatto & Windus, appeared in the summer of 1917. To the war sequence, Nichols had added two sections of pre-war material: 'The Faun's Holiday' and a *mélange* of lyrics like 'A Triptych'. The combination of post-Brookeian heroics and pastorale exactly suited the taste of the time. The *Morning Post* claimed that Nichols 'Both in matter and in manner . . . must rank as the most remarkable of the new soldier poets'. Charles Scott Moncrieff in *New Witness* predicted more long-lasting laurels:

> I confidently foresee that, in schools that are as yet unfounded, the dim-eyed, ill-walking eugenicised scholars will date this epoch – as I use Morte d'Arthur or Gray's Elegy – with the names of Robert Nichols and 'A Faun's Holiday'.

'Poems and Phantasies', the third section of *Ardours and Endurances*, was to have been dedicated to Robert Graves, now recovered from his near-death experience the previous year. Nichols and Graves had met early in 1917, shortly before Graves's return to France. Nichols, as Graves breezily informed Sassoon, was in a private hospital having 'an injection of 606': that is, an injection of salvarsan, the first anti-syphilis drug. Graves, still strongly attached to Peter Johnstone, lectured Nichols on his morals, but found him likeable, literary and 'quite enthusiastic about the right things'. Among the right things was a shared appreciation for Sorley's poems, which Nichols had recently praised in a letter to the *Westminster Gazette*. Graves was also 'absolutely knocked' when he read 'The Assault' although he admitted he had had a bit to drink. With all this literary bonding, Graves was miffed when he discovered that he had been dropped as a dedicatee in *Ardours*, particularly as his replacement was one of Nichols's old university flames.

Nichols dispatched a copy of the book to Marsh who wrote back in raptures. He was so moved by the 'Ardours' sequence that he ranked it with Brooke's sonnets and Julian Grenfell's 'Into Battle'. He did not even demur when Nichols started pitching his theories about rhythmic waves, cups and humps. Marsh had already been considering a third *Georgian Poetry* anthology; Nichols's collection tipped the balance. The new anthology combined trench poems like Sassoon's 'In the Pink' and '"They"' and Graves's 'It's a Queer Time' and 'David and Goliath' with Wilfrid Gibson's sonnet elegy to Brooke and Herbert Asquith's ultra-patriotic 'The Volunteer'. There was new work by regulars like Masefield, Bottomley and de la Mare, together with pieces from Harold Monro's new collection *Strange Meetings* and the remarkable 'Ah, Koelue . . .' speech from Rosenberg's play. The plan was to have a new *Georgian Poetry* out by Christmas. Flatteringly, Marsh asked for twenty pages of Nichols's work. He also passed on a compliment from Masefield that 'Nichols, Graves & Sassoon are singing together like the morning stars'. To be praised by Masefield, to be a major presence in the new *Georgian Poetry* anthology: for Nichols, this was the poetic jackpot.

Rosenberg, after a stint as assistant battery cook and working on roads and railways, was now with the Royal Engineers. He received the request to include the 'Ah, Koelue . . .' speech in July 1917. He agreed of course, although he may have wondered why Marsh chose that extract rather than any of his more recent war poems. In addition to 'Break of Day in the Trenches', he had almost certainly sent Marsh 'Louse Hunting', his 'demons' pantomime' on delousing. He had certainly sent him 'Dead Man's Dump', based on his nightly experience of trundling coils of barbed wire on mule-drawn limbers up to the front line. This was the battle-field as waste land. The poem contained bitterly ironic images – 'the swift iron burning bee / Drained the wild honey of their youth' – and brutally graphic ones: 'A man's brains splattered on / A stretcher-bearer's face'. There were grim half-echoes of Brooke: 'In bleeding pangs / Some borne on stretchers dreamed of home, / Dear things, war-blotted from their hearts.' The final two verses homed in on a typical victim:

> Here is one not long dead;
> His dark hearing caught our far wheels,
> And the choked soul stretched weak hands
> To reach the living word the far wheels said,
> The blood-dazed intelligence beating for light,
> Crying through the suspense of the far torturing wheels
> Swift for the end to break,
> Or the wheels to break,
> Cried as the tide of the world broke over his sight.

Will they come? Will they ever come?
Even as the mixed hoofs of the mules,
The quivering-bellied mules,
And the rushing wheels all mixed
With his tortured upturned sight,
So we crashed round the bend,
We heard his weak scream,
We heard his very last sound,
And our wheels grazed his dead face.

Marsh could take Nichols's theories about rhythm but not Rosenberg's more radical blend of traditional and free verse, and he said so. Rosenberg responded spiritedly that he did not care for regular rhythms and probably blotted his copybook by claiming that Marvell should have 'broken up his rhythms more'. Marsh obviously valued 'Dead Man's Dump' because he copied it out before returning the manuscript. But he did not put it or any of Rosenberg's other newer poems into *Georgian Poetry 1916–1917*, any more than he put in the recently deceased Edward Thomas – although de la Mare offered to step aside. Nor did he find room for anything from D H Lawrence's latest collection, *Look! We Have Come Through!*, though Lawrence pointedly made the offer. Marsh was no prude: he included Sassoon's 'They' with its blunt 'Bert's gone syphilitic'. And he could face horrors. But, although he could tolerate *vers libre*, he was a prosodic puritan with a traditionally tuned ear. He preferred his poetry stirred, not shaken.

Georgian Poetry 1916–1917, dedicated to Edmund Gosse, came out in November 1917. Marsh had arranged the eighteen contributors in reverse alphabetical order to make some of the nine newer, younger contributors more prominent. It was between the pages of this anthology that Rosenberg and Nichols had their improbable meeting. Rosenberg's 'Ah, Koelue . . .' immediately followed Sassoon's eight poems and immediately preceded Nichols's seven. These included 'The Assault' and his pre-war poem about Judas's betrayal of Jesus, 'The Tower'.

The anthology was prominently reviewed, though more coolly, than its predecessors. The *New Statesman* quoted the concluding lines of 'The Assault' but thought Graves's 'It's a Queer Time' more persuasive in its evocation of 'battle, murder and sudden death'. Rosenberg was

barely in the race: 'Mr I. Rosenberg and Mr John Drinkwater also ran.'
The *Times Literary Supplement* reviewer ignored Rosenberg altogether,
but quoted approvingly from 'The Assault' and gave 'Fulfilment' in full.
T S Eliot in *The Egoist* complained of Georgian pleasantness.

In private to Marsh, Bottomley continued to admire the 'Ah,
Koelue . . .' speech: 'if little Rosenberg can ever write twelve consecutive pages as fine as this one page, he will swamp us all except Lascelles.'
Gosse was charmed by Nichols, both in person and on paper, but
merely facetious about Rosenberg: 'Who is Rosenberg? I feel sure he
is a Dane, his verses are so like those which come to me in Danish
from young ladies in Copenhagen.' Rosenberg himself only caught a
quick glimpse of the volume, but told Marsh he was impressed by
Sassoon and admired Nichols's 'The Tower'.

That was in early 1918. Rosenberg was now back in the line in the
Arras–St Quentin sector, after a restless ten-day leave in London
the previous autumn and another spell in hospital. He wrote to Marsh
in late March by the light of a candle stub. His mind hopped from
subject to subject. The platoon was 'very busy just now and poetry
is right out of our scheme'. He had done a bit of sketching, however.
There was still no news about his recent application for a transfer to
the Jewish Battalion in Mesopotamia. The idea of writing a battle song
for the 'Judaens' appealed to him but he could 'think of nothing strong
and wonderful enough yet'. He sent Marsh his latest poem:

> Through these pale cold days
> What dark faces burn
> Out of three thousand years,
> And their wild eyes yearn,
>
> While underneath their brows
> Like waifs their spirits grope
> For the pools of Hebron again –
> For Lebanon's summer slope.
>
> They leave these blond still days
> In dust behind their tread
> They see with living eyes
> How long they have been dead.

By the time the letter was postmarked, Rosenberg was dead. He was killed on 1 April during a German dawn raid. His body was never identified.

9

At Mrs Colefax's

Robert Nichols and Siegfried Sassoon,
15 November and 12 December 1917

On Thursday 15 November 1917, Robert Nichols and Siegfried Sassoon met for the first time, and Sassoon unexpectedly took part in his first poetry reading. Robbie Ross had invited the two soldier-poets to dinner at the Reform Club. It could have been an awkward encounter. Nichols turned up 'dog tired and dog tempered'. He was also apprehensive. Not so much on the poetry front: Sassoon's *The Old Huntsman and Other Poems* (fuelled by its author's very public anti-war protest) had made a decent splash, but it was Nichols's own *Ardours and Endurances* which had been the hit of the season. Edmund Gosse had trumpeted him to the skies in the *Edinburgh Review* ('There is no "promise" here; there is high performance'), while the *Times Literary Supplement* had guaranteed him literary immortality:

> Nothing can prevent poetry like this from taking its place among those permanent possessions of the race which will remain to tell the great-grandchildren of our soldiers to what pure heights of the spirit Englishmen rose out of the great war's horror of waste and ugliness, noise and pain and death!

His poems had been instantly anthologised. There had been the seven in Eddie Marsh's *Georgian Poetry 1916–1917* and eight to Sassoon's

Left: Robert Nichols, 1915
Right: Siegfried Sassoon at Army School, Flixécourt, May 1916

two in E B Osborn's equally prominent and popular *The Muse in Arms*.
This was no mere *succès d'estime*. Sales of *Ardours and Endurances* had
matched the plaudits. The initial printing of 1,000 copies had been
promptly followed by a second 1,000 and in October by another 500
– with yet a further 1,000 in the pipeline for distribution in early 1918.
By November 1917, Nichols had cemented his position as 'the most
remarkable of the new soldier poets', and was widely seen as the
natural successor to Rupert Brooke.

So any misgivings Nichols felt about meeting Sassoon are unlikely
to have been on literary grounds. They were probably more to do
with what Edward Thomas had called 'fighting the keeper', i.e. proving
your mettle. Nichols had seen action, but not much, not recently, and
not for long. His three-week stint at the front hardly counted in com-
parison with Sassoon's record of conspicuous bravery. The fact that
Sassoon arrived at the Reform Club in khaki would simply have underlined the point.

When nervous or apprehensive, Nichols tended to blurt. Sassoon
on the other hand clammed up, especially with socially confident
strangers like Nichols. Besides, Sassoon had his mind on his upcoming
medical board which, despite his unretracted views about the war, he
was desperately hoping would send him back to France. Nor was he
yet sure quite what he thought of Nichols's poetry. In June, he had
told Robert Graves, 'He's *not* as good as Sorley'. Since then, he and
Wilfred Owen had become friends at Craiglockhart, and critiquers
of each other's work. Owen's recent poems like 'Disabled' and
'Anthem for Doomed Youth', no less than his own, offered a far more
disturbing and visceral treatment of the war than anything Nichols had
produced.

Sassoon's reservations might not have gone as far as those of the
anonymous reviewer in the *Nation* who jibbed at Nichols's attempts
to fit 'war's breathlessness, confusion, noise, and meaninglessness to
almost onomatopoeic lines, full of hurried glides, sharp pauses, sudden
irregularities, and phonetic devices'. All the same Sassoon did have
reservations. In a very recent poem, he had taken a quick swipe at
the title, and by implication the quality of feeling, of *Ardours and
Endurances*. This was 'Fight to a Finish', published in the *Cambridge
Magazine* on 27 October. It was a revenge fantasy, in which stay-at-
home journalists line the streets to welcome returning soldiers and

complacently imagine that 'Of all the thrills and ardours War has brought, / This moment is the finest.' At which, the soldiers fix bayonets, 'charge the mob' and make 'the Yellow-Pressmen grunt and squeal'. Sassoon's deliberate choice of the word 'ardours' lined Nichols up for bayoneting along with the journalists.

All in all, the Nichols–Sassoon meeting might have floundered, but for Ross. That '90s survivor with the scarab ring and the jade-green cigarette holder was an expert conversational masseur and soon had the two on good terms. Before long Nichols was talking enthusiastically about poetry in general and about Sassoon's in particular. Their mutual admiration for Sorley's poems probably clinched it. The dinner was an undoubted success.

Sassoon had been hoping – assuming even – that afterwards they would all repair for more talk to Ross's flat in Half Moon Street with its 'old master paintings, antique bookcases, and long table where biscuits, Turkish delight, brandy, and cigarettes were waiting'. Instead, steered by Ross and Nichols, he found himself in Onslow Square, South Kensington, reluctantly attending one of Sibyl Colefax's little parties. Mrs Colefax was a rising society hostess, a 'duchess-snob', who liked to collect literary lions. With Ross as one of her social fixers, she operated a kind of double-bluff system: one guest would be hooked by the promise of another's presence – who might not actually appear – and so on. For this party, war-poet-of-the-moment Nichols and the composer and performer Ivor Novello had obviously formed the original guest-bait, with Sassoon also promised and Ross delegated to net him on the night.

The reason for the two poets' presence was soon clear: they were to give a reading. A table and armchair were placed in the middle of the panelled drawing room, and Nichols stepped forward with his 'thin alert face', apparently quite at ease. He had a very distinctive delivery style. He read for maximum dramatic and emotional effect 'as though absolutely carried away on the wings of his own poetry', and entirely unaware of where he was. Now his voice would be 'bold and resonant', now it would sink 'to a plaintive pianissimo'. When he read the final line of 'The Day's March' – 'I lift my head and smile' – he did exactly that: he raised his head and smiled. Some people loved his delivery; others hated it. That evening it made the increasingly nervous Sassoon uncomfortable and reinforced his uncertainties about the poems themselves. 'He is *the* poet for people emotionally wallowing in the blues', he later reported to Ottoline Morrell.

After Nichols had finished, Ivor Novello played some ragtime numbers. Sassoon became more and more anxious, and annoyed. When it was his turn, he tried to get out of reading altogether until firmly escorted to the table and chair by Ross and Mrs Colefax, and handed a copy of *The Old Huntsman*. Feeling like a pet exhibit and in no mood to be conciliatory, he 'slung a few ugly things' at his audience. His reading style was the polar opposite to Nichols's, being terse, laconic, staccato.

The ugly things were 'The Hero', 'The Rear-Guard' and '"They"'. 'The Hero' showed an officer visiting a grieving mother and telling her 'some gallant lies' about her 'cold-footed, useless swine' of a dead son. 'The Rear-Guard' took the audience into a tunnel 'fifty feet below / The rosy gloom of battle' and described a grimly comic encounter with what turns out to be a corpse, 'whose eyes yet wore / Agony dying hard ten days before'. '"They"' bluntly contrasted the bishop's sub-Brookeian platitudes about war as a spiritually transformative crusade with the troops' own account:

> 'We're none of us the same!' the boys reply.
> 'For George lost both his legs; and Bill's stone blind;
> Poor Jim's shot through the lungs and like to die;
> And Bert's gone syphilitic: you'll not find
> A chap who's served that hasn't found *some* change.'
> And the Bishop said: 'The ways of God are strange!'

Syphilitic was probably not a word often heard in Mrs Colefax's family home, and of course, as Sassoon well knew from Graves, Nichols himself had been having treatment for syphilis. Was he being tough or merely tactless in reading the poem? Sassoon could be both. Whatever he was feeling inside, it did not show. It was his extreme shyness and 'sticking out ears' which most impressed one guest, Lady Cynthia Asquith, while another, Vita Sackville-West, thought Nichols 'a horrid little bounder'.

Nichols himself was soon putting his own gloss on the evening to Graves and Ross. Graves was told how well Sassoon had read and how

effectively his clipped delivery suited his poems. To Ross, Nichols played
the social novice:

> If poetry hadn't been concerned and you Robbie as a friend and leader
> of two untameable poets, I should have been rabbitted – though these
> things put me on my mettle . . .

Then, less disingenuously, he went on: 'However I enjoyed it all enormously', adding as a postscript: 'I say, Sassoon's a noble fellow! I like
him. I must know him better.'

On a personal level, Sassoon returned the compliment. After passing
his medical board on 26 November, he invited Nichols to his mother's at
Weirleigh, and was charmed: 'He is quite different when in town among
a lot of people.' His view of Nichols's poetry, however, did not alter.
'Glory of Women', published in the *Cambridge Magazine* on 8 December,
contained the bitter line 'You crown our distant ardours while we fight'.
This implicitly lumped Nichols along with the women as a crowner of
distant ardours while others, like himself, did the actual fighting. By then,
Sassoon would also have known that, for Nichols, the mini-reading at
Sibyl Colefax's had only been a dummy run. A more elaborate poetry
show, as Nichols termed it, injecting the event with a suitably military
flavour, was in the offing. This was to be a recital for the Red Cross and
would include a substantial cross-section of young modern poets.

By this stage of the war, poetry readings for charity had become part
of the war effort. These readings were very different in character from
the half-hour sessions held a few years earlier in Harold Monro's Poetry
Bookshop. That kind of hard-core reading continued during the war
while alongside there developed the charity recital, organised by
high-society figures like Baroness D'Erlanger and Elizabeth Asquith,
daughter of the Prime Minister. One such recital in April 1916 for the
Star and Garter Fund brought together ten poets, including Belloc,
Binyon, Davies, de la Mare, Newbolt and Yeats. (Yeats apparently 'read
four poems preciously, but really rather beautifully'.) Elizabeth
Asquith's Parnassuses were similarly large-scale affairs – admittance,
£2 2s. – with a raft of poets and going on for quite a time. The Sibyl
Colefax Red Cross reading was to be a modified version of these,
matching them in the number of performing poets, but to be 'smaller,
more *intime*, and above all *shorter*'. Tickets, by invitation, 10s. 6d.

Nichols, with help from Ross, was the major-domo. He picked and approached the poets, and sorted out the logistics of the reading. He was soon writing to Ross with a plan of attack. The venue was again to be Mrs Colefax's with zero hour set for 5 p.m. on the afternoon of Wednesday 12 December. In a letter, Nichols itemised all the essential elements and likely trouble spots, and showed a shrewd grasp of what such a recital would involve:

(a) We must *get at* these poets.
(b) 1. To see if they can come to the real thing.
    2. " " " " " " " " " " " " " rehearsal.
(c) 1. To find out what they're going to read.
    2. How long each piece will take.
(d) What order we're to read in.
(e) How long it's all going to take if we add up all the 2 *c*'s.
(f) How long it *ought* to take.
(g) The certainties and those we shall have to provide understudies for.

The rehearsal was set for the evening of 10 December with poets, poems, running order, all needing to be confirmed well in advance. T S Eliot, two Sitwells, Sherard Vines and Nichols himself were Certs; Aldous Huxley and Sassoon were Possibles; and Iris Tree and Graves were Improbables. Charles Sorley's work was also to be featured. Then Nichols began to have doubts. Vines – a fellow-contributor with Huxley and Iris Tree to the Sitwells' second *Wheels* anthology – might not be so definite after all. Wasn't Tree in America? Perhaps Ross might read for Graves. With ten-plus participants, the time factor would be crucial: how many minutes should each poet be allowed?

Then there was Gosse: 'Edmund the Ever Ready' as Nichols nicknamed him. He was the obvious choice to chair the event, and he would need a gallop – but how long a gallop? The possibilities for catastrophe seemed endless. 'All this makes me nervous,' a jumpy Nichols confided to Ross, 'as we shall dish our applecart as well as upsetting Mrs Colefax's star-climbing wagon, and Gosse into the bargain, if we ain't well organised.' This was Sibyl Colefax's first serious sortie into the charity recital circuit, and she would have impressed on Ross and Nichols that there were to be no hitches.

Nichols was not the only one in a flap about the reading. Gosse

was too. As usual, the pacifying Ross stepped in. He invited Gosse
and his wife to meet the poets over lunch on Sunday 25 November.
Mrs Colefax and Madame Vandervelde, the event sponsors so to speak,
were pointedly not invited, much to Gosse's relief. 'We admire your
discretion in omitting Mrs Colebox and Madame Fan-the-Devil, who
would have reduced me to speechlessness, and probably incivility', he
told Ross. The incendiary nicknames were not just Gosse being facetious: the two hostesses were as formidable as they were mockable –
Virginia Woolf later likened Mrs Colefax to 'a bunch of red cherries
on a hard black straw hat'. Gosse was also worried about the Sitwells,
who were an unknown quantity to him. (What if they turned out to
be pacifists?) He was perfectly happy to chair solid Georgians like
Nichols, Sassoon and Graves, but he had told Mrs Colebox and
Madame Fan-the-Devil that he would leave at once if anyone so much
as mentioned the names of Alfred Douglas or Ezra Pound. Douglas
was a long-standing *bête noire* and was now busy pillorying anyone
who had ever supported Wilde. Pound was a new enemy: earlier in
the year, he had publicly ridiculed Gosse's life of Swinburne as 'the
attempt of a silly and pompous old man to present a man of genius'.

The lunch at Ross's mostly reassured Gosse. He still could not
decide whether the Sitwells were the real thing or not, but he was
won over by their 'beautiful manners' and 'formidable reserve of
humour'. Meeting Nichols only confirmed for Gosse what he had
written in the *Edinburgh Review*. There, bowled over by the 'Ardours
and Endurances' sequence, he had saluted Nichols's 'passionate
grief' and 'melancholy passion'. He had quoted all five stanzas of
'Noon' and the first two of 'Boy':

> In a far field, away from England, lies
> A Boy I friended with a care like love;
> All day the wide earth aches, the cold wind cries,
> The melancholy clouds drive on above.
>
> There, separate from him by a little span,
> Two eagle cousins, generous, reckless, free,
> Two Grenfells, lie, and my Boy is made man,
> One with these elder knights of chivalry.

A poetic cocktail of elegiac homo-erotics, aristocracy and medievalism was one to which Gosse was especially susceptible. He was equally taken with Nichols in person.

Then – serious panic – Gosse found he had mistaken the time of the occasion: he had misread five o'clock as three o'clock. He had a dinner engagement at Grillion's at eight for which he would need to go home to dress. He was adamant: he would be leaving Mrs Colefax's at 6.15 p.m. and not a minute later. Gosse was a past master at creating storms in teacups, and there was probably something self-induced about this particular crisis: his engagement diary also notes a Royal Literary Fund meeting at three o'clock the same day. But amidst all the commotion he got his way over the timing: a maximum of two poems and four and a half minutes per poet.

On 5 December Robert Graves definitively cried off and nominated Gosse to read for him, saying Ross would know which poems. Sassoon was still tossing up whether or not to attend. He was due back up north at Litherland on 11 December and was not at all sure he wanted to come back down to London the following day. On Sunday 9 December, he had breakfast with Marsh at Raymond Buildings and showed him some of his Craiglockhart poems: Marsh cried as he read them. Nichols was also there and that was presumably when Sassoon told him that he would not be appearing at the second Sibyl Colefax reading.

Gosse meanwhile was bombarding Ross with missives. On Monday 10 December, the day of the proposed rehearsal, he still wanted to know if he was to make some introductory remarks. He did agree to read two of Graves's poems. These were 'The Picture Book' (a childhood memory of being terrified by the stories in a German book) and 'The Dead Fox Hunter', about a Royal Welch Fusiliers captain killed near Cuinchy two years earlier:

> We found the little captain at the head;
>   His men lay well aligned.
> We touched his hand – stone cold – and he was dead,
>   And they, all dead behind,
> Had never reached their goal, but they died well;
>   They charged in line, and in the same line fell.

The next day, the day before the reading itself, Gosse was making a fuss about a typo on the flimsy of 'The Dead Fox Hunter'.

Other anxious parties included Osbert, Edith and Sacheverell Sitwell, all three now signed up to appear, and Eliot. For Eliot, in particular, the reading represented a significant step. His literary career was still very much in its early stages. His first collection, *Prufrock and Other Observations*, had appeared (500 copies) in June to a muted response, although Nichols had sent a fan letter. Eliot had also recently become assistant editor of the avant-garde magazine *The Egoist*. Neither venture of course made any money, and he was working full-time at Lloyds Bank. His inclusion in the recital at Mrs Colefax's marked a point of literary-social arrival, and he certainly wanted others to know about it. To his cousin Eleanor Hinkley, he was studiously dismissive: he had been 'invited by a certain Madame Vandervelde, a very dull woman' and the other poets were 'a poor lot . . . the only one who has any merit is a youth named Siegfried Sassoon (semitic) and his stuff is better politics than poetry'. To Pound, he was conscientiously ribald, concerned perhaps that Pound might think he was letting down the avant-garde:

I have been invited by female VANDERVELDE to contribute to a reading of pOETS: big wigs, OSWALD and EDITH Shitwell, Graves (query, George?) Nichols, and OTHERS. Shall I oblige them with our old friend COLUMBO? or Bolo, since famous?

> One day Columbo went below
> To see the ship's physician:
> 'It's this way, doc' he said said he
> I just cant stop a-pissin' . . .

or

> King Bolo's big black kukquheen
> Was fresh as ocean breezes.
> She burst aboard Columbo's ship
> With a cry of gentle Jesus.

★　★　★

So to the afternoon itself: five o'clock, 85 Onslow Square, Wednesday 12 December 1917. The turn-out was impressive. A hundred and fifty invited guests, drawn from the rich and distinguished, packed into Mrs Colefax's drawing room. The final muster of poets, rather different from Nichols's original list, comprised: Gosse, Nichols, Huxley, Viola Tree, Irene Rutherford McLeod, three Sitwells and Eliot. Vines and Sassoon had dropped out. Vines's place was taken by the Australian Irene Rutherford McLeod – the future mother-in-law of Christopher Robin – who had been having a boom with *Songs to Save a Soul, One Mother* and *Swords for Life*. She was also to read for Sassoon. Iris Tree had been replaced by her sister Viola. All three Sitwells, Osbert, Edith and Sacheverell, were to perform. There must have been a programme of the recital but no copies seem to have survived. However, Cynthia Asquith, Arnold Bennett and Huxley all left vivid accounts. Asquith and Bennett both identified Eliot's memorable contribution. The poems carefully stuck into Sibyl Colefax's common-place books provide a strong clue to what some at least of the other poets read.

Gosse, in the chair and reading for Graves, was palpably on edge. Although worried about timing, he, predictably, went on too long. He called the assembled poets bards – a word very much part of his critical vocabulary. 'Too many of our recent rebellious bards fancy that the coach [of the Muses] will drive itself, if only the post-boy sticks his heels hard into Pegasus', he had remarked in that *Edinburgh Review* piece in which he praised Nichols. To make matters worse, Eliot was late: he had had to come straight from work in the City. Gosse publicly ticked him off.

Nichols came next. In a planned and no doubt gratifying surprise, he began with a poem of Gosse's. Then, conscious of time, he probably read two short poems from 'Ardours': 'The Full Heart' and the Brookeish 'Sonnet: Our Dead', followed by Sorley's 'Song of the Ungirt Runners' and 'Expectans Expectavi' (all in Sibyl Colefax's common-place books). He read in thoroughly characteristic fashion. Bennett said he should have been a clergyman. Cynthia Asquith found his performance 'intensely passionate'. Huxley said he 'raved and screamed and hooted and moaned . . . like a Lyceum Villain who hasn't learnt how to act'.

Huxley, who presumably read his own 'Song of the Poplars' since

Sibyl Colefax preserved it, was equally dismissive of Viola Tree: 'a voice so syrupy and fruity and rich, that one felt quite cloyed and sick by two lines'. Irene Rutherford McLeod impressed both Asquith and Bennett. Asquith enjoyed her poems and described her as 'a very remarkable, fierce, rapt girl'. Bennett, perhaps with future copy in mind, noted McLeod down as 'a woman with straight, thin, ruthless lips', thought one of her poems was 'pretty goodish', and liked her reading of Sassoon. (Nichols would have steered her to safe options like the elegiac 'To Victory' or the uplifting 'Absolution'.) The Sitwells, according to Bennett, were '*très cultivée –trop*'; Huxley, noting their extreme nervousness, called them 'the Shufflebottoms'.

Eliot created the biggest stir. He had a jaunty air and appeared in 'sponge-bag' (checked) trousers. He read 'The Hippopotamus'. He told his mother that some of the audience 'didn't know what to make of it', but others clearly did. Cynthia Asquith found it amusing, and Arnold Bennett thought it 'the highlight of the whole occasion . . . Had I been the house, this would have brought the house down!' The poem was not ribald like the verses Eliot had jokingly suggested he might read, but it was far more irreverent than anything else on offer:

> At mating time the hippo's voice
> Betrays inflexions hoarse and odd,
> But every week we hear rejoice
> The Church, at being one with God.

If Gosse left in time to go home, get changed and reach Grillion's by 8 p.m., it must have been a close-run thing. Nine performers on the platform, including himself; another three – Graves, Sassoon and Sorley – hovering as ghostly presences. Then all the inevitable getting up, sitting down, opening books, finding places. Even if they started on the dot of five o'clock, to have wrapped up by six-fifteen would have been no mean achievement. But perhaps they did, and, at the same time that Huxley was off getting pleasantly squiffy with the Sitwells and Lady Cynthia was at the Trocadero with dashing Brigadier Freyberg, Gosse was enjoying his dinner, and Nichols drawing a huge sigh of relief.

Because it had been a memorable occasion, and a notable personal triumph for Nichols. He had been largely responsible for making it happen. The great and the good had turned up. So had the poets. There had been Gosse's spat with Eliot but apart from that everything had run smoothly: no apple-carts had been dished; no star-climbing wagons upset. As a performer, too, Nichols could justifiably feel he had been the most prominent figure: he had read five poems, more than anyone else. His old friend Philip Heseltine had told him back in July that he left 'the Lawrences and Hodgsons and Abercrombies and de la Mares – not to mention the hysterically-lamented Brooke . . . a very long way behind'. That afternoon at Sibyl Colefax's re-affirmed his position, among the younger poets, as leader of the pack.

Back in France, the war had stalled again. At dawn on 20 November, in a surprise initiative, 476 tanks, followed by infantry, broke through on an eight-mile front at Cambrai. At first, hopes were high for significant gains after the months of mud and slaughter at Passch-endaele. But on 30 November the Germans counter-attacked and by 7 December they had recaptured virtually all the ground that had been lost. Another instance of cool madness, as Nichols might have put it.

With hindsight, it is tempting to see that reading at Mrs Colefax's on 12 December as a watershed in English poetry: the afternoon the Modernists – Eliot, the Sitwells, Huxley – routed the Georgians / War Poets – Nichols & Co. But this is one of those convenient distortions we like to make. In fact, it would take Eliot several more years to become accepted as the equal of Hardy and Yeats. The Sitwells would have their moment but quickly become a fascinating literary sideshow, and Huxley would soon give up poetry for novels. Back in December 1917 Nichols not only looked like the young poetic front-runner; he looked modern, even modernist – although the term was not yet in use. The expressionist free verse of his 'The Assault' was more obvi-ously new than anything in Eliot's *Prufrock* volume, and much of his other verse was considerably freer than the strict quatrains and iambic tetrameters of 'The Hippopotamus'. As for Huxley, if he did read 'Song of Poplars', its pastoralism would have sounded remarkably similar to that of Nichols's 'A Faun's Holiday'. In late 1917, Graves was calling Nichols, Sassoon and himself 'we three inevitables'. Of the three, at the time, there would have been no doubt as to who seemed the most inevitable.

10

The Physic Garden

Wilfred Owen and Siegfried Sassoon, Thursday 15 August 1918

When Owen and Sassoon parted in Edinburgh on 3 November 1917, both were ultimately headed back to France and the front, although it would take them months to get there. The sealed envelope Sassoon gave Owen that evening contained £10, Robbie Ross's address in Half Moon Street and a note saying: 'Why *shouldn't* you enjoy your leave? Don't mention this again or I'll be very angry. S.S.' Means, entrée, permission: that was the code, and the open sesame to the literary and social world Owen had dreamed of so long.

His letter to Sassoon two days later – half fan-letter, half love-letter – was giddy with prospects. He was to meet Ross on the 9th. He had been 'always a mad comet' but now that Sassoon had fixed him, he would 'swing out soon, a dark star in the orbit where you will blaze'. Sassoon was 'Keats + Christ + Elijah + my Colonel + my father-confessor + Amenophis IV in profile'. He loved Sassoon 'dispassionately, so much, so *very* much'. He even anticipated, and discounted, Sassoon's smile on reading the letter.

Owen did meet Ross on the 9th, at the Reform Club, and found himself lunching with giants: H G Wells and Arnold Bennett. Wells – 'bayonet-coloured eyes' above a 'brown-sandbag' of a moustache – was in good form and confiding, while Owen and Bennett talked

Left: Wilfred Owen, Hastings, late August 1918
Right: Siegfried Sassoon at Garsington, 1916

about Sassoon. Owen felt he had more than held his own. Then there was dinner with Ross at the Reform and talk at Half Moon Street – with probably some reading of his poems – till one in the morning. He and his poems went down well, Owen proudly informed his mother. A few days later in the Poetry Bookshop he was flipping through Graves's *Fairies and Fusiliers* and exchanging a wink with Harold Monro when a customer began inquiring about Sassoon. Suddenly, overnight, he had made it, and he knew whom to thank. 'Oh! world you are making for me, Sassoon!' he enthused on 27 November, neatly adapting the last phrase of Sassoon's poem 'At Carnoy': 'O world God made!' By then, he was in Scarborough, back with the 5th (Reserve) Battalion of the Manchester Regiment on light duties.

Meanwhile Sassoon was digesting some unexpected news. Graves, now an instructor in North Wales and effectively *hors de combat*, was engaged to be married. His fiancée was eighteen-year-old Nancy Nicholson, the feminist daughter of William Nicholson the painter. Graves was careful how he presented this big change in emotional direction. The heterosexual Nichols was told to clear his mind of any misunderstanding about Graves's predilections. Homosexual friends were told how boyish Nancy was as though she was not really a woman at all. Sassoon was even offered a personal apology.

That was all simmering away in the background. More pressingly, on 26 November, Sassoon was passed fit for General Service. He still openly held to his anti-war views but had decided it was his personal, as opposed to patriotic, duty to return to 'the sausage machine', and Rivers duly primed the board. After a fortnight's leave – visiting his mother, hunting and seeing friends – he reported to the 3rd Battalion of the Royal Welch Fusiliers and saw out the rest of the year at Litherland. He anticipated what awaited him all too soon in the trenches. 'I must try to think as little as possible', he told himself. 'And write happy poems.' Then added: '(Can I?)'.

Owen at Scarborough was still taking stock. His job, a relatively menial one, was to supervise a bevy of domestic staff in the hotel where the officers were billeted. Off duty, he sat by his fire in a 'five-windowed turret' room in his purple slippers, devouring Graves, Nichols, classical and English elegists, Wells and Bennett, and reflecting on the immensity of what had happened to him and of what lay ahead. 'I am held peer by the Georgians', he wrote his mother triumphantly on New Year's Eve. '. . . The tugs have left me; I feel the great swelling of the open sea taking my galleon.'

In the poems he was writing, he was developing his recent discovery of pararhyme. One poem urged Sassoon – in lines Owen later recycled – to 'turn back to beauty and to thought' and survive because

> Beauty is yours, and you have mastery;
> Wisdom is mine, and I have mystery;
> We two will stay behind and keep our troth.

'Miners' began with a newspaper account of a colliery explosion, read as Owen sat by his own coal fire, and flamed out to the subject always on his mind:

> I thought of all that worked dark pits
>   Of war, and died
> Digging the rock where Death reputes
>   Peace lies indeed.

He finished 'Miners' in half an hour, sent it to *The Nation* where the poem appeared soon afterwards. To Owen's delight, he was paid £2 2s.

It was Owen not Sassoon who attended Graves's wedding on 23 January 1918. Graves had been writing to him about his poems, full of praise but also old pro tips like 'Best thing, I find, is never to marry two colloquialisms in the same line'. The invitation to the wedding in Piccadilly and the reception at Nancy's family house at 11 Apple-Tree Yard marked a further confirmation of Owen's new literary and social acceptance. 'Graves was pretty worked up, but calm,' Owen told his mother. 'The Bride, 18 years old, was pretty, but nowise handsome.' Graves later claimed that Nancy had been hopping mad, having only just read the marital vows and discovered exactly what she was letting herself in for. Owen's wedding gift was eleven apostle spoons with apparently a note to the effect that the twelfth had been court-martialled for cowardice and was to be executed. The most significant contact he made at the wedding was Charles Scott Moncrieff, a sub-Wildean poet and translator lamed at the Somme and the warm reviewer of Nichols. That evening at Half Moon Street, Scott Moncrieff was there again and clearly took a shine both to Owen's work and to Owen himself.

Sassoon could probably have attended the wedding if he had really tried. He was now in Limerick, drilling and lecturing troops and under orders for Egypt. He had wanted France and urged Marsh, Rivers and others to pull strings. Fortunately for him they could or would not: the 2nd Battalion of the Royal Welch Fusiliers suffered severe casualties around Ypres. To dull his mind, he reverted to his fox-hunting self, riding regularly to hounds. Some of his poems too reverted to pre-war type and yearned for 'Dim wealds of vanished summer' and 'league-spread, quiring symphonies'. If Owen was now consciously leading a kind of double life – khakied soldier by day, purple-slippered poet by night – Sassoon had put one side of his life on hold. His booklist for Egypt underlined the point: Hardy, Pater, Crabbe, Trollope, Surtees, Scott – but also *War and Peace*.

Owen's Scarborough reading suggests he was preparing himself to write more anthems and elegies for doomed youth. And so he was but, ironically, his easy acceptance into Ross's world, heavy with 1890s aestheticism and coded homosexual references, complicated his sense of poetic duty forged at Craiglockhart. He had taken to haunting second-hand furniture shops, and this found a temporary equivalent in the Wardour Street *faux*-medievalism of a poem like 'Page Eglantine':

> Nay, light me no fire tonight,
>   Page Eglantine;
> I have no desire tonight
>   To drink or dine;
> I will suck no briar tonight,
>   Nor read no line;
> An you be my quire tonight,
>   And you my wine.

At the same time he was probably working on poems like 'Conscious' about a wounded soldier waking up in hospital: 'there's no light to see the voices by . . . / There is no time to ask . . . he knows not what.' A kind of inner battle was going on for Owen's poetic soul: whether to bear witness to war-suffering and if necessary return to the front (Sassoon) or to follow a more Wildean, libertarian path and, if at all possible, survive the war (Ross, Scott Moncrieff). One manifestation of Owen's emergent Wildean side was an odd lecture to his mother, written in New Testamentese, about not denying his younger brother Colin 'the thing he craves', as Owen felt she had denied him 'the Doll that would have made my contentment. And my nights were terrible to be borne.' On 12 March with the inner battle still in progress, Owen was sent to the Northern Command Depot at Ripon, housing around 30,000 troops. 'An awful Camp,' he informed his mother on arrival, '– huts – dirty blankets – in fact WAR once more. Farewell Books, Sonnets, Letters, friends, fires, oysters, antique-shops. Training again!'

Sassoon was now moving more rapidly towards the war, if only to a Middle Eastern sideshow. He left Southampton on 11 February and after a marathon nine-day train journey through France and Italy – Trollope, Hardy, Pater, 'fir-clad hills', vineyards, a 'flat, lavender sea', olive trees – reached Taranto. His companions bored him. He thought his travel sketches and landscape poems no good. He caught a cold. He longed for the heroic. He did not find it in Alexandria nor with the 25th Battalion of the Royal Welch Fusiliers to which he was posted, before moving into Palestine. The most excitement he had was to go out birding with the medical officer. In his journal he noted seeing nearly sixty different species, including a Cretzschmar's Bunting and five kinds of warbler.

Elsewhere there was drama enough. On 21 March Germany launched a massive offensive in the Somme area and achieved a major breakthrough. There were horrendous casualties on both sides, retreat and desperate defence by the Allied forces, and the serious prospect of a German victory. Soon Owen and Sassoon were hearing of the fall of towns which they had helped to take and/or hold in previous years. 'They are dying again in Beaumont Hamel, which already in 1916 was cobbled with skulls,' Owen told his sister. The same month Robbie Ross's flat was raided by the police under the Defence of the Realm Act, following a smear campaign by the homophobic, conspiracy-mongering MP Noel Pemberton Billing.

News of the attacks on Ross hit Sassoon hard and presumably Owen too in Ripon where he was putting in a major creative burst. He had found himself a room in a nearby cottage where he could slip away to write. Here he worked away on drafts and new poems. The most haunting, and haunted, of these was 'Strange Meeting' with lines recycled from that Scarborough poem to Sassoon:

> It seemed that out of battle I escaped
> Down some profound dull tunnel, long since scooped
> Through granites which titanic wars had groined.

Down below the soldier-speaker came across sleeping, groaning figures, one of whom sprang up and recognised him, and the speaker suddenly realised that he was in Hell. The second figure gave a despairing inventory of all that he had lost – future, hope, pursuit of beauty, laughter, compassion, the chance to reveal 'the truth untold, / The pity of war, the pity war distilled', the chance, after the war, to find the words, the truths, to heal the survivors. The second figure then joltingly revealed his identity, and the poem broke off:

> 'I am the enemy you killed, my friend.
> I knew you in this dark: for so you frowned
> Yesterday through me as you jabbed and killed.
> I parried; but my hands were loath and cold.
> Let us sleep now . . .'

The enemy soldier – whom the speaker had killed the previous day, and who presumably also killed him – was his double. He expressed all Owen's deepest aspirations, fears and regrets. 'Strange Meeting' was Owen's anthem to his own doomed youth, his *petit testament*.

Besides a ghostly, Dantesque encounter with the enemy who was really yourself, the poem was a strange meeting on various other levels. The title fused a phrase from Shelley's *Revolt of Islam* – 'all / Seemed like some brothers . . . whom now strange meeting did befall / In a strange land' – with the title of Monro's latest volume, *Strange Meetings*. The form and nature of the admonishing exchange evoked the Romantic visionary fragment (in particular, Keats's 'The Fall of Hyperion') but also, closer to home, the gruesome underground

encounter in Sassoon's 'The Rear-Guard'. The language reverberated
with echoes from the Bible, Keats, Shelley, Wordsworth, Sassoon, and
Owen's own poems. The lines 'I went hunting wild / After the wildest
beauty in the world' even hinted at Owen's recent sorties into
dangerously Wildean zones. What clinched the overall effect, and gave
the poem its highly individual stamp, was the wrenching, displacing
pararhyme: groined/groaned, hall/Hell, tigress/progress, chariot-
wheels/wells, friend/frowned.

And all the while, Owen was inexorably inching his way up the six
divisions of military fitness. In April he reached level four. By early
May he was at level three.

At the same time Sassoon was writing his own (second) 'Testament'
on board ship, bound at last for the front and, as he imagined, his
death. The lines contained their own miniature strange meeting:

> For the last time I say – War is not glorious,
> Though lads march out superb and fall victorious, –
> Scrapping like demons, suffering like slaves,
> And crowned by peace, the sunlight on their graves.
>
> You swear we crush The Beast: I say we fight
> Because men lost their landmarks in the night,
> And met in gloom to grapple, stab, and kill,
> Yelling the fetish-names of Good and Ill
> That have been shamed in history.
>   O my heart,
> Be still; you have cried your cry; you have played your part.

Orders had come through a few weeks earlier, and Sassoon was building
himself up for what lay ahead. The battle scenes in *War and Peace*
helped, also in a different vein *Howards End*, whose author he had
narrowly missed in Alexandria. 'I fear they'll do me in this time,' he
wrote E M Forster from the ship, 'or else send me off my chump.'
Imminent danger prompted him to be more frankly homo-erotic in
his journal. He noted 'young Roberts running about with nothing on
but a pair of tight shorts – a sort of Apollo' and the men 'leaning
against each other with their arms round one another – it is pathetic
and beautiful and human'. On 7 May Sassoon's ship docked in

Marseilles. He told Graves he had left him £250 a year in his will and
suggested Nichols should write his elegy. A week later he was up
north, earnestly training his company in the Forest of Crécy near
Abbeville, and feeling 'rather ghost-like in the familiar country and
happenings'. He could hardly have known it, but he was returning to
the Western Front at a vital stage. The German offensive was still
powering forward, and in a month German soldiers would again be
a mere forty-five miles from Paris. Yet with General Foch now in
command of the Allied armies in France and France itself filling up
with hundreds of thousands of American troops, the tide of the war
was about to turn.

Back in England Owen kept no intimate journal. The nearest equivalent
was his often daily correspondence with his mother, and he could
hardly be forthcoming about his sexual preferences with her. However,
he did come close to dropping his guard at home in early April with
his naval brother Harold on what both knew might be their last time
together. The brothers sat up talking all night over endless coffees and
cigarettes. Perhaps Harold had long suspected his brother's tempera-
ment. Alternatively, hearing of his connection with Ross and his milieu
and learning of Pemberton Billing's smear campaign, Harold might
have put two and two together. At any event he brought up the topic
circuitously by mentioning a case of indecent behaviour between two
seamen. Owen, as if puzzled, replied that he too had wanted to canvass
the 'disgusting subject' of homosexuality, thinking his brother might
have some understanding of it from his naval experience, and adding
with a significant look: 'But of course you sailors are all heterosexual
by nature.' Owen continued that he had heard there was a good deal
of that sort of thing between the troops in France and he was not
sure how he would cope, faced with 'such a situation'. Then he changed
the topic: 'However, we obviously can't help each other so let's talk
of other things.' That at least was one of Harold's later accounts of
the conversation. In a more probable version, Harold asked Owen
directly whether he was homosexual, and Owen denied it. However,
he did profess a theoretical interest in the subject since so many intelligent men seemed to be that way inclined.

   Whatever Owen did or did not tell his brother, his sex life became
more complicated soon afterwards on the weekend of 18–19 May.

Scott Moncrieff was now working at the War Office, and Owen spent the afternoon there on Friday the 17th. Scott Moncrieff broached the possibility that he might be able to get Owen assigned to a job lecturing to a cadet battalion. Furthermore, as Owen discovered, Scott Moncrieff had just written a piece for *The New Witness*, mentioning him in the same sentence as Sassoon, Graves and Nichols as one of 'Our younger fame'. The possible ticket to survival and the literary leg-up were genuinely meant but had an ulterior motive: Scott Moncrieff made a pass at Owen some time later over the weekend. Whether the pass was accepted or rebuffed remains unclear though Scott Moncrieff's Shakespearean sonnet, dated by Owen as Sunday the 19th, implies rejection: 'Nor blame head heart hands feet that, overpowered / Fell at thy feet to draw thy heart to me.'

It was also a crowded weekend for Owen on the literary front. Osbert Sitwell was invited round to Half Moon Street especially to meet him, and Owen's new poems were enthusiastically received. Ross proposed having them typed up and sent to Sassoon's publisher Heinemann, who would then almost certainly send them to Ross for an appraisal. It looked virtually signed and sealed. Owen hoped for a volume the following spring.

Back in Ripon, he worked on a rough table of contents of nearly thirty poems together with some doubtfuls, scrawled notes for a preface, thought about an overall title and listed those to receive a copy: Sassoon came first, followed by Graves. Almost all the poems were ones he had written since meeting Sassoon, including 'The Chances', 'Dulce et Decorum Est', 'Anthem for Doomed Youth', 'Miners', 'Strange Meeting'. A couple, 'Futility' ('Move him into the sun – / Gently its touch awoke him once') and 'Hospital Barge', he sent to *The Nation* where they appeared on 15 June – the day Vera Brittain's brother Edward was killed in action on the Italian Front. Beside the column of individual titles Owen wrote a parallel column headed Motive, suggesting that, in imitation of Nichols's *Ardours and Endurances*, Owen was arranging the poems so as to tell an exemplary story of feeling. His own story began with Protest, moved through Cheerfulness, Description and Grief, and culminated in Philosophy – though the heaviest emphasis was undoubtedly on Protest. The notes towards a preface – very much a rough draft with crossings-out and second thoughts – read like a free verse memorandum to himself, occasionally modulating into blank verse:

> This book is not about heroes. English Poetry
> is not yet fit to speak of them . . .
> Above all I am not concerned with Poetry.
> My subject is War, and the pity of War.
> The Poetry is in the pity . . .
> All a poet can do today is warn.
> That is why the true Poet must be truthful . . .

One rejected title for the collection was *With Lightning and with Music* (too Shelleyan?); another was *English Elegies* (too bland?). Eventually Owen settled on the uncompromising *Disabled and Other Poems*. Perhaps this was in ironic anticipation or commemoration of himself being passed fit for General Service, as he was on 4 June. The following day he returned to Scarborough for more extensive training. At the War Office Scott Moncrieff continued his efforts to obtain Owen a home-based instructorship. Things looked promising till late in the month when orders from higher up decreed that all the fit were required in France. That news more or less coincided with the publication of Sassoon's new collection *Counter-Attack and Other Poems*, which included many of the bitter poems Owen knew from Craiglockhart, and a letter from Sassoon himself, containing 'Testament'. Owen, a better-than-average pistol shot, concentrated on 'the hideous faces of the Advanced Revolver Targets' and started to count down the days.

Sassoon was concentrating on his company and preparing them for the trenches. They moved from Cauchy to Magnicourt to Harbarcq, only a few miles from all too well-known towns like Arras and Basseux. He felt gratified when, at an inspection, his company was picked out for praise. He dreamed of battle charges, of losing his company who turned into lost hounds. He read de la Mare and Whitman, went to the front for three days of observation. On 20 June, when Owen was still hoping for an instructorship, Sassoon's company moved to Saint-Hilaire. He heard a sermon from the Deputy Chaplain General who called Christ the '*Warrior Son of God*' and compared the British army to early Christians. It reminded him of the jingoistic sermon he had satirised in '"They"', but ironically the boys seemed to enjoy it.

Before dawn on 10 July he was at the front for real, taking over trenches in the boggy Saint-Flouris sector. Wired and exhilarated, almost the first thing he did was to dump his equipment, tunic and helmet, and head out into no man's land with a bayonet for a recce of the opposing enemy lines. Slipping into a trench, he even encountered four members of what he took to be a machine-gun team, before sensibly bolting back to his own side when one of them caught sight of him. Night patrols in no man's land were strictly against orders for company commanders but he was out again at one o'clock on the morning of 13 July with a corporal and grenades, attacking a machine-gun post about 600 yards away. Two hours later, still unobserved, they were fifty yards or so from the post, when the German machine-gunner happened to loose off a few rounds. Sassoon and Davis the corporal chucked their grenades and 'retreated with the rapidity of a pair of scared badgers'. On the return journey and now out of sight of the enemy trenches, Sassoon took off his helmet and stood up to look back at the German lines. A moment later he fell, hit in the head by a rifle shot, mistakenly fired by one of his own troops. As he lay bleeding on the ground, he found himself thinking that he should 'say something special – last words of dying soldier'.

A fortnight later Owen had some momentous news to tell his mother: 'Siegfried is in London, the victim of a British Sniper.' Sassoon's book, his near-death experience, a burst of letters from the hospital in Lancaster Gate restored Sassoon as 'the Greatest friend I have', and cleared Owen's mind. He knew what he had to do. 'Now must I throw my little candle on [Sassoon's] torch, and go out again,' he wrote his mother on 30 July. He put his name forward for the next draft for France, where Allied forces were once more starting to make significant gains. On 10 August, he told his mother he was to have a medical the following day. He reaffirmed his identification with Sassoon, refocusing the final line of the latter's 'Testament': 'I am glad. That is I am much gladder to be going out again than afraid. I shall be better able to cry my outcry, playing my part.' This was no doubt partly to cheer up himself and his mother, but he

meant it. He soon knew 'Testament' by heart, and the poem became
his credo.

As Owen had guessed from his letters, Sassoon was not in good
shape. A verse letter to Graves caught his situation and state of mind.
It began ominously:

> Dear Roberto,
> I'd timed my death in action to the minute
> (The *Nation* with my deathly verses in it).
> The day told off – 13 – (the month July) –
> The picture planned – O Threshold of the dark!
> And then, the quivering songster failed to die
> Because the bloody Bullet missed its mark.

Endless visitors ('when MarshMoonStreetMeiklejohnArdoursand-
enduranSitwellitis prevailed'); sleeplessness; swipes at Graves's betrayal
('Yes, you can touch my Banker when you need him. / Why keep a
Jewish friend unless you bleed him?'); survivor guilt: the lines jumbled
and jumped in rhymed free verse quite unlike Sassoon's usual honed
mode. He knew his war was over.

Owen had the medical, and failed it (cardiac valves); Scott
Moncrieff tried again to swing the instructorship. Owen had some
leave due in any case and on Wednesday 14 August was in London.
The following day he and Sassoon saw each other for the first time
in eight and a half months. It was high summer, and Sassoon was
allowed out of hospital for the day. They passed the warm, blue
afternoon with Osbert Sitwell. He had arranged a private recital for
them by the celebrated harpsichordist and clavichordist Violet
Gordon Woodhouse, who for a couple of hours delighted them with
her playing of 'Bach, Mozart and the early English composers'. Back
in Chelsea they sat in the cool beneath the mulberry trees in the
seventeenth-century Physic Garden opposite Sitwell's house in Swan
Walk. Sitwell laid on a splendid tea, with raspberries and 'ices of
incredibly creamy quality'. After tea they sat once more in the garden.
Sassoon and Owen went on to dinner with Meiklejohn at the Reform
Club, before Owen escorted Sassoon back to Lancaster Gate. This
was their one chance for a private chat. It was probably then that
Owen mentioned Scott Moncrieff's renewed efforts on his behalf,

also his desire to play his part. Sassoon said he 'would stab him in the leg if he tried to return to the Front'. There was an inadequate goodbye on the hospital steps.

Scott Moncrieff's efforts failed – Owen's supposed cowardice in France in spring 1917 may have been a factor – and on 31 August he was, as he wrote Sassoon from Étaples, 'in hasty retreat towards the Front'. From the Reception Depot in Amiens, he asked his mother for:

I Pears Soap.
I Euthymol Toothpaste.
I Refill Battery.
2 Boxes <u>Non Safety</u> Matches.
2 pair Madoxes 2/6 socks.
The gloves.
20 Players Navy Cut or more if possible.
Horlicks Tablets.
<u>No</u> Chocolate, unless room is left.
? Handkerchiefs.

On 22 September, now in D Company of the 2nd Manchesters, he sent Sassoon his mother's address: 'I know you would try to see her, if – I failed to see her again.' He also revised drafts of 'The Sentry' and part of 'Spring Offensive', together with a new poem, the Sassoonish 'Smile, Smile, Smile', which satirised recent speeches by George Roberts, the Minister of Labour, and the French Prime Minister, Georges Clemenceau.

On 1 October he was in action in the attack on the Beaurevoir–Fonsomme Line, just south of Joncourt – the Allied advance now in full swing. When his company commander was wounded, he took command, captured a machine-gun and turned it on the enemy. 'I lost all my earthly faculties, and fought like an angel,' he told his mother, adding that he had been recommended for a Military Cross – which was later approved. He had kept his nerve under fire, and been seen to do so. Furthermore his men liked and trusted him, as he knew from censoring their letters: '"he is a *toff* I can tell you. No na-poo. Compree?" Interpreted: "a fine fellow, no nonsense about him."'

Owen added a pencilled conclusion to 'Spring Offensive', the final, abrupt question reaffirming his self-appointed task:

> But what say such as from existence' brink
> Ventured but drave too swift to sink,
> The few who rushed in the body to enter hell,
> And there out-fiending all its fiends and flames
> With superhuman inhumanities,
> Long-famous glories, immemorial shames –
> And crawling slowly back, have by degrees
> Regained cool peaceful air in wonder –
> Why speak not they of comrades that went under?

Early on 4 November he was killed (perhaps on the canal bank, perhaps on a raft) as, under heavy fire, his battalion tried to cross the Oise–Sambre Canal. A week later the Armistice was signed.

But what if Sassoon's and Owen's fates had been reversed? What if Sassoon had been killed by friendly fire on 13 July 1918 and Owen had survived the crossing of the Oise–Sambre Canal and lived to see, in Larkin's lines, 'the end of the Chatterley ban / And the Beatles' first LP'?

In Sassoon's case, all his premonitions of dying in poems, letters and diary entries, as he moved back towards France, would have quickened with post-Brookeian pathos. *Counter-Attack and Other Poems* would bulk even larger than it does, sharp with promise unfulfilled. The final poem in the collection, 'Together', in which, out hunting, Sassoon imagined the ghostly presence of his dead sporting friend Gordon Harbord, would have acquired a special poignancy. Some readers would have taken the poem as a self-epitaph with a subliminal loading on the words 'morning' and 'good-night' in the closing lines:

> I shall forget him in the morning light;
> And while we gallop on he will not speak:
> But at the stable-door he'll say good-night.

On the posthumous appearance of 'Testament', the coda – 'O my heart, / Be still, you have cried your cry; you have played your part' – would have been much quoted.

Nichols would, no doubt, have written an elegy, though Owen's and Graves's would have been more memorable. There would have been reminiscences – from Marsh perhaps and Graves, but not from Owen. Sassoon's moral as well as physical courage would have remained a beacon to future peace movements. There would have been speculation about his poetic future. Would he have been able to sustain the class-anger of his bitterest war poems into the jazz age? Some, as Stephen Maguire did at the time in *The New Age*, would have predicted a reversion 'to the pleasures of an English country gentleman, Tory mild'. Would the homo-erotic strain in his work have flowered into something more subversive? The prose potential of the diaries would have been debated.

If Sassoon had died, more would certainly have been made of why exactly he stood up bare-headed in no man's land. The oddest lines in his verse letter to Graves are those opening ones:

> I'd timed my death in action to the minute . . .
> And then, the quivering songster failed to die
> Because the bloody Bullet missed its mark.

These have not been – but could be – read quite literally: that having proved himself he deliberately exposed himself to fire from either side: was he really as out of sight of the German trenches as he later claimed? Be that as it may, a Sassoon, dead at thirty-one, would still now be best known as a war poet. And had he died then, by intention or by accident, it is still hard to imagine him filling quite the literary space that Owen has come to occupy.

If on the other hand Owen had survived, the hypothetical future seems temptingly wide open – or does it? One possible scenario has *Disabled and Other Poems* as the poetic sensation of 1919, followed by a successful American reading-and-lecture tour such as Nichols and Sassoon enjoyed. But what then? The Half Moon Street circle and its literary patronage effectively evaporated with Robbie Ross's death in early October 1918. The Sitwells could have partly filled the gap. They had asked Owen for poems for their modernist annual *Wheels* in 1918 and indeed included seven – 'Strange Meeting', 'The Show', 'A Terre', 'The Sentry', 'Disabled', 'The Dead-Beat' and 'The Chances' – in the 1919 edition of the annual. This marked Owen's

first concerted appearance on the literary stage. It is also reasonable to imagine Owen appearing in either or both of *Georgian Poetry
1918–1919* and *Georgian Poetry 1920–1922*. Marsh had not taken to the
poems Graves excitedly sent him in early 1918 – these probably
included 'Disabled' and 'A Terre' – but pushed by Graves, Nichols
and others, and charmed by the author himself, he would probably
have relented.

Which suggests an Owen developing somewhere between the
Georgians and the proto-modernists – but not embracing Eliot's or
Pound's more radical poetics. What would such an Owen have made
of *The Waste Land*? Andrew Motion in an intriguing 'what if' imagines a surviving Edward Thomas reading Eliot's poem with cautious
enthusiasm. At a stretch one can imagine the same of Owen: that
he would have gone beyond Sassoon's somewhat baffled if admiring
reaction to what he called Eliot's 'intellectualities in verse'. At the
least, a Sitwellian-Georgian Owen would have significantly altered
the literary landscape of the 1920s and afterwards.

A less dynamic scenario cannot be altogether discounted. On 5 May
1918 at Ripon, Owen noted a list of his literary plans:

> 1. To write blank-verse plays on old Welsh themes.
>   Models: Tennyson, Yeats, 1920.
> 2. Collected Poems. (1919)
> 3. Perseus.
> 4. Idyls in Prose.

Item 2 is all right; the others are dismaying. But, as the poet James
Fenton pointed out in a brilliant essay on Owen's poetic development,
'When reasoning about our creativity, we cannot assume that causality
is going to behave in the way causality normally behaves'. Fenton's
point is that it took 'a complicated set of forces' – including Sassoon,
the war and his sexuality – to release Owen from his own earlier work
and poetic aspirations, and to get him to forget about Poetry with a
capital P. Just as one cannot be sure how Owen's beloved Keats,
whose career his own curiously paralleled, would have developed, nor
can one be sure with Owen. It is impossible to tell with any certainty
what would have happened to him in a post-war world once that force
field ceased to operate.

In another scenario altogether, Owen's lost poems, of whatever kind, matter less than a cancelled future in which, had he lived, he might have been happy.

11

Good-bye to All That

Edmund Blunden, Robert Graves and Siegfried Sassoon, November 1929

Robert Graves's autobiography *Good-bye to All That* was published by Jonathan Cape on 18 November 1929, price 10s. 6d. Graves was thirty-four. The book lived up to its title. It told the story of his life in unusually intimate detail in page-turning prose. Graves debunked the upper-middle-class world he grew up in, and omitted or relegated family and old friends. As he later admitted, he deliberately included the 'things that people like reading about'. He included poets, prime ministers, travel, sport, also 'school episodes, love affairs (regular and irregular), wounds, weddings, religious doubts, methods of bringing up children, severe illnesses, suicides' – and above all battles. *Good-bye* was meant to be a bestseller – and it was, supposedly selling 30,000 copies within a month of publication. The book particularly upset two of Graves's old friends, Edmund Blunden and Siegfried Sassoon.

Blunden had received an advance copy for review in *Time and Tide*. He was a natural choice. During the war he had served as an officer with the Royal Sussex Regiment, spending altogether two years at the front and gaining a Military Cross. In 1928, a year before Graves, he had published his own war memoir, *Undertones of War*, to considerable acclaim. He also had a solid reputation as a poet in the pastoral

Left: Edmund Blunden, 1929
Right: Robert Graves, frontispiece to *Good-bye to All That*, 1929

line. He was known for his gentleness, and people often felt protective towards him. In appearance, Blunden looked remarkably like a small bird: short, slightly hunched from asthma and with a beaklike nose. Virginia Woolf called him 'a London house sparrow, that pecks and cheeps'.

Blunden found Graves's book infuriating. On the title page he inserted his own subtitle: 'or, the Welsh-Irish Bull in a China Shop'. That was on 7 November; he inscribed the date on the flyleaf in his elegant calligraphic hand. By then he had probably already peppered with comments the margins of more than half of the 448 pages of his review copy – now in the Berg Collection of the New York Public Library. These comments ranged from the portentous to the catty to the pernickety. He regularly copy-edited Graves's text, correcting his phrasing, punctuation and quotations.

On 11 November Blunden wrote to Sassoon. He told him *Good-bye* contained a 'bombastic and profit-seeking display of your personal affairs'. Sassoon marched off to Jonathan Cape to look at a copy. What he read enraged him, and he promptly demanded two last-minute excisions, which he obtained. At some point, he and Blunden added further remarks to Blunden's copy. What had brought the three old friends to this pitch of acrimony? And what was all the fuss about?

One of the passages Sassoon demanded be removed was a paragraph in which Graves described how in 1916 he had stayed at 'the house of a First Battalion friend' whose brother had died at Gallipoli. During the night he was awakened by 'sudden rapping noises' and 'a diabolic yell and a succession of laughing, sobbing shrieks'. This, it turned out, was his friend's mother trying through spiritualism to get in touch with her dead son. Graves did not specifically identify the friend or his grieving mother, but the paragraph came right in the middle of an extended section about Sassoon, and, whether or not anyone else made the connection, Sassoon himself was bound to recognise the painful episode. Besides his mother was still alive and could easily have read it. Sassoon's annotation in Blunden's copy read simply: 'To me, this passage is unforgivable.'

The other excised piece was his previously unpublished verse letter to Graves from July 1918, beginning 'DEAR ROBERTO, / I'd timed my death in action to the minute'. What Sassoon minded, as much as the theft, was the poem's evident hysteria. The voice in his best-known war poems (whether bitter or compassionate) was usually under tight control; here it was palpably falling apart.

Those two abuses were bad enough but Sassoon was also riled by Graves's account of his 1917 anti-war protest. He found himself in the role of courageous, misguided dupe, only saved from utter disaster by his old friend's energy and ability to pull strings. Graves claimed to have been convalescing on the Isle of Wight when he read Sassoon's public statement in a newspaper. He promptly got himself passed fit (though he wasn't) and located Sassoon in a Liverpool hotel, awaiting almost certain court martial. He persuaded Sassoon that 'his letter had not been given and would not be given the publicity he intended; so, because he was ill, and knew it', he should consent to appear before another medical board (he had already boycotted one). Graves then fixed the medical board so that Sassoon was sent to Craiglockhart, the hospital for shell shockers outside Edinburgh where he met Wilfred Owen and his doctor and mentor W H R Rivers.

That was Graves's version. Sassoon was furious:

> I didn't consent 'because I was ill & knew it!' I consented because R. lied to me. The assistant-adjutant told me everything 6 months later. His words were, 'If you'd refused the next Medical Board, nothing could have prevented you being court-martialled.'

According to Sassoon, Graves had taken an oath on the Bible that whatever Sassoon's actions they would simply put him in a mental asylum. In other words, he had only consented to the medical board because Graves swore that his protest was entirely pointless. Sassoon admitted that 'This well-meaning lie saved me from a lot of trouble & enabled me to come into contact with Rivers', but his annotation to Blunden's copy concluded uncompromisingly: 'R. has misrepresented all this so as to improve his own share in it.' To add insult to injury, Sassoon was trying to write his own account of his protest in *Memoirs of an Infantry Officer*, the sequel to his lightly fictionalised *Memoirs of a Fox-hunting Man* (1928). His old friend was stealing his thunder.

★   ★   ★

Blunden had nothing so dramatic to complain of, but he too was far from happy with his portrayal in *Good-bye*. He was a more recent friend of Graves's, meeting him first in 1919. Sassoon had been the catalyst. Blunden had sent poems and an appreciative note to Sassoon, then literary editor at the left-wing *Daily Herald*. Sassoon warmed to the poems and to Blunden as a person, and put him in touch with Graves. Graves also liked the poems and took some for a literary magazine he was co-editing. The friendship was sealed that October, when Blunden and Graves took up the Oxford scholarships they had won before the war and became part of an anthology of poets living on Boar's Hill; others included Robert Bridges, John Masefield and Robert Nichols. Poetry, similar literary values, extensive war service and war damage, university studies, domesticity (both were fairly recently married), a way to make in the post-war literary world: on the face of it, Blunden and Graves had a good deal in common.

However, from the first, there were tensions. Graves liked to play the expert with his poetic contemporaries. 'War poetry is played out,' he advised Blunden in an early letter, '. . . Country Sentiment is the most acceptable dope now, and this is the name I've given my new poems.' This was good news for Blunden as country sentiment was very much his dope too. However, he may not have cared for Graves's insouciant invitation: 'Have you anything else in the "brishing-hook-bine-head" vein?'

Graves was always an inveterate giver of advice to other poets. Shortly after meeting Nichols in 1917, he was dishing it out: 'it seems such a rotten stunt for you to sit in a *kimono* to view constellations quietly, quietly burning, and read Bridges.' The same happened to Wilfred Owen. The thing about Graves though was that he could take advice as well as give it. He was suitably grateful for Sassoon's assistance with that *Country Sentiment* volume. Blunden was different. He minded when Graves and Nichols took the blue pencil to his work. He minded even more when Graves seemed to claim credit for it – in *Good-bye*, Graves referred to helping Blunden with the publication of his first full-length collection *The Waggoner and Other Poems*. (Blunden, like Sassoon, had begun with a number of small, privately printed collections.) In the margin of his review copy of *Good-bye*, Blunden tartly noted: 'ie rewriting & rearranging my verses'. That was not the only occasion. In 1921 Blunden was complaining to Sassoon that he had shown Graves some new poems: 'his critique takes the form of a good many revisions for the worse (which I indulged him, and afterwards expunged), and the general platitude: "you've written too much".'

Friends, Blunden and Graves may have been; they were also literary rivals. Throughout the 1920s one or both of them brought out a new collection almost every year. This would not have mattered had their literary reputations kept pace with each other. To begin with, they seemed to. Both appeared in 1922 in the fifth *Georgian Poetry* anthology, Eddie Marsh's swansong. Blunden, the first-timer, had six poems, Graves, the old-stager, nine. The volume's highlight, however, came from another old-stager, D H Lawrence, with 'Snake'. By then, it had turned out that country sentiment was not for Graves after all, and he had become preoccupied with metaphysical concerns and the exploration of psychological states – the word 'lost' haunts the poems like a refrain. Old friends like Sassoon and Marsh confessed them-selves puzzled, and Graves found himself explaining defensively that a poem like 'The Feather Bed', an overheated dramatic monologue about an abandoned lover, was written 'for ten years hence when knowledge of morbid psychology will be commoner than now'. Even a more explicit poem like the Imagistic 'Angry Samson' stumped Marsh, though it should have been clear enough that here Graves was having a go not only at an increasingly indifferent public but also at those, like Sassoon perhaps, who considered him 'pillow-smothered / And stripped of his powers', i.e. poetically emasculated by domesticity:

> O stolid Philistines,
>   Stare now in amaze
> At my foxes running in your cornfields
>   With their tails ablaze . . .

Annoyingly for Graves, it was increasingly Blunden at whom the stolid Philistines were staring in amaze. His Cranfordian 'Almswomen', dedicated to Graves and his wife Nancy, was an early favourite: 'At Quincey's moat the squandering village ends, / And there in the almshouse dwell the dearest friends / Of all the village, two old dames . . .' Other poems in *The Waggoner* were less reassuring, as Blunden in his own way tried to exorcise his demons. The menacing

'The Pike', one of several fish poems, obliquely evoked the war through the word bastion ('The moss-green bastions of the weir'); 'The Estrangement' explicitly redeployed trench images and practices to embody Blunden's sense of post-war alienation back in an England which should have been pastorally restorative:

> A hounded kern in this grim No Man's Land,
> I am spurned between the secret countersigns . . .
> The very bat that stoops and whips askance
> Shrills malice at the soul grown strange in France.

Elswhere, in survivor-guilt-wracked poems like 'Third Ypres: A Reminiscence', it seemed the war was still going on: 'But who with what command can now relieve / The dead men from that chaos, or my soul?'

In 1922 Blunden published his second post-war collection, *The Shepherd and Other Poems of Peace and War*, to appreciative reviews. Graves told Blunden the book contained 'some lovely poems'; but told Marsh it only contained 'four or five real poems' and the collection was full of 'self-pity and selfishness, and this Clare reincarnation delusion'. Graves was alluding to Blunden's fixation with John Clare, the nineteenth-century nature poet. Blunden did much as editor and critic to restore Clare's standing after nearly a century of neglect but, disturbingly, he also strongly identified with Clare's sad life-story. Clare had died in an asylum after decades as an inmate.

The Shepherd was awarded the Hawthornden prize, worth £100. Graves claimed to despise such literary prizes, but the win obviously rankled. In 1925 he brought out a longish satirical poem called *The Marmosite's Miscellany* under the pseudonym John Doyle – though his authorship was no secret. This contained a section which took a swipe at several of his literary contemporaries, including Blunden:

> *'Blunden wore the sunset hues of a stranded bream,*
> *A shoal of Oxford minnows followed upstream,*
> *Edward Marsh was poised on the edge of a sofa,*
> *Hardy dribbled his umbrella,*
> *Belloc danced a tarantella,*
> *Aldous Huxley juggled up a skull and a loofah.'*

Blunden cannot have liked being labelled a stranded bream, nor much placated by the explanation in the Notes that 'the sunset hues suggest that Mr Blunden is the last dying glory' of an outmoded brand of 'Natural History verse'. In a further dig, a later stanza ironically recommended '*Fish for the Society's annual prize*'.

The Marmosite's Miscellany came out while the always hard-up Blunden was in Japan as Professor of English at Tokyo University. But it is hard to imagine he did not read the poem. Sassoon certainly read *Miscellany* and enjoyed it: it resembled his own somewhat arch post-war satirical vein and, besides, he was not one of the targets. Blunden was, and he had a skin too few.

But Blunden's animus towards Graves and his autobiography was not just on account of old literary slights. *Good-bye* brought back other grudges from Boar's Hill days. Graves stated at one point that he and Blunden 'would talk each other into an almost hysterical state about the trenches'. Blunden's annotation had an undertow: 'Not so much: R.G. would not talk about the war and the furious N.N. [Nancy Nicholson, Graves's wife] always broke in with some snub when she heard conversation going that way.' Blunden had never cared for Nancy. His letters from the early 1920s show that he resented what he saw as Graves's and her interference in his marriage, also their comments to others about an inherited liking for the bottle. Graves tried, not altogether convincingly, to smooth things over: 'All I ever said was that you have an "inferiority complex" . . . concerned with your father's shortcomings as I had with my mother's . . . The news that you and Mary are happy together makes my heart leap for joy'.

Blunden's reactions – both at the time and in retrospect – were partly prompted by a bad conscience. His and Mary's marriage was never that happy. She refused to go to Japan with him, and when he returned in 1927 it was with a Japanese secretary-cum-mistress. By 1929 the marriage was in serious trouble, being dissolved in 1931 – and, whether inherited from his father or not, Blunden did have a drinking problem. Nancy might be conscientiously blunt and Graves conscientiously tactless, but here they had twice hit the spot, and it still hurt.

Sassoon too found Nancy hard to take. He used to complain that she monopolised his old friend. This was no doubt true, but also disingenuous. In June 1922 he admitted to his diary that, with Graves, 'there was some vague sexual element lurking in the background of our war-harnessed relationship. There was always some restless passionate nerve-racked quality in my friendship with R.G.' He was jealous of Nancy, even sexually jealous of her. Part of his and Graves's close wartime bond had been based on their shared homosexuality. Graves had been in love with Peter Johnstone, Sassoon with David Thomas. In addition, Graves had shown a lively curiosity about which of their poetic contemporaries might or might not be 'so'. Then in early 1918, he had married Nancy. Sassoon felt the marriage as a personal betrayal and never adjusted – nor perhaps tried very hard to adjust – to the new situation. Nancy's marked coolness towards him complemented his hostility towards her.

A further complication was that, post-war, Sassoon belatedly started to sleep with men as well as fall in love with them. This secret life he – largely or entirely – kept from Graves so that by the late 1920s when the now forty-something Sassoon was heavily entangled with the difficult and much younger Stephen Tennant, Graves knew little or nothing about it. By the standards of the time, he had been remarkably frank in *Good-bye* about his Charterhouse love for 'Dick' (Peter Johnstone), whereas few readers of Sassoon's *Fox-hunting Man* could have guessed the similar nature of his feelings for David Thomas – also given the name Dick.

But although Graves was open about his earlier attachment, he was also careful to quarantine himself off from it by presenting his homosexuality as simply a public-school-induced condition, a temporary phase he had now left behind. This, in effect, amounted to a coded goodbye to that once-central strand in his friendship with Sassoon. Blunden obviously noticed something. On the page where Graves described his devastation when 'Dick' was picked up for soliciting, Blunden observed: 'actually R.G. had, when I knew him, rather a liking for homosexual topics.' The implication was that Graves had not put that aspect of his past behind him as quickly or as firmly as he liked to make out.

With Blunden, Sassoon felt no such complications. Much as he liked and admired Blunden, he did not fancy him: 'it is a kinship of the mind; the gross elements of sex are miraculously remote.' Which meant that consequently Sassoon felt no jealousy towards Mary Blunden who, in any case, he thought, 'showed considerable adroitness in her creating of a favourable impression with me'.

Then there was Laura. From early 1926, Graves lived in a *ménage à trois* with Nancy and the charismatic young American poet Laura Riding. The original idea was that Riding would provide sympathetic female company for Nancy and intellectual and literary stimulus for Graves. Initially the unconventional household worked well enough. This was during Graves's brief stint as Professor of Literature at Cairo University: he and Nancy were by then desperate for money, the salary was £1,400 and the actual teaching minimal. In Egypt, Nancy's health picked up, and she began drawing again; Graves found Riding's directness liberating and her utter certainty about her own opinions intoxicating. However, a combination of heat, haunting and job-hatred led to Graves's resignation from the professorship after only six months and a return to England.

Back in England, the 'three-life' (Riding's term) soon became more like the two-plus-one-life when Graves and Riding started collaborating over more than just literary projects and became lovers. Eventually Nancy took the by now four children off to Cumberland while Graves and Riding took a flat in St Peter's Square, Hammersmith. Riding then increasingly became the centre of Graves's emotional, intellectual and literary life. He became high priest to the goddess, knight-at-arms to her Belle Dame Sans Merci. Riding liked to refer to herself as Finality, and friends and family who did not accept her supreme authority were reprimanded and usually dropped. The illusion of a threesome with Nancy was maintained through visits – which meant in practice Nancy and the children coming to London and staying nearby on a barge. Money remained tight until in a friendly gesture T E Lawrence nominated Graves as his biographer. *Lawrence and the Arabs* (1927), knocked off in a couple of months, was soon selling like hot cakes, at one point 10,000 copies a week.

In February 1929, the three-life transformed itself briefly into the four-life with the inclusion of a handsome young Irish poet, Geoffrey Phibbs, a fan of Riding's poetry. However, Phibbs kept running away, and Graves or Nancy would be dispatched to bring him back. Things fell apart in spectacular fashion in the St Peter's Square flat early on Saturday 27 April. The previous night there had been a prolonged and heated debate about the quartet's future. The following morning Phibbs declared that he was '*not* going to continue to live with or near Laura'. She promptly swallowed Lysol and jumped out of the third-floor window, shouting 'Goodbye, chaps.' Graves followed suit, throwing himself out of a window on the floor below. Both landed on a concreted-over garden area but astonishingly survived. Graves was relatively unhurt, but Riding had bent her spine, and broken her pelvis and several vertebrae.

It was partly to meet Riding's hospital bills – money again in short supply – that Graves decided to write his autobiography, completing it in three months. Riding herself was nowhere mentioned in the main body of the book, yet Graves managed semi-covertly to turn the whole enterprise into an act of homage to her. He placed Riding's enigmatic poem 'World's End' at the beginning and a short 'Dedicatory Epilogue to Laura Riding' at the end. He thus made Riding's presence bracket his own story, turning that story into a parenthesis in the face of her Finality – what he called in Riding-speak 'your true quality of one living invisibly, against kind, as dead, beyond event'. By the time the book appeared, and Sassoon and Blunden were angrily annotating it, Graves and a mostly recovered Riding had left the country and were setting up house in Deyá in Mallorca.

Neither Blunden nor Sassoon could stand Riding. T E Lawrence described the Riding-dominated Graves as 'bewitched and bitched'. They would have heartily agreed. Blunden was in Japan when she came on the scene. On his return to England in 1927, he tried to pick up the threads with Graves but found his Riding-worship and Riding's own self-importance insupportable. Flickers of hostility appear in his *Good-bye* annotations. The name Laura is written alongside Graves's use of the phrase 'a lot', implying she was partly responsible for what Blunden considered Graves's cheaply journalistic style. Alongside the phrase 'vulgar glosses', he wrote 'Vulgar Laura?'. Vulgar was one of Riding's favourite critical put-downs, but Blunden probably also meant that he found her vulgar. Perhaps most tellingly, where Graves briefly alluded to his *Poems (1914–1926)*, Blunden noted: 'All his nicest things being disapproved of by L. Riding.'

Sassoon would have concurred. After Riding's appearance, he mostly maintained contact with Graves by letter and continued to help with money, even buying Graves a Morris Oxford to take to Egypt. But, despite some effort on both sides, he and Riding did not hit it off. He thought her poetry boring; she thought his clumsy. He avoided encounters as much as he had when Graves's world revolved around Nancy. None of his annotations in Blunden's copy of *Good-bye* refer to Riding, but she and the book were clearly integrally and upsettingly associated in his mind. He eventually found a novel way of sublimating his distress, as Robert Nichols discovered on a visit. Into his copy of *Good-bye*, Sassoon 'pasted . . . cuttings of a magazine of the early nineties – pictures of an advanced young lady in bloomers riding a bicycle etc with Laura Riding in black print letters beneath. The book is in fact a roaring farce.' It might have been better for Blunden if he could have transformed some of his anger and hurt into surreal humour. His obsessive annotation suggests he simply could not let it go.

Over and above their personal grievances and sense of betrayed friendship, Blunden and Sassoon had a larger bone to pick with *Good-bye*. They objected to Graves's portrayal of the past – more particularly, his refusal to share their mythic sense of the war.

Blunden's memoir *Undertones of War* and Sassoon's *Memoirs of a Fox-hunting Man* were nostalgic, elegiac, consciously literary. Their success had in part been the appeal of their underlying story: that the war had shattered a previously existing pastoral world. Not that in either Blunden's or Sassoon's case this story was entirely untrue. Blunden – from the more modest background, his parents were schoolteachers – had enjoyed an idyllic country childhood in Kent of fishing, cricket, orchards, hop-gardens, and oast-houses. He had loved his boarding school Christ's Hospital – also the *alma mater* of Coleridge, Charles Lamb and Leigh Hunt – and left it in July 1915 as Senior Grecian (head boy), with his Oxford scholarship. He had then taken a commission in the Royal Sussex Regiment, and been posted to France in spring 1916.

That was where *Undertones* picked up the story. Blunden cast himself as 'a harmless young shepherd', pitched into the alien dangers of army life. The memoir took the reader from the Béthune–

La Bassée canal area to the Somme and Thiepval Wood to Pass-chendaele, with Blunden variously acting as field works officer, intelligence officer and signaller. Trench life was fully represented – the mud, rats, gas and whizz-bangs, the reconnaissance and wire-mending patrols at night in no man's land, the friends and comrades blown to bits: the 'gobbets of blackening flesh, the earth-wall sotted with blood, with flesh, the eye under the duckboard, the pulpy bone'.

But it was not all horror. In deliberate counterpoint, there was the great natural beauty of France. Blunden was stirred by the picturesque villages in which he had been billeted, the changing face of the seasons: 'our garden was lovely, with flowering shrubs, streaked and painted blooms, gooseberry bushes, convenient new gaps and paths, and walks between evergreen hedges – "unsafe by day", as the notice-boards said'. Annequin was 'friendly, and near it lay the marshy land full of tall and whispering reeds, over which evening looked her last with an unusual sad beauty, well suiting one's mood'. Givenchy 'with its famous keep and huge crater was no sinecure, but some memories of our incarceration there have an Arcadian quality about them.' If not quite paradise lost, the wartime France Blunden so lyrically evoked was certainly paradise under extreme threat. This was equally true of the world of the war-related poems Blunden included as a supplement to *Undertones*, and even more so of two very recent poems, 'Report on Experience' – 'I have seen a green country, useful to the race, / Knocked silly with guns and mines, its villages vanished' – and the just published 'The Sunlit Vale':

> I saw the sunlit vale, and the pastoral fairy-tale;
> The sweet and bitter scent of the may drifted by;
> And never have I seen such a bright bewildering green,
>> But it looked like a lie,
>> Like a kindly meant lie.

The pastoral vision of France stood in for Blunden's pre-war world, which he could only re-enter imaginatively.

Sassoon's *Fox-hunting Man*, first published anonymously in 1928, was self-evidently a lament for a pre-war pastoral world. The narrator George Sherston, Sassoon's surrogate self, openly longed for that lost world of rural certainties, as in the nostalgic 'Flower Show Match' section. Here, very appealingly, Sassoon re-created the archetypal village cricket match, stocked with local characters such as a peg-legged umpire, a one-eyed, bewhiskered wicketkeeper, and an eccentric fast bowler. In a heart-stopping finish, the young narrator, 'an awkward overgrown boy', helps to win the game. Sassoon's reminiscences of his/Sherston's triumphant point-to-point victories and Jorrocks-like exploits on the hunting field, were equally sepia-tinted:

> With my heart in my mouth I followed Mr Gaffikin over one fence after another. Harkaway was a bold jumper and he took complete control of me . . . The gallop ended with the huntsman blowing his horn under a park wall while the hounds scrabbled and bayed rather dubiously over a rabbit-hole. There were only eight or ten riders up at the finish . . .

Into this apparently safe, timeless existence erupted the war. The final sections transported the narrator to the trenches and confronted him with death: 'A sack was lowered into a hole in the ground. The sack was Dick. I knew Death then.' Sassoon had quite deliberately produced a prose equivalent of those *Et in Arcadia Ego* paintings, placed in a typically English setting. The effect was undeniably charming and poignant, but entirely different from the angry, class-renegade poems with which he had first made his name.

It was Graves who publicly blew Sassoon's cover as the author of *Fox-hunting Man*, outing him in October 1928 in the *Daily News* (another source of annoyance). In a snappy piece he attributed Sassoon's anonymity to his 'divided mind' about his fox-hunting self, and claimed that a proper autobiography – one which also included the future poet of *Counter-Attack* – would have been more balanced. The problem, according to Graves, was that Sassoon left 'his readers to decide whether the book is sincere or ironical'. As a passing shot, he suggested that Sassoon himself was often divided in just this way. He claimed that Sassoon's 'The Kiss' – 'To these I turn, in these I trust – / Brother Lead and Sister Steel' – had really begun as a sincere tribute to 'the persuasive Bullet-and-Bayonet lecture' of a famous 'fire-eating staff-lecturer'. The poem had only later come to look ironic in the light of Sassoon's subsequent war poems.

Graves's own autobiography was not going to leave it up to any reader to decide or wonder. He took the role of the jaunty iconoclast, sceptical of the illusions with which others sustained themselves. For him, there was no lost or threatened pastoral world to mourn. He portrayed the pre-war world as rotten with gentlemanliness, belletrism and the public school ethos: 'It is only recently that I have overcome my education,' he claimed. His account of the war itself was more detailed and sparer than Blunden's and Sassoon's – they both complained about his factual inaccuracies. He did not present the war as a mythic event; it was simply an appalling experience to be survived as best one could. Sceptical, debunking, informal: *Good-bye* seemed as modern as Eliot's *The Waste Land*, Aldous Huxley's novels and Evelyn Waugh's *Decline and Fall*. In a flash, *Good-bye* made *Undertones* and *Fox-hunting Man* look old-fashioned, out of date.

Blunden's *Time and Tide* review appeared on 6 December, two and a half weeks after *Good-bye*'s publication. His anger was apparent. He immediately identified himself as one of those whom Graves had tidied up and put in the graveyard of 'All That'. Then he hit back. He charged Graves with incoherence, egotism and a muddled memory. His prime example of egotism was the way Graves had appropriated Sassoon's story: 'attention is concentrated on Sassoon the Rebel of the Western Front, with Mr Graves now directing the rebellion, now hovering, a Guardian Angel, over his friend'. Graves, Blunden remonstrated, had nothing to say about Sassoon's great kindnesses, nothing to say about his qualities as a poet. He mentioned Graves's unscrupulous use of Sassoon's 1918 verse letter – which must have bewildered readers when they looked for it and found only asterisks.

As in his private annotations, Blunden corrected various references to himself. He and Graves had not talked much of the war in the Boar's Hill days nor had there been a race between the war-damaged veterans to set down their war reminiscences. Blunden had written *Undertones* during his three years in Japan 'not to solve nervous problems, but to record men whom I missed'. He took a swipe at Graves's 'passion for amending all poems, his own, or mine, or yours' and at Graves's prose style: 'If Mr Graves includes his slip-shod prose in "All That", the valediction has its merits.' Coming from someone usually generous about other writers' work, the review reaffirmed just how much *Good-bye* had caught Blunden on the raw. His sour dismissal of Graves and his book broke the friendship. It was over thirty-five years before the two poets met again and were reconciled.

Sassoon did not publicly review *Good-bye*, but he did write to Graves in Mallorca, and there was a brief exchange of letters, riddled with recrimination and riposte. Some of the disagreements were little more than debating points. Why had Graves been so rude to Edmund Gosse and had Gosse deserved it? Had Thomas Hardy really said that *The Iliad* was 'in the *Marmion* class', i.e. as good as Walter Scott's poem *Marmion*, and, if so, what exactly had he meant by the remark? Other altercations were more substantive. Sassoon complained, as he had in his annotations to Blunden's copy, about Graves's inaccurate and journalistic version of his 1917 anti-war protest. He also objected to Graves's sensationalism – such as his claim that officers in his company used to ride sixteen miles into Amiens to visit a brothel: 'I challenge you to produce three names . . .' Graves answered that he would correct the 1917 material if Sassoon wanted him to but thought Sassoon emerged with more credit than he did. He defended his racy style – mentioning in passing Blunden's 'mean little remarks in *Time and Tide*' – and duly produced the names of three brothel-visiting officers. Then he retaliated: 'It doesn't take long to fuck; but perhaps you don't know about that.' To which Sassoon retorted: 'Isn't it sometimes dependent on the taste, capacity, etc., of the participants?'

Sassoon brought up Graves's attack on *Fox-hunting Man* in the *Daily News*. Graves countered that where Sassoon had been serious, rather than quaint, *Fox-hunting Man* was 'a good book'. At least, he slipped in, *Good-bye* would not be winning the Hawthornden Prize, as *Fox-hunting Man* had done. Sassoon admitted that when *Good-bye* appeared, he had been working on *Memoirs of an Infantry Officer* and 'your Auto-biography . . . landed on my little edifice like a Zeppelin bomb'. That was his own fault, Graves replied. If Sassoon, who was always making out he was so generous with his money, had only responded to Graves's cry for financial help in the aftermath of Riding's attempted suicide, *Good-bye* would never have been written, and the Zeppelin bomb would never have exploded.

Underneath the jabs and jibes there were seriously hurt feelings on both sides. Each felt the other had betrayed the friendship. Graves was typically the blunter of the two. Sassoon, he said, had sacrificed friendship for loyalty – to Gosse and Hardy: 'I had given you every chance to come up to scratch after the Gosse business; you failed me badly.' Later in the same letter he elaborated further: 'The friendship that was between us was always disturbed by several cross-currents; your homosexual leanings and I believe some jealousy of Nancy . . . finally your difficulty with the idea of Laura.' Sassoon was less than candid in his response, conveniently forgetting or ignoring what he had written in his diary in 1922. He had never been jealous of Nancy, he said; he had felt affection for Graves but never been physically attracted to him.

It was Stephen Tennant – at the time alternately delighting and tormenting Sassoon – who showed the shrewdest grasp of what was really wounding Graves: 'he is hurt and sullen at S. ignoring him.' Which raises the possibility that at some profound level Graves too was jealous. Throughout the 1920s it had been Graves who had tried the harder to maintain the friendship. For long periods, Sassoon had kept his old friend at a distance, retreating into what he called his Enoch Arden complex. But not with Blunden. Sassoon had always kept up with him. It was Blunden who had brought *Good-bye* so dramatically to Sassoon's attention. The row over *Good-bye* had many layers, but one of them was rivalry over Sassoon's friendship. Graves felt that Blunden had usurped his rightful place.

When Graves hit another financial crisis in 1933, he wrote again to Sassoon, and another bout of accusation and exculpation briefly ensued. Then there was silence for twenty years. In the 1950s, they finally buried the hatchet, and when Graves decided to bring out a revised version of *Good-bye*, he made sure to inform Sassoon. Sassoon replied, hoping that the book would 'remind the present generation of what 1914–18 was for those who endured it'. He went further. He attributed his past anger to his state of mind when writing *Memoirs of an Infantry Officer.* 'All that you wrote about me was entirely generous,' he said, '– beyond my deserts.'

After the bust-up over *Good-bye*, Blunden went on to have an active and distinguished academic and literary career. He was a Fellow and tutor in English at Merton College, Oxford (1931–42), Cultural Liaison Officer with the British Mission in Japan (1947–50) and Professor of English at Hong Kong University (1953–64). I was a junior lecturer in the English Department at HKU in the mid-1970s and for a couple of years had Blunden's old desk, a relic I failed to value as I should have done. Blunden had taught a number of my colleagues, and I heard various stories about him.

One Chinese colleague used to say a little tartly that Blunden had gathered round him a cohort of former students from his Merton days, and that there had been considerable jealousy among the admiring acolytes. Another, Jack Lowcock, had more poignant anecdotes to tell. Blunden and his third wife Claire used to invite students to their flat for breakfast on Sunday mornings. At the first breakfast Jack attended, he was keen to ask Blunden about R C Sherriff's *Journey's End*, having played the leading role, Stanhope, in a recent school production. But when he brought up the play, Blunden simply said 'It wasn't like that' and deflected the conversation to other topics. Jack also recalled that Blunden could not bear the idea of killing anything living, not even the ever-present cockroaches. His strongest memory, however, was of a lecture of Blunden's on First World War poetry. After a while, Jack noticed that the tears were streaming down Blunden's face, and he realised with a jolt that Blunden was not talking about literature, something remote and safe; he was talking about his friends and contemporaries, and at that moment he was back there with them in the mud and the fear.

Blunden never did say goodbye to the war, any more than Sassoon. Almost anything could bring it to mind. Watching Duleepsinghji score a century for England against Australia in 1930 in his first test match, Blunden noticed how the batsman used each pause in play to look at the pitch. This at once prompted the thought: 'So the tunnellers listened under the trenches for minute messages of danger.' Asked in a 1964 interview 'what kind of experience' was 'likely to contain the germ of a poem', he replied: 'I think something quite accidental disturbs something else. It's like digging in the sand and hitting a land-mine or something.' As he admitted in another late interview: 'My experiences in the First World War have haunted me all my life and for many days I have, it seemed, lived in that world rather than this.'

12

Strange Hells

Ivor Gurney, Helen Thomas and Edward Thomas, circa *Summer 1932*

Ivor Gurney and Edward Thomas never met in life. The two did, however, have a number of vicarious encounters around 1932, when Thomas's widow Helen visited Gurney at Stone House, the City of London Mental Hospital in Dartford. By then, Gurney had been a patient at Stone House for almost ten years.

Whether he should ever have been committed still provokes heated debate. There had been warning signs like the breakdown before the war. Then the relative equilibrium produced by the extreme conditions of the war itself. Then the gassing and convalescence in England, the talk of suicide and a further breakdown in 1918. After the war, however, the signs at first looked more promising, and it seemed as though the third spectre's prediction that Gurney would 'live one hour of agony' might prove unfounded. He went back to the Royal College of Music, studying composition with Vaughan Williams. His first collection of poems, *Severn & Somme*, was reprinted in January 1919, and a less enthusiastically received successor, *War's Embers*, appeared that May. But, on the personal front, things were not so stable. Gurney soon reverted to a version of his peripatetic pre-war existence, becoming again a cuckoo in the homes of friends and relations in London, Gloucester and High Wycombe.

Left: Ivor Gurney – the asylum years
Right: Edward Thomas at Wick Green, 1913–14

Over the next four years, he worked for brief spells as a church organist, a cinema pianist, and a farm labourer. Eddie Marsh even fixed him up a post in the Gloucester tax office. Nothing lasted. During this period he produced poems in furious bursts, but although a number were published in magazines like *The Spectator* and J C Squire's *London Mercury*, Gurney failed to find a publisher for a third collection, which might have secured his reputation.

He was also turning out settings of songs and poems at a great rate. He set traditional ballads, poems by his contemporaries (Housman, Edward Thomas, Graves, de la Mare and others) and a few of his own. His friend and benefactor Marion Scott recalled him singing his own version of 'Twa Corbies' 'with gruesome intensity'. Some of these settings were published, both before and after he officially dropped out of the RCM in July 1921.

The poems written in the immediate post-war years, and typed up by Gurney's sister Dorothy, brimmed with details of the natural world: 'The gnats go plaining by the sedges'; 'Now are there green flames springing by washed roads'; 'There the gorse sea with yellow foam / Holds tracks to guide the sheep-boy home'. Many seemed in search of an inner England, 'A type of England by the intellect / Not hindered and not faulted' as he put it in 'A Farmer's House'. This imaginary, historical-pastoral country of spring and autumn, of renewal intercut with depression, was lovingly but hectically evoked. The lines jumped with sudden syntactical contractions: 'Long shines the line of wet lamps dark in gleaming'; 'First he loves baffle streams and dull the bright'. There were sudden archaisms – 'kine', 'conies', 'ancientry' – and idiosyncratic coinings: 'fire-mutter', 'moisted', 'homelongings', 'mentorises', 'infire'. Abrupt leaps and fractures of feeling, too, into something darker, as in the Imagistic 'April Gale':

> The wind frightens my dog, but I bathe in it,
> Sound, rush, scent of the Spring fields.
>
> My dog's hairs are blown like feathers askew,
> My coat's a demon, torturing like life.

Or the more Thomas-like 'Cold Dusk', with its frayed rhymes and disquieting owl:

Now the red sun goes under
To a thousand foemen,
And dusk brings mystery
To all that Roman
Camp, height and common.

I am the trespasser
With thistles and waste things.
It is right to fear.
An owl cries warnings
From the dim copse near.

Some poems displayed an almost metaphysical wit, like 'Daily' which likened the constant repairing of emotional hurt to mending punctures on a bicycle:

If one's heart is broken twenty times a day,
What easier thing than to fling the bits away,
But still one gathers fragments, and looks for wire,
Or patches it up like some old bicycle tyre.

Other poems imagined place in terms of specific human responses to the surrounding landscape. In 'The Square Thing', the church was St Mary's at Norton Green, a few miles outside Gloucester, with a notable medieval perpendicular tower. The poem contained a number of characteristic Gurney oddities of phrasing and diction:

At Norton Green the tower stands well off road
And is a squareness meaning many things;
Nearest to us, the makers had abode
Beside the Northern road of priests and kings.

Men of a morning looked away to Wales
Or wavy Malvern under smoothy roof;
And said, 'That we have seen such hills and vales
Our churchkin here must give men certain proof.'

And so from virtue mixed of sky and land
They raised a thing to match our equal dreams.
It was no common infire moved their hand,
Building so squarely among meadow streams.

The poems made up an impressive body of work. And there was an audience for pastoral poetry, as Edmund Blunden was discovering with the success of *The Waggoner* (1920) and *The Shepherd* (1922). Gurney in fact appealed to Blunden for help with finding a publisher for his third collection.

Gurney's increasingly erratic behaviour and strange requests alarmed his friends, supporters and family. In one all-too-probable story, a policeman was called to the family home where Gurney was staying. He came in and found everyone acting normally until Gurney took him aside and asked if he had such a thing as a revolver about him as he wanted to shoot himself. Gurney's family tried their best, but found it hard to sympathise with what often seemed like a wilful refusal to settle down and earn a living like everyone else. There was also some predictable envy and resentment at Gurney's arty London friends and their influence. His brother Ronald took a tough line: 'I am convinced that nothing on earth will do Ivor much good till by Iron Discipline he has had his natural obstinacy and stubbornness broken down.'

In September 1922, following various suicide attempts, Gurney was declared insane and committed to Barnwood, a private asylum near Gloucester. After two escapes and recaptures, the medical superintendent Arthur Townsend recommended to the faithful Marion Scott that he be moved to Stone House in Dartford ('an eminently suitable place'). The idea was that, away from his beloved Gloucester, Gurney would be less likely to try to run away. On 21 December he was driven by hire car to the second largest private mental hospital in England. He was 32 years old.

At the time he himself complained of 'a twisting of the inside', of hearing voices, 'pains in the head', being tormented, physically and mentally, by telegraphy, electricity, wireless. Dr Steen, the Medical Superintendent at Stone House, diagnosed his condition as 'Delusional Insanity (Systematised)'. Gurney's biographer Michael Hurd, writing in 1978, translated the diagnosis as 'paranoid schizophrenia'. Since then, others have seriously argued for bi-polar disorder (manic depression) and, mostly on the basis of malarial therapy Gurney received in 1923, for syphilis. Whatever the true nature of his condition, it is tempting to think that he might have recovered some equilibrium, would at least have been happier, had he not been locked up. Equally, he might simply have shot or poisoned himself as he had threatened to do.

The regime at Stone House seems on the whole to have been reasonably humane. Dr Steen believed in the efficacy of fresh air, and in the warmer weather patients' beds were moved outside to verandas. Some of the staff had had training at war hospitals and had experience of neurasthenics. (Gurney was drawing a war pension on the basis that he was a shell shocker.) Private patients like him had better food, were allowed to wear their own clothes, and he seems to have had his own room. There was a bowling alley, a mini-golf course, cricket, football, hockey teams, but no evidence that Gurney took any part in these sporting activities despite having once been quite keen on both cricket and football. There were workshops, a cinema, musical evenings, entertainments.

Stone House was the first asylum to have a wireless, and Gurney could have heard the BBC broadcast of his setting of his own 'Strange Service' on 7 December 1926, and 'Severn Meadows' on 1 April 1932. He sometimes played one of the several grand pianos. He drank a lot of tea, walked about with his head in a book. He wrote desperate letters to the police, to Lloyd George; though it is not clear that these were ever sent. He continued to write poems and music in frenetic bursts. He ran away once, a couple of weeks after being transferred to Stone House. By the late 1920s, he believed he had written Shakespeare's plays and composed Beethoven's and Haydn's music. Sometimes he could sound entirely lucid.

There were sad oases of hope. In 1925, one member of the staff, Dr Randolph Davis, persuaded Gurney's friends that he could cure Gurney. His plan was to kidnap Gurney from Stone House, rent rooms in London and treat him on a one-on-one basis – paid for by Gurney's friends. It turned out to be a scam: Davis had serious debts and was hoping to use Gurney as a cash cow. The following year a Harley

Street specialist was approached, and in 1927 a Christian Scientist prac-
titioner, both to no avail.

Gurney's main standby all through his years at Stone House was Marion
Scott. His £2-a-week pension did not quite cover the hospital's weekly
charge of two guineas (plus an additional charge of £2 a quarter for
clothing, etc). By arrangement, Marion Scott made up the shortfall.
She regularly sent him money, cigarettes, chocolate, biscuits and books.
She took him out for drives, to the seaside, to a production of *A
Midsummer Night's Dream* at the Old Vic. She collected his endlessly
growing pile of manuscript material, sent poems to Squire, music to
Music and Letters and to the publishers Stainer & Bell. There were
small successes – clutches of poems continued to appear from time
to time in the *London Mercury* – but no third collection.

Over the years, Gurney's poems and letters to Scott show the
development of an increasingly personalised, inner geography. Towns
and districts are anthropomorphised, favourite writers and composers
evoked. This letter of 10 November 1932 is fairly typical. To read it is
like encountering a novel form of shorthand in which by an imaginative squinting a kind of meaning seems to fade in and out of view.
The handwriting is confident and well-formed though not always easy
to decipher:

Dear Miss Scott
I regret this winter weakness so / unless there is a Thames Vicarage
way of civilisation –
and may the name of Cirencester bring more luck than Latin or
German verse to England – of which so many noble things were
told: and, I think, piteous after victory also . . .
Before Armistice Day, to salute the victory of Loos, and to thank for
(1913) –
It is part of the luck and magnificence of (Mr) Thomas Carlyle: to
be able to write so –
and lets Ireland speak with freer tongue of what is before Her . . .
the performance of the Beethoven G Major Concerto, delighted me
last night . . . at its best . . . (Here is Hell), and the transformation of
Wm Goethe is so beautiful: like spring at Arras or Rouen . . . or like
the change at Aubers Ridge. (3).

(Perhaps even a Stanford may reflect with satisfaction on such changes of war . . .)

Of Armistice Day, as to how Hampstead (noble) and Oxford and Buckingham write of it . . . for the Pacific West cannot often restore Germany, etc, and the news from the Atlantic obscure still.

(But I think such account must please the friends of Carlyle.)

However, [than?] the present English fortune, I think, the William Hazlitt writers deserved far better . . . (Here praising the publication of <u>Dickens</u>.) and thanking for Cambridge honour . . .

Will you please send me more money, and a small handbook on London (if there are good ones). To read of what Chelsea, and Aldgate stand for . . . and what the Mississippi can like to praise still – (the fame of J W H Turner, at least . . .) and so may [Hodow?] (for Minnesota) arise anew from a magnificent dark forest . . .

It is painful to think of North Italy, worse still of Herzgovina [*sic*] . . .

Please remember me to Gilly Potter (Linlithgow, [they say?]) and for the great-ceiling's sake – (at the South East).

I hope Louisville & Nash are his courteous friends/and so Nikolas [Lenan?] now writes; forgetting all ages in his pride of conquest; (and for the City of London shield North . . .)

A difficult tale, but I hope that [<u>Noltebrohm</u>?] will make a very grand one of it . . . / and greater glory than William Shakespeare (etc) is not known.

With best wishes and honour

Ivor Gurney

Edward Thomas had long been an important figure in Gurney's mental landscape. Amongst the music Scott sent to Stainer & Bell was Gurney's *Lights Out* sequence (1926), settings made over the years of six of Thomas's poems: 'The Penny Whistle', 'Scents', 'Bright Clouds', 'Lights Out', 'Will You Come?' and 'The Trumpet'. Altogether Gurney set around eighteen of Thomas's poems. He had probably first become aware of him as a poet in late 1917 with the posthumous publication of *Poems* – around the time he mentioned being shown 'the unquiet face of E.T.' by Thomas's friend J W Haines. By January 1918, Gurney was telling Scott that the poems rewarded multiple rereadings. He enthused to her about their 'living subtlety' and 'half-lights', 'the deep-in sadness of [Thomas's] lovable mind', and particularly revered 'The Owl'. 'The Lock-keeper' in *War's Embers* is dedicated to Thomas's memory.

One jerky but coherent letter from Stone House to Scott seems to refer to Helen Thomas giving permission for publication of the *Lights Out* sequence (the letter is undated and unstamped, but ink and handwriting suggest a 1925 date):

> To Miss M M Scott
>   Thanking her so much
> and thanking Mrs Edward Thomas too, so honoured; and you for sending her the two volumes of my verses: in which sudden out of unruffled blithering every now and then the voice of young Gloucestershire speaks.

Another undated letter contained the cryptic comment: 'ET is not (it is Hell).' This could simply be registering the hellish realisation of Thomas's non-existence or perhaps Gurney's struggles to complete his setting of Thomas's poems. He had set the poem 'Lights Out' in 1919. It is not hard to see why its depiction of an irresistible path into the dark and silence should have continued to appeal to him:

> . . . There is not any book
> Or face of dearest look
> That I would not turn from now
> To go into the unknown
> I must enter and leave alone
> I know not how.
>
> The tall forest towers;
> Its cloudy foliage lowers
> Ahead, shelf above shelf;
> Its silence I hear and obey
> That I may lose my way
> And myself.

A poem called 'Sounds', subtitled 'After E. Thomas', also dates from the 1925–6 period, when Gurney experienced another poetic surge.

'Sounds' was the last piece in a collection he put together in a brown-and-blue marbled exercise book and entitled *Best Poems*. On the title page below his name and his service and other details, he wrote '*First war poet* (He does truly believe)'. 'Sounds' was a list poem, which loosely strung together his favourite places and composers. Other poems flickered in and out of reminiscences of the war. 'Strange Hells' – 'There are strange hells within the minds war made' – re-created a moment of release in the trenches through song, 'that blither of tune: / "Après la guerre fini"'. 'The Silent One' recalled another trench-incident when an officer with 'a finicking accent' apparently asked Gurney to crawl through a non-existent hole in the wire – '"Do you think you might crawl through there; [Gurney's name crossed out] theres a hole"' – Gurney declined:

> 'I'm afraid not, Sir.' There was no hole, no way to be seen,
> Nothing but chance of death, after tearing of clothes
> Kept flat, and watched the darkness, hearing bullets whizzing –
> And thought of music – and swore deep heart's deep oaths.
> (Polite to God –) and retreated and came on again.
> Again retreated – and a second time faced the screen.

It was Marion Scott who, around the summer of 1932, suggested that Helen Thomas should visit Gurney. There were apparently several meetings. On the first, the two women took the train down from London. They were shown in by a warder. Doors were unlocked and locked. They came across Gurney in a corridor, 'a tall gaunt dishevelled man clad in pyjamas and dressing gown'. Scott made the introductions, and Gurney looked at Helen Thomas fixedly and silently took her hand. She had brought flowers and gave them to him: he accepted the flowers in silence with the same fixed look. The first thing he said was: 'You are Helen, Edward's wife and Edward is dead.' To which she replied: 'Yes, let us talk of him.'

They went to his bedroom, 'the only furniture was a bed and a chair'. Gurney placed the flowers on the bed as there was nowhere else to put them. The room itself was 'bare and drab', totally devoid of anything that could be used as a sharp implement. Gurney commented on Helen's 'pretty hat'. The conversation turned to her husband. She later recalled that although Gurney's conversation 'was generally quite sane and lucid, he said suddenly, "It was wireless that killed Edward", and this idea of the danger of wireless and his fear of it constantly occurred in his talk'. They talked about the Gloucestershire countryside with which Gurney particularly associated Thomas. Before Helen left, they went to another room where Gurney played the piano for her and Marion Scott and for a 'tragic circle of men who sat on hard benches built into the walls'.

On Helen's next visit, she brought with her some of her husband's old Ordnance Survey maps of the West Midlands and Welsh border. What happened next was a kind of miracle, a strange meeting indeed. Gurney laid the maps out on the bed:

> and he and I spent the whole time I was there tracing with our fingers the lanes and byways and villages of which Ivor Gurney knew every step and over which Edward had also walked. He spent that hour in revisiting his home, in spotting a village or a track, a hill or a wood and seeing it all in his mind's eye, with flowers and trees, stiles and hedges, a mental vision sharper and more actual for his heightened intensity. He trod, in a way we who were sane could not emulate, the lanes and fields he knew and loved so well, his guide being his finger tracing the way on the map . . . he had Edward as companion in this strange perambulation and he was utterly happy . . .

The maps, which still survive, support Helen Thomas's account. For there, in pencil at the top of Ordnance Survey Sheet 81, is 'Shows my home St Mary's' – St Mary's being the church at Norton Green that Gurney had written about with the distinctive tower in 'The Square Thing'.

In 1937 Gurney's health, never robust, went seriously downhill. In November, he was found to have pleurisy and TB. He lived long enough to receive but not to look at proofs of an edition of *Music and Letters*, put together by Marion Scott and the composer Gerald Finzi, and devoted exclusively to his work. On being shown the volume, he simply said: 'It is too late . . .' He died at 3.45 a.m. on the morning of 26 December 1937 and was buried five days later near Gloucester at Twigworth. The words on his tombstone, now mottled and lichen-eaten, read:

To The Dear Memory
Of
Ivor Gurney
Musician And Poet
A Lover And Maker
Of Beauty
1890–1937
Beside The Waters Of Comfort.

In late August 2007, I visited what remains of Stone House with my friend, the historian David Kynaston. It was a hot day and a sharp walk uphill to the hospital from the station. The gates were open and no one apparently about, so we walked in. On the left was what had once been the star-shaped Airing Court for the male patients (now a small wilderness), then a wide lawn with big, shady trees – pines, a copper-beech or two. There was a bit of breeze and it was pleasant to stroll around where Gurney must have walked endlessly, his head in a book.

On the right was the main building, the imposing façade still intact and looking remarkably like a nineteenth-century school or prison. The many windows were all boarded over. The whole was overlooked by a tall tower, which would have made a good observation post but was apparently purely ornamental. We walked across the front, past the wing for male patients, past the dining room, past the female patients' wing, and round the back. More boarded-up windows. Grass in cracked concrete. There was a chapel, St Luke's, separate from the main building. A back gateway gave on to a largish yard between the chapel and the administration wing of the hospital. By the back door stood a van; dogs were barking inside it. A man appeared and came towards us. He turned out to be the security guard, a grey-haired man in his fifties with a northern accent. For a moment we wondered if he was going to order us off the property, even set the dogs on us. In fact, he was very friendly and communicative. He knew a good deal about the hospital, past and present, sections of which, he said, had been in use for drug and alcohol cases until very recently. He hadn't heard of Ivor Gurney. He told us that in a few weeks the whole place would be closed up for renovation. The main building was to be made over into expensive residential flats, but keeping the façade as it was a listed building.

His main job, he said, was preventing 'travellers' from coming in at night and stripping the lead from the roofs (the only thing left still worth stealing). So far he had been successful. But, he added, he didn't much like being there at night – and nor did the dogs.

13

Hope Divine

Vera Brittain and Siegfried Sassoon, 13 January 1937

On the evening of Wednesday 13 January 1937, the Central Hall, Old Market, Bristol was packed. A large crowd had come to hear 'Dick' Sheppard, the charismatic founder of the Peace Pledge Union (PPU), and two of the PPU's most celebrated supporters, Vera Brittain and Siegfried Sassoon. According to one newspaper account, 900 Bristoleans had already signed the PPU's pledge: 'We renounce war and never again directly or indirectly will we support or sanction another.' Several local newspapers covered the event, though the brief report in the *Bristol Evening World* was almost entirely dwarfed by a half-page ad for the final fortnight of the James Phillips & Sons furniture sale. The rally fared better in the *Bristol Evening Post*.

Before the main gathering, there had been a 'tea-table conference' at which it was agreed to divide up the various districts of the city into peace teams. A moment of drama occurred while the crowds queued outside the hall. Seventy-nine-year-old George Barwood collapsed and was taken to hospital, where he was found to be dead on arrival. Inside the hall, it was announced that Sheppard would not after all be appearing. He had flu, and his place would be taken by his second-in-command Canon Stuart Morris.

Left: Vera Brittain, 1934
Right: Siegfried Sassoon, early 1940s

Morris began with the rearmament question, arguing that it was 'a premeditated policy of the indiscriminate mass murder of civilian populations'. Peace could only be achieved when people created the the right conditions. It was obvious that 'if goods do not cross frontiers, sooner or later armies must'. He urged the need for immediate negotiations before another war broke out.

Brittain followed Morris. What had made her a pacifist, she said, was not propaganda, but 'experience of life, or rather of death'. She talked of her time as a VAD after the battle of Cambrai in late 1917, nursing the early casualties from mustard gas. She had visited the area again in 1933, and the ground where the gas shells had fallen was so polluted that it had become completely barren. War, she insisted, was not inevitable; it was perpetuated by human volition.

She hit out at the current League of Nations, calling it 'merely a camouflage for the alliance of one group of Powers against another'. Nevertheless if the idea of the League could be developed and its organisation reformed, she hoped that a cure for war might one day be achieved. The next war, she predicted, 'would be a matter of skulking in dug-outs and not heroism on the field'. She pointed out that the cost of three bombardments in France during the Great War was the equivalent to funding a national maternity service for twenty years. In what sounds like a final peroration, she rousingly asked the audience 'to work as long as you have breath against the waste that is war. England needs the lives of her young people – not their deaths.'

Sassoon was next. He read nine poems, some from the Great War and some more recent work in a more peaceful vein. Exactly what he read is not known, but his presence and the effect of his reading overwhelmed Brittain. She listened 'with reddening nose, mopping my eyes'. He seemed, she told a friend, 'an epitome of the war generation at its gentlest and most pathetic'.

Very different paths had led Brittain and Sassoon to that peace platform in Bristol. But, for each of them, the immediately preceding years had been full of emotional and literary triumphs and disasters. The apparently confirmed homosexual Sassoon had, at the age of forty-seven, suddenly got married and become a besotted father. Brittain had discovered a long-concealed secret about her dead brother, and had lost her father and her dearest friend. She had also become a famous writer while Sassoon's poetic star had waned.

The year 1933, for both, marked a turning point. In late May, Sassoon's spoilt, sick lover Stephen Tennant finally broke with him – typically via a third party. The devoted Sassoon was distraught. Yet, within a couple of weeks he had met twenty-seven-year-old Hester Gatty, and by December he had married her. The initial meeting was arranged by a match-making female friend. The occasion was a pageant at Wilton House to commemorate the tercentenary of George Herbert's death. Sassoon had been persuaded to take part as an Elizabethan bard: a photograph shows him looking distinctly strained in ruff, doublet and baggy pantaloons. Hester, like Sassoon, was on the rebound. Poetry would bring them together.

In fact, it didn't. The first meeting was rather a non-event. Sassoon certainly noticed Hester – 'Miss G looked delightful in a lavender coloured silk dress (Charles 1 period)' – but displayed no further interest in her. Not so Hester. She preserved an oak sprig he had been holding as a personal treasure, and in early September she took the initiative. Sassoon was leasing Fitz House, an old, stone-flagged, mullion-windowed house in Teffont Magna, near Salisbury. Hester installed herself in the local inn, on the pretext of painting scenes of the village. The move worked: an encounter led to dinner, led to confidences and love, led to an engagement in November. (Stephen Tennant on hearing the news took to his bed for the next five months.) On 18 December 1933, the couple were privately married by a Canon Gay at Christchurch Priory, near Bournemouth. A dozen friends and relations were present. One was T E Lawrence – by then, known as Aircraftsman Shaw – who turned up on his motorbike Boanerges. Within a year, Sassoon and Hester had settled on their own 220-acre estate, Heytesbury House, on the borders of Salisbury Plain. In October 1936, after an earlier miscarriage, they were celebrating the birth of their son George. 'O Hester, you must redeem my life for me', Sassoon had written in early October 1933; three years later, it seemed as though she had.

On 28 August 1933, days before Hester made her decisive move, Brittain published *Testament of Youth*. Like Byron, she woke up to find herself famous, but, unlike Byron, she had waited a long time for fame. Married in 1925 to the political theorist George Catlin, she had spent much of the 1920s trying, and failing, to turn herself into a successful novelist: neither her Oxford nor Buxton novels, *The Dark Tide* (1923) and *Not Without Honour* (1924), had quite worked. More particularly, she had tried to write a novel based on her own war experiences and those of her war dead – fiancé Roland Leighton, brother Edward, and their friends Victor Richardson and Geoffrey Thurlow. This project went through umpteen drafts and versions with titles like 'The Pawn of Fate', 'Folly's Vineyard', 'The Incidental Adam', 'The War Generation' and 'Youth's Cavalry'. This, she knew, was her subject, her story, but how to tell it?

The breakthrough came in late 1928. She had been reading Blunden's recently published *Undertones of War* and thought it 'grave, dignified but perfectly simple and straightforward'. She caught herself wondering: 'Why shouldn't I write one like that?' What had failed to work as fiction might work as autobiography. The late 1920s had seen a boom in war novels and memoirs, and Brittain was soon immersing herself in these. With typical application, she treated *Undertones of War*, Graves's *Good-bye to All That* and Sassoon's *Memoirs of a Fox-hunting Man* and *Memoirs of an Infantry Officer* as how-to manuals. She found Sassoon's way of objectifying his material particularly helpful.

Brittain's study of Blunden, Graves, Sassoon and others prompted the reflection:

> Why should these young men have the war to themselves? Didn't women have their war as well? They weren't, as these men make them, only suffering wives and mothers, or callous parasites, or mercenary prostitutes ... Who will write the epic of the women who went to the war?

The answer was clear: she would. She had her very detailed diaries. She had Roland's letters, also her brother's and Victor's. Her letters to them had been preserved. The raw material was ready and waiting. Even so, the book took three years to write: she now had two small children, a household to run, a journalistic career to maintain, and a demanding position to uphold as a spokesperson on women's issues.

In the end, it was only thanks to a time-releasing, £500 annuity from her father that she was able to finish *Testament of Youth*, as she eventually called her memoir.

On publication, the book struck an immediate chord. 'Oh, *what* a head-cracking week!' she told her diary. 'Reviews, reviews, reviews, & reviews again. Never did I imagine that the *Testament* would inspire such great praise at such length, or provoke – in smaller doses – so much abuse.' Letters of appreciation poured in, requests for articles. Everyone wanted to know her. The first printing of 5,000 sold out in a week and within a fortnight a further 10,000 had been sold. (In October, the book proved a similar hit in America.) As Brittain had hoped, *Testament* provided the largely untold story of the women's war, both on the Home Front and on active service in hospitals. It also provided a tragic love story, one with which many could still identify.

She unashamedly enjoyed the sudden whirligig of fame. She gave talks up and down the country, wrote articles, and did a hugely successful lecture tour of the United States – falling in love with her American publisher George Brett in the course of it. She started a new novel, *Honourable Estate*, a multi-generational portrayal of changing attitudes by and towards women from the 1890s to the 1930s. Her hour had come.

While Brittain's literary stock rose, Sassoon's fell, at least as a poet. A gradual muffling had overtaken his poetry. The slangy attack and cartoon directness of wartime poems like 'Does it Matter?', 'The General' and 'To Any Dead Officer' had long gone. Even the baroque facetiousness of *Satirical Poems* (1926), which the young Auden admired, had evaporated:

> July proceeds. In ante-prandial strollings
> I note the Season's climax. Cabbage-green,
> Lush from humidity of cloud cajolings,
> Predominates the vegetative scene . . .

The late 1920s and early 1930s saw Sassoon struggling to recover a 'poetry that springs direct from the heart'. Too often the results sounded like this quatrain from 'Elected Silence':

> How solitude can hear! O see
> How stillness unreluctant stands
> Enharmonized with cloud and tree . . .
> O earth and heaven not made with hands!

Poetically, the war had brought out the best in him. It had been his subject and, in prose, remained so, as *Fox-hunting Man* and *Infantry Officer* clearly showed. But, in his poetry, even the war in time failed to fire his imagination, as 'War Experience', from 1929, acknowledged:

> somewhat softly booms
> A Somme bombardment: almost unbelieved-in looms
> The day-break sentry staring over Kiel Trench crater.

By 1934, in 'Ex-Service', he was reduced to echoing his own lines: the biting 'And speed glum heroes up the line to death' from 'Base Details' had become the shambling 'But most went glumly through it / Dumbly doomed to rue it'. The drop in poetic heat was palpable.

The fact was that, by the mid-1930s, Sassoon had become a poetic back-number. This was the decade of Auden, MacNeice, Spender and Day-Lewis – MacSpaunday as the poet Roy Campbell wittily called them. Their knowing tone, abrupt syntactical compressions, cryptic warnings of social and psychological breakdown made Sassoon's poems seem naively old-fashioned. And he knew it. Early 1936 saw him taking some mild revenge. In 'Aunt Eudora and the Poets', a *faux*-review of *The Year's Poetry 1935* in *The Spectator*, he hauled out opening and closing stanzas by Auden, William Empson, Ronald Bottrall and Rex Warner, and had 'Aunt Eudora' complain of their flatness, spurious metaphysics and 'pretentious verbiage'. He followed this up with 'Educating Aunt Eudora' – ostensibly a review of de la Mare's *Collected Poems* – and got a lengthy and rather po-faced response from the poet and anthologist Michael Roberts. In June, Sassoon rounded things off with 'Querkes, Farmonger and Dusp' in which 'Aunt Eudora' reminisced about a forgotten arty trio of painter, composer and poet, whose grandiose ambitions had only been matched by their absence of talent.

Sassoon had had his bit of fun, but all he had really demonstrated was that his prose was now livelier than his poetry. The point was further brought home in September 1936 by the success of the third and last volume of his George Sherston chronicles. His previous poetry collection *Vigils* (1935) had created little attention; *Sherston's Progress* was greeted with acclaim and sold well. Sassoon badly needed something to reaffirm his vocation and standing as a poet.

Testament of Youth brought Brittain other consequences along with fame. In it, she had written movingly about her brother's death on the Italian Front, shot in the head by a sniper on the morning of 15 June 1918, after helping to repulse an enemy attack. She had also written at some length about her attempts to find out more about his death from his commanding officer, Colonel Charles Hudson – wounded in the same attack and awarded a VC. Back in 1918, Brittain had tracked Hudson down to a hospital near Park Lane and found him suspiciously evasive. Eager to think the best of her beloved brother, she portrayed Hudson in *Testament of Youth* in less than flattering terms: 'a stiff young disciplinarian, impregnated with all the military virtues but limited in imagination and benevolence'. She strongly implied that he saw her attentions as husband-hunting and even that he might have taken credit for honours that rightly belonged to her brother.

Hudson, understandably nettled by his depiction in *Testament of Youth* and feeling that Brittain deserved to know the truth, got in touch with her in the summer of 1934. The story he had to tell was not at all what she had expected. Edward and another officer had been having homosexual relations with their men. This was clear from a letter from the other officer to Edward, picked up by the censor at the base. Hudson, according to his own account, was ordered to keep things under wraps while investigations proceeded. But he felt uncomfortable about doing so and, on 14 June, privately dropped a heavy hint to Edward, who 'turned white'. The next day Edward was killed. On hearing of his death, Hudson immediately assumed that – to avoid the court martial and disgrace which would undoubtedly have followed disclosure – Edward had either shot himself or deliberately courted death. Sixteen years later, he still felt responsible for whatever had happened. Brittain reassured Hudson in a letter, dismissing the notion that her brother would have countenanced suicide in any form.

However, her inclusion of a similar death in action under similar circumstances in *Honourable Estate* suggests her real reaction. To find out the truth after so long must have been a devastating shock, not least the discovery that, for all their closeness, her brother had been leading a secret life.

Other devastations soon followed. Her father's health and spirits had not been good for years. He had frequently talked about suicide and in the early hours of 2 August 1935 he drowned himself in the Thames near Richmond. When his already much-decomposed body was found three days later, Brittain's husband George discouraged her from seeing it, but told her the face looked 'black and red and swollen like the bruised face of a prize-fighter'. Her father had apparently been much preoccupied with a favourite song, 'The Diver', and with thoughts of 'how dreadful it must be at the bottom of the sea'.

Worse still was the death the following month of her dearest friend Winifred Holtby. Their friendship had been forged at Oxford after the war. Following university, they had shared lodgings, thoughts, feminist politics and literary aspirations – Winifred was the more prolific and successful novelist. When Brittain married George, she assured Winifred that she still loved her best but needed them both. 'The ideal life,' she wrote to Winifred while on honeymoon, '. . . seems to me that in which I come into daily contact with both him and you.'

If this ideal wasn't always achieved, or achievable, Winifred certainly remained the most important person in Brittain's life and was a semi-regular member of the household. George accepted the situation, and the children knew her as Auntie. Then in 1932 Winifred was diagnosed with Bright's disease (renal sclerosis). Although her condition seemed to stabilise over the next two years, by 1935 she went into a serious decline and died in a nursing home on 29 September, with Brittain holding her hand.

Over the years there has been much written about the Brittain–Holtby friendship, and about how exactly to characterise it. Brittain always denied the relationship was a sexual one. 'I am wholly a heterosexual person,' she claimed, 'without an atom of homosexuality in my make-up.' This was not what several thought at the time and others have thought since. Some have argued that theirs was a lesbian relationship, pure and simple, but one which could not be publicly acknowledged. Some that it was, in effect, a lesbian relationship but that one or both of the participants may not have been aware of the true nature of their feelings. Then there are those who say Brittain was not a lesbian but Winifred was – or was an unconscious one. And so on. Such discussions have their interest, reminding us, if nothing else, that people in the past had emotional lives quite as complicated and conflicted as our own. Brittain fell in love with at least two men and married a third – with whom she had two children and shared most of her adult life. Yet, without sensing any contradiction, she knowingly loved Winifred more deeply than any of these men.

Her brother, Edward Brittain, seems to have seen himself as exclusively homosexual, but did Sassoon see himself like that? While clearly predominantly homosexual, he does seem to have genuinely fallen in love with Hester – and for a few years at least had a full marriage. He certainly turned into a proud and doting father. This must complicate, to some degree, one's sense of his sexual make-up. Brittain's and Sassoon's stories – Graves's and Brooke's too – are a reminder that while sexuality is sometimes a matter of either/or, it can also be a matter of both/and.

On one of the last times Brittain saw Winifred, she noted in her diary: 'As I came out of the home leaving Winifred dying & unconscious, a newspaper placard confronted me: "Abyssinia Mobilises". Everything that Winifred and I had lived & worked for – peace, justice, decency – seemed to be gone.' One of the organisations the two friends had assiduously worked for was the League of Nations. But by the mid-1930s Brittain had come to feel that the League though admirable in principle was in practice ineffectual or, as she was to tell her Bristol audience, 'merely a camouflage for the alliance of one group of Powers against another'. She began to look for a different kind of peace forum. This she eventually found in 'Dick' Sheppard's PPU.

Sheppard was a former vicar of St Martin-in-the-Fields and now a canon at St Paul's Cathedral. A noted speaker and broadcaster on peace and poverty issues, he had the common touch, the ability to strike up an instant rapport with individuals he met and crowds he lectured to. In October 1934, he initiated what was to become the PPU with an open letter in the press. The letter urged men – the peace movement already commanded widespread support among women – to send him a postcard with the pledge: 'We renounce war and never again directly or indirectly will we support or sanction another.' Within weeks, Sheppard had been deluged with tens of thousands of postcards. This overwhelming response led to a peace rally at the Albert Hall in July 1935 – 7,000 attended – and in May 1936 to the formal inauguration of the PPU. A couple of months later, women too were invited to join.

Various factors drew Brittain to Sheppard and his movement. One was undoubtedly the fact that he and Winifred had been on friendly terms. This connection was underlined by Sheppard taking Winifred's memorial service at St Martin-in-the-Fields. In her diary, Brittain noted with approval: 'Canon Sheppard said that because those who were left must carry on the struggle, we would end the service by singing "Jerusalem"', adding that the hymn had been her choice. On 3 October 1935, Mussolini duly invaded Abyssinia, and League of Nations sanctions proved no deterrent.

A three-week trip to Germany in the late spring of 1936 saw a further sharpening of Brittain's desire for significant pacifist action. On 28 March, she heard Hitler address an audience of 10,000 in Cologne. With his clenched fist and breast-beating, he struck her as more a 'religious maniac' than a 'wily diplomatist'. His fanaticism was frightening, but Goering had been even scarier in Charlottenburg, Berlin, the previous day. His speech had been 'like the letting loose of some enormous impersonal force'. '"Germany is going to rearm," he told the fervent crowd. "Pacifism is a phrase – what matters is honour & freedom."' Applause punctuated his words 'like the roar of a titanic waterfall'.

A couple of months later, in blazing June heat, Brittain found herself addressing a large peace gathering near Dorchester. She and the other speakers, of whom Sheppard was one, were seated on an elevated platform under 'a striped sun umbrella'. Awaiting her turn, Brittain watched Sheppard, a chronic asthmatic, inhaling 'oxygen from a rubber apparatus'. When he spoke, she registered that he too was no mean demagogue, able to 'play on the emotions of a crowd with a master's skill' – if for quite other purposes than Hitler or Goering.

Afterwards she travelled back with Sheppard on the London train. Brittain was not always the easiest in company but, during a lengthy conversation, Sheppard impressed her by his 'deep humanity and magnetic charm'. She was also taken by his utter informality: 'with his coat thrown on the table and shirt-sleeves rolled up, he resembled a tipsy cricketer going home at the end of a too enjoyable afternoon.' This meeting certainly nudged Brittain closer to the PPU though it was not until early January 1937, a few days before the Bristol rally, that she officially joined the union. It was apparently reading Bertrand Russell's *Which Way to Peace?* which finally tipped the balance.

The cricket-mad Sassoon would have enjoyed Brittain's description of Sheppard as like a tipsy cricketer. He himself had been involved with the emergent PPU rather longer and had read at the first Albert Hall rally in 1935. Wisely, his contributions always mixed the old and the new. The old included the joyful 'Everyone Sang'; the new, the heartfelt but awkward 'Credo', which imagined a spiritually improved humanity whose hallowed ground would be the war's 'dumb forgotten dead' and in whose eyes would 'shine my deathless hope divine'. In 1936, Sassoon gave no less than five 'peace' readings. For one, in November again at the Albert Hall, he specially wrote 'A Prayer from 1936'. In the poem the only voices audible to those in the hell of the modern world are the voices of the 'tyrant and the politician', calling for rearmament and war.

Such readings, including the one with Brittain in Bristol the following January, affirmed to Sassoon that, back-number he might be, but he remained *the* war poet. He was, as Brittain acknowledged, a piece of walking history. Together, they spoke for a large constituency of those who had lived through the horror of war – and couldn't bear for it to happen again. But, ironically, that Bristol reading was one of the last Sassoon gave for the PPU. He was starting to move away from an entirely pacifist position just at the time when Brittain was becoming ever more closely involved. A year later, and it is unlikely their paths would have crossed.

'Dick' Sheppard died suddenly at his desk in late October 1937. The PPU continued its work under his deputy, Canon Morris. Sassoon and Brittain both enshrined Sheppard's personal importance to them in their work. Sassoon wrote a short elegy published in December 1937 in the *St Martin's Review*, its essence encapsulated in the couplet: 'You and your work for Christ, for whom you died, / In long remembrance live beatified.' After the Second World War, Brittain used Sheppard as the model for Robert Carbury, the pacifist vicar hero of her last novel *Born 1925* (1948).

14

No Fire Brigade Was Needed
for the Thames

Robert Nichols, Robert Graves,
Siegfried Sassoon, Autumn 1943

In late 1917 Robert Graves had been cheerfully anticipating the poetic future of 'we three inevitables' – Nichols, Sassoon and himself. But things had not gone according to plan. After the war, Sassoon soon became poetically *passé* but eventually reinvented himself as a cele-brated war-memoirist in prose. Graves, though very productive as a poet in the 1920s and '30s, was to have his greatest successes with prose: first with *Good-bye to All That* and then with his two Roman novels, *I, Claudius* and *Claudius the God*, both published in 1934. After his marriage to Hester, Sassoon increasingly retreated into the past, re-creating as the squire of Heytesbury a version of his pre-war world. Graves, with Laura Riding, had also retreated, and during the 1930s turned himself into the magus of Mallorca.

But what had happened to Robert Nichols, the third of the inevit-ables, the poetic star of 1917, the heir to Rupert Brooke?

In September 1918, after an unsuccessful attempt to re-enlist, Nichols had gone to the States on a lecture tour. He lectured at Yale, Vassar, Cornell, Chicago, Nashville, Pittsburgh and elsewhere. He talked

Left: Robert Nichols by Catherine Dodgson, 1935–6
Right: Robert Graves at Galmpton, 1943

about the effects of war and about recent British war poets, concentrating on Sassoon, Graves and Sorley. He told the *Boston Evening Transcript* shortly before the Armistice that Sassoon was his greatest friend among his contemporaries and that, of those who had died young in the war, Sorley's was the greatest disaster for English literature. He obviously hadn't lost any of the theatricality so apparent at the Sibyl Colefax readings in November and December 1917. It was 'with a shaking voice and with outstretched, nervous hands' that he told a Nashville audience:

> The love of officers and men is the one beautiful thing which developed . . . War makes no man finer. It is a process of defilement, a time when you wait and lurk to kill your neighbour, as he is waiting and lurking to kill you. To say that such as that makes a soul better is blather.

While he was away, Nichols reaffirmed the poetic triumvirate in a playful new poem, 'Winter Overnight', written in New York. This snowy pastoral continued the affectionate verse letters which had passed between Graves, Sassoon and himself during the war. Here Nichols contrasted his and Graves's very different versions of heaven. His own heaven was solitary and Marvellian:

> just so white, so bright, so still,
> As this white air and that white hill,
> Wherein sight's fixed and sound is caught
> Into one pure celestial thought.

Graves's heaven was boisterous and busy with children:

> Bright-eyed, red-cheeked, with towsled hair,
> My cherubs foray here and there,
> Cracking the sky with jolly shout;
> Bandying the brittle snow about . . .

Sassoon was brought in at the end to – or fail to – adjudicate between the two: 'Both heavens are good – but of the two . . . / Judge for me, World, now: which would you?' This was not just wishful thinking

on Nichols's part; Graves at least still fully shared the vision of the
big three. When Eddie Marsh's fourth anthology, *Georgian Poetry
1918–1919*, appeared, the poems Graves picked out for special praise
were Nichols's 'The Sprig of Lime' and Sassoon's 'Everyone Sang'.

Back in England, Nichols embarked on a wild affair with rebellious heiress and cultural trophy hunter Nancy Cunard. It was mostly
melodrama and ended in tears. On one occasion she smacked his
face in public; on another, Nichols pulled out a pistol, tossed it at
Cunard's feet and begged her to stop him shooting himself. When
he wrote a sequence of love sonnets about the affair, and published
them in *Aurelia and Other Poems* (1920), Cunard was not amused. 'Lord
had I but known what I was starting, when I got hold of that young
man,' she confided to her diary; ' . . . He is mad, no doubt of it, and
very, very common, but thinks he is a genius instead of which he is
really a shocking poet.'

Not all the reviewers of *Aurelia* thought so badly of the poems.
The *Morning Post* continued to tout Nichols as 'the greatest of the
"Georgian poets"' and hoped that he might still 'become the Keats of
a new century'. *The Times Literary Supplement*, which had previously
installed Nichols among the immortals, now, however, backed off.
Gosse had already administered a private wigging. 'Flattery and excitement and the silly criticism of an adoring circle of admirers have
completely turned you, for the time being, out of the true path,' he
wrote Nichols in July 1919, warning him that he was 'on the brink of
poetical bankruptcy'.

In 1920 Nichols joined Graves, Blunden and the other poets on
Boar's Hill near Oxford. Graves and his wife Nancy fully expected
Nichols to stir things up, and so he did. He would suddenly appear
with a fog-shattering laugh, Blunden later recalled, 'tall and thin and
quick' in a mulberry-coloured suit. He would hold forth on Goethe.
He would complain that 'Oxford was full of *little* writers' and, swooping
on the other poets' poems, would get out his blue pencil and make
annotations and corrections – his illegible handwriting flew across the
page. When Hardy attended an undergraduate production of scenes
from *The Dynasts*, Nichols shook hands with the old poet, 'bowing
over him with a suggestion that it might be Goethe who was welcom-
ing the seer of Wessex'. Boar's Hill was a magical time for Nichols:
the evenings with Graves and Blunden had, he claimed, 'some of the

romance' of the Pre-Raphaelite circle producing *The Germ* or 'that Leigh Hunt and his friends must have known when Keats was at Hampstead'.

But, as quickly as Nichols appeared, he was gone. In 1921 he took up a professorship in English Literature at Imperial College, Tokyo. It was partly the money. The university was offering him just over £1,000 a year, a significant increase on his father's £240 allowance. In Japan, he lectured on Shakespeare, Meredith and Whitman, but to judge by the amount of literary journalism he turned out for the *Japan Advertiser*, he cannot have been overburdened with teaching. The other reason he took the job was that he wanted to marry Norah Denny.

Nichols and Norah had probably first met in 1916 when, still on sick leave, he was sent by the Red Cross to recuperate with a Mrs Denny in Sussex. Or they could have met via musical circles through Norah's uncle Roger Quilter. However they met, her family did not at all approve of the match: an impoverished, sick, unstable poet was not at all what the affluent Dennys – their money made from bacon – had in mind for their daughter. Marry they did, nevertheless, during Nichols's leave from Japan in July 1922. The ceremony took place in St Martin-in-the-Fields with 'Dick' Sheppard officiating. Norah's father refused to attend altogether, and her mother stayed in the vestry throughout the service; but the literary and musical worlds turned up in force: the Sitwells, Elgar, Masefield, Huxley, Ronald Firbank, Marsh ('in a top-hat and tears'), Nichols's fan Cynthia Asquith, with her husband Beb. Roger Quilter gave Norah away. Sassoon, in a 'black coat (minus abhorred tails)' and wearing 'a tie that had enough in it to be a little Radical', was best man.

Graves was not invited to the wedding and complained to Blunden that Nichols had not even sent 'a piece of his cake or a slice of his father-in-law's prime bacon'. At first the marriage was a success. This was no doubt mostly because Norah was happy to play helpmate to the genius. As she later wrote in a newspaper article entitled 'On Being the Wife of a Poet': 'To begin with, she must be of the kind who really enjoys playing second fiddle.'

Nichols left Japan in 1924 and was succeeded by Blunden. He may have left under a cloud – not unlikely, given his capacity for scrapes. But he did not leave empty-handed. He had completed his first play there, *Guilty Souls*, published in 1922, and started a new one, *Komuso*, at which he tinkered for years. *Guilty Souls* began, in Nichols's words, 'with two solicitors and a deed box' and ended with 'two guilty souls and God'. The play, long on dialogue and short on action, revolved around embezzlement, guilt and revenge. Nichols's aim was a metaphysical thriller that would stir an audience 'with the thrill of a crooked soul's attempted escape from God'. Whether such a thrill would or could be achieved has never been put to the test. What made *Guilty Souls* notable was its sixty-seven-page introduction, a leisurely disquisition on the need for a 'Moral Renaissance', led by the 'passionate few'. Here for the first time Nichols had hit on his most natural form of composition: the preface.

After Japan came Hollywood, and another bright beginning. Nichols and Norah landed full of hopes that he would find work as a scriptwriter. Douglas Fairbanks Sr eventually took him on at a salary of $150 a month; but Nichols no more got the hang of Hollywood than he had of Japan. He turned out various treatments, co-authored another play, *Twenty Below*, and wrote articles for *The Times* on 'The Future of the Cinema'. None of the scriptwriting led to anything, and Nichols soon exemplified that later Hollywood witticism: 'Forgotten but not gone'. By the time the couple returned to England in 1926, the closest he had come to making his mark was being a consultant on Fairbanks's *The Black Pirate*. In practice, this meant he had helped with the night trial and the scene in which the hero walks the plank.

Back in England the couple settled in Winchelsea where Norah's relenting parents bought them a house. Nichols had another misfire with *Under the Yew* (1928), a gothic tale about gambling, set in the late eighteenth century. But then, unexpectedly, he had another moment in the sun. This was with *Wings Over Europe: A Dramatic Extravaganza on a Pressing Theme*, co-written with Maurice Browne. The idea itself was promising. Francis Lightfoot, a brilliant young physicist and nephew to the British Prime Minister, has succeeded in splitting the atom. He reveals this momentous news to the Cabinet, imagining his breakthrough will free mankind from all material needs and herald a new utopia. He gives the Cabinet a week to release the news and organise the beneficial consequences. The Cabinet is predictably appalled and plans to imprison Lightfoot. He returns a week later and, fearing the Cabinet's reaction, has made contingency plans: to blow up the earth. Before he can do so, however, he is shot on stage by the Secretary of State for War. A final stage direction underlined the meaning of the title: 'The roar of aeroplanes fills the entire theatre', the harbinger presumably of world destruction.

Wings Over Europe premièred in New York in December 1928, was well received, ran for ninety performances and went on tour. It opened to mixed reviews in London in April 1932, the month before the atom really was split. Aldous Huxley in Time and Tide thought the play a 'very interesting and spirited dramatic fable'; the Observer called it the 'prose epitome of the Socialist Song-Book'. Wings Over Europe, to Nichols's intense disappointment, closed after a fortnight.

When Graves's Good-bye to All That appeared in November 1929, Nichols, like Blunden, was a natural choice to review it: the Listener gave him a column and a half. His relations with Graves had also taken a nose-dive with the entry of Laura Riding into Graves's life. Nichols had invited Graves to Winchelsea around the time of his review and suggested he bring Laura Riding. He made the mistake of referring to Riding as 'your lady'. This led to a swift ticking-off from Graves, followed by another from Riding. When Nichols renewed his invitation with an apology, Riding sent him an eight-page tirade in her best mind-numbing manner: 'It is one of the laws of the universe that you will have to accept: that when you make an observation about me you get a statement back. It just happens.' That, and Graves's and Riding's flit to Mallorca, effectively ended the friendship with Graves, though the two kept tabs on each other from a distance.

None of this stopped Nichols from giving Good-bye the thumbs up. He praised Graves's humour, skill and integrity, and called the book brave and good-tempered. He endorsed the account of public school life while conceding it would 'startle many and horrify some'. He commended the war narrative, 'nonetheless vivid for being extremely direct and matter-of-fact'. He regretted that a writer who had 'written more good poetry than any living Englishman under forty' was unable to earn his living in the post-war world. This was handsome, particularly since Graves had dismissed Nichols himself in a single paragraph: 'Another poet on Boar's Hill was Robert Nichols, still another neurasthenic ex-soldier, with his flame-opal ring, his wide-brimmed hat, his flapping arms and "mournful grandeur" (the phrase is from a review by Sir Edmund Gosse).' Graves even denied the legend he had so assiduously promoted back in 1917 of Nichols, Sassoon and himself as 'the new Three Musketeers'. Blunden noticed, and noted crisply in the margin of his copy of *Good-bye* that back then Nichols was 'almost worshipped by R.G., & considered by R.G. as with S.S. and himself forming the Big Three of poetry'. Nichols noticed too but made no comment in his review. He was hurt though. In one of his weekly letters to his old mentor Henry Head, he kept insisting that he didn't reproach Graves for 'not remembering or not counting me among his friends'.

The 1930s saw three other occasions when Nichols almost re-established himself as a significant literary figure. The first was the inclusion of his 1918 poem 'Dawn on the Somme' in Arthur Bliss's choral symphony and war requiem, *Morning Heroes*. Nichols attended the première at the Norwich Festival on 22 October 1930. He arrived at the venue after a bone- and nerve-shaking train journey and a ghastly dinner at the hotel: 'My wild duck had been a marathon runner and had evidently tried to do a bolt while half-cooked.' But the perform-ance itself was impressive and moving. When the artillery came in and 'the cries of War! War!', he 'began to twitch like an automaton' and later started to cry. Wilfred Owen's 'Spring Offensive' was, he thought, 'perhaps the most moving thing in the whole work'. He thought his own 'Dawn on the Somme' – a phrase from which gave *Morning Heroes* its title – opened well, but the sopranos 'had nothing left for the "Who arise, arise" on to the end which is one crescendo from f to fff'. *The Times* approved but *Morning Heroes* gave no fillip to Nichols's standing, and any boost to his self-esteem was soon blotted out by an act of literary assassination from an old acquaintance.

The assassin was Osbert Sitwell, the scene of the crime a short story 'Alive – Alive Oh!'. In the story a Georgian poet Joseph Bundle has a boom during and just after the war, but when he fails to die young in the approved Keatsian manner his stock falls and sales plummet. Literary oblivion is only averted when Bundle, apparently gravely ill, goes to Italy and duly dies. At once his reputation and sales soar, and his widow becomes rich. But it has all been a hoax, and years later Bundle is discovered by the narrator, alive and well in Calabria. The story appeared in Sitwell's collection *Dumb-Animal and other stories* in 1930. Nichols saw himself as Bundle, and was as furious as Sassoon and Blunden had been reading *Good-bye to All That*.

In fact, Bundle was not an individual portrait but a composite. Sitwell had literally bundled him together from various Georgians including John Squire, Sassoon, Graves, and especially Blunden – Bundle had 'a special line in birds, fresh-water fish, and . . . old people in alehouse and workhouse', and – an obvious giveaway – his name was a near-anagram of Blunden's. But Sitwell had undoubtedly borrowed some details from Nichols: Bundle was a gunner, fell from a roof, had early success, was likened to Keats, and suffered a sharp decline in reputation and sales in the post-war period. Woundingly, Sitwell had parodied specific Nichols phrases and poetic features in Bundle's best-known poem. This was quite enough for someone as self-absorbed as Nichols, and he took revenge in kind. The result was *Fisbo*, a satire in heroic couplets of a would-be poet, whose name subliminally recalled Osbert's. The poem appeared in October 1934 in a limited, signed edition of 1,000 copies, price 7s. 6d.

The poem sent up 1920s and '30s celebrity culture, in particular the contemporary literary scene. Fellow-Georgians – described as 'sticking to their guns' – were exempt, also T S Eliot, but not Ezra Pound. The Sitwells' poetic pretensions were, surprisingly, only given a quick generic spank:

> That precious harp, most fair of all fair things,
> Which, when some sort of Sitwell smites the strings,
> 'Sobs out' (ah me!) 'its crystal syrupings' . . .

When Fisbo fails to get his own satire published, he is rescued by publicity agent Max S Fitzgammon who soon lays down the modern poetic law:

> *Abolish Imagination; eschew Passion;*
> *Syllables must not dance – it's out of fashion.*
> *The music should be flat; the sense yet flatter;*
> *Should such persist, they should out-mad the hatter.*

Fisbo learns his lessons well, particularly '*Let us be known*: that is the only *credo*' and eventually becomes a household name, much touted in the popular press.

The reviews were glowing. The *Manchester Guardian* saluted the poem as the revenge of the vanishing Georgians on the 'new bardolatry': 'There was a dragon to be slain and it is a Georgian who has slain it.' Marsh was ecstatic. 'It's a really magnificent piece of satiric writing, full of poetry and wit,' he told another vanishing Georgian, Francis Brett Young. Within a month, 700 copies had been sold, and Nichols must have thought he had finally cracked it.

But no. *Fisbo* was another fizzer, and Graves's lack of interest – 'I haven't read *Fishboo* [*sic*],' he told Marsh bluntly – soon became the norm. The truth was the poem was far too long, far too diffuse – always Nichols's besetting sin. Dryden needed only 200 lines to demolish Shadwell in 'Mac Flecknoe', Pope a mere twenty-nine to skewer Sporus in 'Epistle to Dr Arbuthnot'. Nichols took around 4,500 lines to fail to nobble Fisbo. His jibe at Fisbo's satire proved true of his own: 'No fire brigade was needed for the Thames.'

His third opportunity was W B Yeats's *Oxford Book of Modern Verse* (1936). The anthology contained nine of Nichols's poems, including four of the 'Aurelia' sonnets and 'Don Juan's Address to the Sunset', an extract from an unfinished play. This was a serious strike rate among his fellow-Georgians and war poets. Blunden scored six, Sassoon four, and Brooke one. Graves, Owen, Thomas and Co were not featured at all: Owen's omission, which has been commented on ever since, was due to Yeats's dictum that 'passive suffering is not a theme for poetry'. Even before publication, however, Nichols was unhappy about the poems Yeats had chosen and feared the worst. He was right. The anthology was panned, and his own work barely mentioned.

Nichols's health, about which he had long complained, continued to seesaw wildly (at one point he had a kidney removed), and his domestic life went into sharp decline when Norah left him. She finally got fed up with playing the faithful helpmate to someone who was proving increasingly less faithful to her. When he eventually fell for the very much younger Vivienne Wilkinson in 1934, Norah took off, and the couple got divorced. With ups and downs, the affair with Vivienne lasted the rest of Nichols's life, although it was still Norah who typed up the manuscripts.

The outbreak of the Second World War found Nichols in debt and muddle, living in the south of France. When Germany occupied France in 1940, he escaped to England and settled down in modest circumstances in Cambridge. In June 1942 Collins brought out *Such Was My Singing*, his selected poems. This contained generous servings from *Ardours and Endurances* and *Aurelia*, together with gobbets from *Fisbo* and the Don Juan play, and other uncollected lyrics. The introduction, a defence of Nichols's poetic practice, was a modest twenty-five pages long. Responses were muted. The *New Statesman* wondered 'why so energetic a poet, so volubly conscious of a high purpose, should, after all, have so little work to select, from', while the *Adelphi* saw Nichols

> standing defiantly on the bridge, but quite sure that his ship – the ship of bourgeois values, if you like, or the ship of humanist culture – will pull through somehow, unaware, one suspects, of the extent to which it has already sunk.

But he was not finished yet. The following year Nicholson & Watson brought out his delayed *Anthology of War Poetry 1914–1918*. The anthology, which contained fifty-four poems in all, was a bringing together, a meeting of Nichols's favourite war poems and former friends.

Brooke was represented by the five war sonnets, Owen by four poems (including 'Spring Offensive' and 'Anthem for Doomed Youth'), and Sorley simply by 'All the hills and vales along'. Nichols's staunchest friend Sassoon was awarded thirteen poems, including 'To Any Dead Officer' and 'Reconciliation' but few of the really bitter ones. Blunden had nine poems and Graves eight. Graves's recent 'Recalling War' with its tough ironies and mocking echoes of Brooke was the surprise selection and arguably the highlight of the entire collection:

> Entrance and exit wounds are silvered clean,
> The track aches only when the rain reminds . . .
>
> Fear made fine bed-fellows. Sick with delight
> At life's discovered transitoriness,
> Our youth became all-flesh and waived the mind.
> Never was such antiqueness of romance,
> Such tasteless honey oozing from the heart.

Nichols restricted himself to two entries – 'Battery Moving Up' and
the post-war 'Epic Wind' as an inspiriting epilogue: *'Blessëd be those for
England died, / Blessëd by those for her shall live!'* There was no Thomas,
no Rosenberg, no Gurney. The poets were arranged, in imitation of
Nichols's own once celebrated 'Ardours and Endurances' sequence, to
tell an exemplary 'muse in arms' story of the war: early patriotism
(Brooke); movement towards action (Sorley, Nichols); actual combat
(Graves and Blunden); disillusionment (Sassoon); elegiac regret
(Owen).

The fifty pages of poems were however swamped by the eighty-
three-page preface. Dated January 1940, this took the form of an
imaginary conversation between Nichols and a young friend, Julian
Tennyson. Tennyson – a real person, later killed in Burma – had just
been called up, and Nichols imagined the two of them debating their
very different attitudes to their respective wars. The main point of
the preface was of course for Nichols to expound his views about the
Great War. He slowly teased out a number of elements he had come
to feel were integral to the combatants' experience – especially that
of his own volunteer generation of 1914. These elements included the
volunteers' almost total ignorance of modern warfare, the deep bonds
of battalion loyalty, the absolute squalor of life at the front, the largely
disregarded significance of psychological trauma, the change of spirit
after conscription and the Somme, and the impassable gulf between
combatants and non-combatants.

The poets were adroitly woven into the unfolding discussion.
Brooke's sonnets were praised as 'a just, dazzling and perfect expression of what we all felt'. Sorley's rejection of Brooke was noted as a
significant turning-point in the poetry of the war as was his lead in
expressing 'the pity and exaltation felt by an officer in the presence
of the men he commands'. Owen's *'Apologia pro Poemate Meo'* was
approvingly cited as evidence of the 'fellowship . . . exclusive,
passionate and fiercely scornful' which developed among the troops:
'Bound with the bandage of the arm that drips, / Knit in the webbing
of the rifle-thong'. Sassoon was saluted as 'the first poet to blow the
gaff' on the estrangement between the troops at the front and those
back in England, and as 'A man of quite exceptional moral as well as
physical courage'. Nichols's major reservation about the poets of the
Great War was their lack of 'Elevated beauty having a tragic tone'.

The only poems that had come close to sounding the true tragic note were Blunden's 'Zero' – 'It's plain we were born for this, naught else' – and Owen's 'Spring Offensive':

> But many there stood still
> To face the stark, blank sky beyond the ridge,
> Knowing their feet had come to the end of the world.

The anthology was a totally lopsided affair, but Desmond MacCarthy was right to call the preface 'the best piece of prose Mr Robert Nichols has written, and extremely interesting'. It was also Nichols's swansong; he died in Cambridge on 17 December 1944. The cause of death was heart failure, the end-product perhaps of the syphilis Nichols had contracted nearly thirty years earlier. When Marsh heard the news, he wrote to the novelist Charles Morgan (evoking Keats to the last):

> It's tragic to think of his last moments, if he realized that he would never live to trace the shadows of the symbols that crowded his brain. I never had much belief in *Don Juan*, but some of his projects were very fine – if only he had been able to concentrate on one of them.

Nichols received some warm obituaries, and a memorial service was held on 3 January 1945 in the Church of All Saints, Margaret Street. The order of service included Gluck, Mozart, Bach, two psalms, and readings from St John's Gospel, Job, Timothy and Corinthians. Two of Nichols's poems were read out: a short lyric – 'The wood is still; I do not hear / A single bird-song grieved or gay' – and 'Don Juan's Address to the Sunset': 'Exquisite stillness! What serenities / Of earth and air!'. The reader was John Laurie, the Scottish actor who played the grumpy crofter in Hitchcock's *The 39 Steps*, and later the equally grumpy Fraser in *Dad's Army*.

Two old friends also wrote tributes. In fact, Graves had already written his the year before Nichols's death. The military historian Basil Liddell Hart had been reading Nichols's *Anthology of War Poetry* and asked Graves about its compiler. Graves's summary of Nichols's character and career was cruel, funny but not inaccurate:

Robert . . . was an unbalanced undergraduate in 1914 who pelted
Lloyd George with mangolds and pheasants at the Union . . . Then he
went to the war, spent 3 weeks with the Gunners in a quiet part of
the line, fell off a roof, went home as shell-shocked, slept with 17
prostitutes in 3 weeks and got a bad dose. As his mother was in the
looney-bin and he himself was always pretty unsettled, this did him
no good; he recovered, was a terrific comet of success in poetry in 1917,
went to the USA to lecture, told frightful lies about his war service
and involved me in them, was always having passionate terrible love
affairs . . . Then he played the genius for a bit, went to Japan, Tokyo
University, as Professor, did something awful and was saved from
destruction by a medical certificate . . . Went to Los Angeles to be a
copy writer in Douglas Fairbanks's circus. . . . Married a Miss (Bacon
– rich) Denny, a niece of Roger Quilter. Became a prosperous poet at
Yew Tree Cottage, Winchelsea; lost a kidney; became such a bore that
wife left him recently . . . Is now rather living on past glories. His chief
gift is musical. I like him but he is too much of an embarrassment to
have about . . .

Blunden's 'In Memory of Robert Nichols' was kinder. Fittingly, it
contained a line from Nichols's own 'Farewell to a Place of Comfort':

> 'The bell is sounding down in Dedham Vale',
> And merry Robert in his snow-wrapt grave;
> O come again, join star and nightingale –
> But truth turns wintry now. Let tempest rave.

That was not quite the end; Nichols had one final, posthumous stab
at fame. In November 1955 the Arts Theatre Club put on his long-
gestated Japanese play, *Komuso*, after a successful radio broadcast the
previous year. Honor Blackman played Karin, the doomed heroine,
with whom the three male characters – all versions of Nichols himself
– are in love. *Komuso* ran from 8 November till 11 December. Kenneth
Tynan was the most generous reviewer, calling the play a 'jewel-
scattered ruin'. The *Financial Times* had a field day: 'Paul Eddington
plays a howling cad in a topee who gives his hostess an unaccustomed
nip of gin, seduces her in an earthquake and appears in the last act
in riding breeches and boots – or did one dream it?' Milton Shulman's

verdict was the most telling. While agreeing the piece 'richly deserves the neglect that the years have heaped upon it', he felt it was 'a well-meaning play earnestly groping for some significance that is constantly eluding it'. That last phrase, slightly adapted, might stand as Robert Nichols's sobering epitaph: *A well-meaning poet who earnestly groped for some significance that constantly eluded him.*

15

Sacred Intimacies

David Jones and Siegfried Sassoon, 15 July 1964

David Jones and Siegfried Sassoon met on only one occasion. They had lunch together and a 'longish talk' on Wednesday 15 July 1964. The lunch was organised by a mutual friend, the retired civil servant and courtier Sir Alan ('Tommy') Lascelles, and took place at his apartment in the Old Stables at Kensington Palace. Coincidentally, the date marked the forty-eighth anniversary of Jones's evacuation back to England with a Blighty.

On the face of it, Sassoon and Jones had a good deal in common and to talk about. Both had served in the Great War in the Royal Welch Fusiliers and written at length about their war experiences. Although neither had been a natural soldier – Sassoon much preferred derring-do in no man's land to commanding a company, and Jones described himself as 'a parade's despair' – both had retained a kind of soldier self, and a way of speaking liberally sprinkled with army slang. Both saw themselves as in some sense outsiders or at least not entirely English: Sassoon because of his Jewish ancestry, Jones because of his Welsh. Both, perhaps as a consequence, had created improved versions of an older England: Sassoon by pastoralising his childhood and adolescence in *The Old Century and Seven More Years* (1938) and *The Weald of Youth* (1942), and Jones by drawing on a mythic Romano-Celtic past in his epic poem *The Anathemata* (1952).

Both, too, were Catholic converts, another indication perhaps of a

Left: David Jones in his sixties
Right: Siegfried Sassoon, 'The Great Dictator'

shared desire to connect themselves with an older, alternative England. Jones had been received into the Church in 1921, aged twenty-five, Sassoon in 1957 in his early seventies. In fact, it was probably as a consequence of his conversion that Sassoon came across Jones as a poet. In 1957 he had taken instruction from Dom Sebastian Moore, a monk at Downside Abbey. Moore had made a special study of Jones's work, and seems to have encouraged Sassoon to read *The Anathemata* and, more particularly, Jones's seven-part prose-poem about the war, *In Parenthesis* (1937). Sassoon had certainly read these because, a fortnight before the lunch, he told Lascelles he thought Jones 'undoubtedly a man of genius'.

If the two had a good deal in common, there were sharp differences. Sexuality, class, education and material circumstances, for instance. Sassoon was predominantly homosexual but married, and an oppressively adoring father; Jones was timidly heterosexual, once briefly engaged but unmarried. The upper-middle-class Sassoon had gone to Marlborough and Cambridge, the lower-middle-class Jones to Brockley Road School in outer London and Camberwell School of Art. Sassoon had been an officer in the war, Jones a private. Sassoon was rich; Jones had a Civil List pension of £150 a year, the odd royalty and reviewing cheque, and survived on hand-outs from a small, intensely loyal band of friends and admirers. Sassoon lived at Heytesbury House with fifty-two rooms and 220 acres, Jones in a succession of one-room dug-outs, as he called them. His current dug-out was a small, darkish, ground-floor room in the Monksdene Residential Hotel, at the bottom of Harrow Hill. The amenities were a gas ring and a kettle. Meals were served on a tray.

The lunch came about following a stray remark by Jones to Lascelles, and it says a good deal for Lascelles's diplomatic and organisational skills that he managed to make it happen. Something else Sassoon and Jones had in common was a strong reclusive streak, so that both were in the habit of holing up like hermits. In Jones's case, this tendency was partly caused, partly reinforced, by his acute agoraphobia. By this stage of his life, he went outside as little as possible and would often cancel engagements rather than face a panic attack. Friends and visitors usually had to come to him. That Jones actually made it to the lunch suggests how keen he was on the meeting.

Sassoon was a bit more sociable and used to make hair-raising car trips across country to see fellow-convert friends like Lady Katharine Asquith at Mells or for a cricket net at Downside on Wednesday afternoons. He would, however, hibernate at Heytesbury for long periods. When he did invite visitors, he could be an unpredictable host. The novelist Anthony Powell and his wife were asked to tea in the autumn of 1963. They arrived to find no one about and no reply to repeated knocking and bell-ringing. They eventually climbed in through a half-open window and found themselves in a sizeable drawing room where 'Life seemed to have stopped perhaps half a century before'. Sassoon then 'suddenly appeared from nowhere', as though in 'a dream world'. He seemed entirely unfazed by his guests' unorthodox entry, asked them whether they thought the place Tennysonian, and, when they readily agreed, proposed to make tea.

Given his agoraphobia, Jones almost certainly arrived at the Old Stables by taxi. Initially there was a bit of a kerfuffle finding the place, but eventually it was located 'at the end of an avenue parallel to "Millionaires' Row"'. The day was a scorcher, and after lunch Lascelles suggested they should all sit in the garden. Jones demurred, saying: 'Well, if you don't mind, I'd prefer to stay in this room as I loathe sitting in gardens.' So Lascelles took himself, his wife and the other lunch guest outside, leaving the two elderly poets alone in the cool, quiet study where they talked for an hour and a half.

They made a strongly contrasting pair. The seventy-seven-year-old Sassoon was tall, thin, with 'a timeless craggy Jewish face', and false teeth. He was by then pretty unbending, as the Powells had discovered the previous autumn, watching Sassoon make the tea. The kettle was on the floor, plugged into the skirting-board, and Sassoon, clearly unable 'to bend from the waist', leant down towards it 'at an ominously acute angle. It seemed impossible that he would be able to maintain his balance, then straighten himself, but he brought about that manoeuvre successfully, and made the tea.' This physical inflexibility seemed, to Powell, to mirror other inflexibilities: 'Siegfried Sassoon belonged to another era, another civilization than one's own.' Powell completed his snapshot with the telling point that for 'Captain Sassoon . . . the first war was still in progress'.

Jones was sixty-eight, short, and deaf in the left ear. His once baby face was wizened, and he spoke in a light, slightly querulous voice. He had always been something of a valetudinarian, and his friend William Blissett recalled his saying that 'what for his friends is a cold, for him is the Black Death'. Now, in addition to the agoraphobia and the deafness, there was eye-trouble, insomnia and memory loss. Also, since the early 1930s, he had suffered recurrent periods of depression and breakdown. He nicknamed these Rosy (after neu*rosis*). Rosy had returned for a time the previous year, and at the lunch he was probably heavily medicated: Nardil for the agoraphobia, and a serious cocktail of other anti-depressants, including Nembutal, Trofanil phenobarbitone, Drinaryl and Librium.

The combination of Sassoon's false teeth and Jones's deafness introduced an element of comedy to their conversation, as well as pathos. Uncomfortable with his dentures, Sassoon spoke 'very softly without opening his mouth'. When talking, he tended to turn his head sideways and to avoid looking at the other person. The result of all this was that both men had their work cut out. Sassoon, something of a monologist, seems to have done most of the talking while Jones strained to hear what he said, only catching half of it and having to guess the rest. He was understandably reluctant to ask Sassoon to repeat himself – or to speak up. This was no doubt partly politeness, but also the effect of the past and particularly the war. Powell had grasped that, for the last fifty years or so, Sassoon had on some level always remained Captain Sassoon. And if he was Captain Sassoon, that made Jones once again Private Jones, and no private would dream of asking a captain to repeat himself. Not of course that they would have used their old army ranks. So what, one wonders, did they call each other? Siegfried and David seems unlikely on a first meeting for two men of their generation. Mr Sassoon and Mr Jones would have been too tophattedly Victorian. They probably just used surnames: Sassoon and Jones.

Initially, they talked about mutual acquaintances. Then Jones broached the two topics closest to his heart. He began with 'the fate of the Latin rite'. This was a subject much debated by Catholics in the 1960s as the successive sessions of 'Vatican II' slowly proceeded. Where you stood on 'all this vernacularisation of the Mass', in Jones's phrase, was a burning question. He himself had strong views. Only days earlier, he had delivered a lengthy polemic in a letter to a friend. 'Liberal' Catholics, he claimed, were 'making the same mistake as those classical dons' who argued that the point of learning Latin and Greek was to help people 'to think clearly, to write clear English, to become competent civil servants or what not':

What the dons ought to have said was that the classics were an integral
part of our Western heritage and should be fought for on that ground
alone. Our Church leaders have even more reason to guard that heritage
– for it is saturated with the sacral. It's not a matter of knowledge but
of love. It's a terrible thought that the language of the West, of the
Western liturgy, and inevitably the Roman chant, might become
virtually extinct.

To Jones's surprise, Sassoon hardly seemed aware of the whole contro-
versy. This is quite possible. Equally, he may simply not have been
prepared to discuss his private beliefs with a new acquaintance. He had
been mortified when, not long after his reception into the Church, he
had been conned into an off-the-record interview by a reporter, only
to find his conversion and other 'most sacred intimacies' all over the
Sunday Express. Besides, for Sassoon, belief in the Old Faith, as he liked
to call it, was not so much a matter of intellectual argument and public
discussion but more one of unconditional personal surrender to a
higher authority.

Jones also tried to steer the talk towards *poiesis*, but without success.
'We seem *all* to live in separated worlds', he later reflected of this and
his previous conversational misfire:

> and as far as I could make out, his particular literary outlook offered
> few openings that I could infiltrate to discuss the things that most
> occupy my mind. It was *not* that we disagreed, but never seemed to
> get engaged on the central issues.

Poiesis – literally 'creative production' – was one of Jones's favourite
terms for the art of making. Another favourite was *anamnesis* for 'the
recalling of things past'. The latter he especially valued because of its
Eucharistic connotations. If he tried words like *poiesis* and *anamnesis*
on Sassoon, who was allergic to any hint of pretension, it is no wonder
he drew a blank. However, with poetry he would probably have drawn
a blank anyway.

If Sassoon had felt poetically old-fashioned in the 1930s, thirty years
later he felt like a dinosaur. He continued to publish regular collections of his poems, both in small, private editions and commercially
with Faber & Faber. These were largely ignored although a youngish

Philip Larkin made appreciative noises about *Sequences* (1956) in the *Manchester Guardian*. Sassoon, he wrote, 'remains one of the few living English poets whose poems are sustained by the depth of feeling in them, and for this he deserves praise and allegiance'. Sassoon returned the compliment when he read Larkin's *The Less Deceived*, telling Edmund Blunden he thought the poems 'very accomplished'. It is not hard to see why Larkin should have appealed to Sassoon. His particular blend of directness and pared-down lyricism, his metrical inventiveness, his use of traditional forms, all made him seem like a delayed Georgian, still abiding, like Sassoon, by Eddie Marsh's fifty-year-old injunctions. Indeed, taking that hint about allegiance, Sassoon probably saw Larkin as one of his poetic descendants.

Jones's *In Parenthesis* and *The Anathemata*, however, rocketed the reader into quite another poetic universe. His work was governed by entirely different conceptions of poetry. Whereas Sassoon cared deeply about traditional forms and prosody, Jones, like Eliot and Pound, was an out-and-out modernist, writing in layered, often cryptic fragments, which readers were expected to puzzle away at and piece together as best they could. This was how he described *The Anathemata* in a 1954 radio talk:

> I was explicitly concerned with a re-calling of certain things which I myself had received, things which are part of the complex deposits of this Island, so of course involving Wales and of course involving the central Christian rite and mythological, historical, etc., data of all sorts. These were, so to say, my 'subject matter'.

The plumbing of such complex deposits made entirely different demands on the reader from, say, Sassoon's charming mid-1950s poem 'Cleaning the Candelabrum', which was also about recalling the past:

> While rubbing up the ring by which one lifts it,
> I visualise some Queen Anne country squire
> Guiding a guest from dining-room to parlour
> Where port and filberts wait them by the fire:
> Or – in the later cosmos of Miss Austen –
> Two spinsters, wavering shadows on a wall,
> Conferring volubly about Napoleon
> And what was worn at the Assembly Ball . . .

Jones's earlier *In Parenthesis* was considerably more accessible. It had a clear narrative thread and an identifiable Everyman figure and anti-hero in Private John Ball. The original 1937 edition had a remarkable frontispiece, showing a large, composite, half-naked figure, part soldier, part civilian, entangled in barbed wire and surrounded by smashed, broken trees with inserted vignettes of rats, a mule, duckboards and troops engaged in various tasks. The story followed the fortunes (largely misfortunes) of B Company from its departure for France in December 1915 to its disastrous engagement at Mametz Wood in July 1916, where Private Ball was wounded and lay among the dead, waiting for the stretcher-bearers to find him. In other words, the poem provided an amplified and embellished account of Jones's own early experiences in the war. The seventh and final section, 'The Five Unmistakable Marks', described the attack on Mametz Wood. Here, after the slaughter, the Queen of the Woods – at once Welsh deity, Earth Mother, Virgin Mary and death – 'cut bright boughs of various flowering' and went among the fallen, British and German, real and legendary:

> Some she gives white berries
>   some she gives brown
> Emil has a curious crown it's
>   made of golden saxifrage.
> Fatty wears sweet-briar,
> he will reign with her for a thousand years.
> For Balder she reaches high to fetch his.
> Ulrich smiles for his myrtle wand.
> That swine Lillywhite has daisies to his chain – you'd hard-
> ly credit it.
> She plaits torques of equal splendour for Mr Jenkins and
> Billy Crower.
> Hansel with Gronwy share dog-violets for a palm, where
> they lie in serious embrace beneath the twisted tripod.
> Siôn gets St John's Wort – that's fair enough.
> Dai Great-coat she can't find him anywhere – she calls
> both high and low, she had a very special one for him.
> Among this July noblesse she is mindful of December wood
> – when the trees of the forest beat against each other because
> of him.

> She carries to Aneirin-in-the-nullah a rowan sprig, for the
> glory of Guenedota. You couldn't hear what she said to
> him, because she was careful for the Disciplines of the Wars.

Jones could be undeniably difficult, arguably more so than Eliot
and Pound, because his range of reference, including, as above, Welsh,
Arthurian, Norse, German and other allusions, was even less familiar.
Also, unlike Eliot and to a lesser extent Pound, he had not yet been
picked up by academia and subjected to serious exposition and exegesis.
Not that Jones himself saw it quite like that. Writing in 1952 to his old
friend René Hague about *The Anathemata*, he said: 'I know it's a bit
of a bugger on the surface; but underneath it's pretty straightforward
really, compared with most modern "personal experience" and "psychological" kinds of poetry.' To Sassoon, however, Jones's work was more
than a bit of a bugger. He told the nun Dame Felicitas Corrigan, one
of his key confidantes, that *The Anathemata* was 'quite beyond him'.
The most he could claim for *In Parenthesis* was that it was 'an important war record' but it did not speak to him like Edmund Blunden's
Undertones of War. This was kinder than Robert Graves who called *In
Parenthesis* 'a war-book by Joyce out of Eliot' and accused Jones of
plagiarism.

Yet, if he could have allowed himself, Sassoon might have found
some poetic common ground with Jones. In his own way he would
have concurred with Jones's depiction of the poet as a rememberer.
He would have agreed that it was a part of the poet's 'business to
keep open the lines of communication . . . by handing on such fragmented bits of our own inheritance as we have ourselves received'.
The problem was the fragmented bits of Jones's inheritance were so
very different from Sassoon's. Jones's were mythic and Eucharistic;
Sassoon's were mystical and nostalgic. As Sassoon had put it in 'The
Trial', he was 'Zealous to walk the way of Henry Vaughan', and that
remained true even after his conversion.

So with Sassoon having struck Catholicism and poetry off the conversational agenda, all that was left for the two to talk about was the war,
and books about the war. They discovered a strong, shared admiration
for *Undertones of War* while having reservations about Graves's
Good-bye to All That. Sassoon and Graves had had their rapprochement
in the mid-1950s, and Sassoon now spoke affectionately of his old friend.

He had not forgotten the old feud about *Good-bye to All That*, however, and reiterated that the book was 'full of inaccuracies and heightenings and roundings out'. He also mentioned Blunden's personal copy with all its marginal comments and annotations.

This perhaps gave Jones the cue to point out an error he had noticed in *Good-bye to All That*. Graves regularly had officers refer to the Germans as Fritz. As Jones remembered it, the officers tended to say Boche, while the other ranks used Fritz or Squarehead. That kind of detail was precisely the sort to appeal to Sassoon, and Jones could well have brought it up. However, he almost certainly did not mention Graves's highly speculative history of the muse, *The White Goddess* (1948), although he had read that too. In theory, this exposition of a supposedly lost tradition was very much in Jones's imaginative territory, but he was frustrated by the book's lack of proper referencing which made its leads hard to follow up. Another war book which Sassoon did lavishly praise and recommend was Dr J C Dunn's little-known *The War the Infantry Knew, 1914–1919*, published anonymously in 1938. Dunn had been a long-serving and decorated medical officer in the Royal Welch Fusiliers and a close friend of Sassoon's.

Inevitably, though, the main topic of conversation was the war itself. This was the real bond, establishing for all Sassoon's and Jones's differences an overriding point of interest and connection. Even after so long, both could recall with great accuracy events, names, people, places, anecdotes, turns of speech. Soon they were raptly exchanging 'details of trench life at various times and in various sectors'. That both had been in the Royal Welch Fusiliers (Sassoon in C Company of the 1st Battalion and Jones in B Company of the 15th Battalion) and had served in the Mametz Wood area naturally lent an extra frisson to their reminiscences. In fact, at some point, these reminiscences must have led to the great revelation of the afternoon. This was that it was Jones's battalion which had relieved Sassoon's on the evening of 5 July 1916. So the two had been in exactly the same part of the line at exactly the same time, forty-eight years before. They had very likely passed each other or caught a glimpse of each other during the hand-over. A goose-bumpy discovery.

That, in fact, was Sassoon's 'day out bombing the Prussian Guard', as he nonchalantly termed it to Dame Felicitas. Determined to knock out an enemy sniper, Sassoon had single-handedly rushed a German trench, throwing a couple of Mills bombs as he approached. Reaching the trench, he found the numerous occupants in retreat, unaware that 'they were being attacked by a single fool'. Sassoon watched them disappear and – still at heart a fox-hunting man – put his finger in his right ear and 'emitted a series of view-holloas'. He then looked about the trench and, according to Graves, read a book of poems before running back to the British lines. Later on, he received a severe telling-off from his commanding officer for failing to consolidate the trench and failing to notify anyone of its capture. Sassoon was left in no doubt that he had 'made a mess of the whole affair'. Some or all of this would have been familiar to Jones from *Memoirs of an Infantry Officer* and *Good-bye to All That*, but Sassoon very probably rehashed some version of the exploit for his benefit, however self-deprecatingly. That very evening of 5 July his battalion – now down to less than 400 men – had been relieved by a new Royal Welch Fusiliers battalion of around double the number, among whom had been Private Jones.

It is hard to imagine that Jones too did not offer some account of what befell him in the aftermath of the hand-over – though, again, Sassoon would have had some idea from *In Parenthesis*. On 10 July Jones's battalion took part in a large-scale attack on Mametz Wood. The following day he was hit in the left leg, the bullet passing directly through the calf. It was, he told René Hague:

as if a great baulk of timber or a heavy bar of some sort had struck me sideways, in fact I thought a ponderous branch of one of the trees of the wood had been severed by shrapnel and had fallen across my leg but couldn't account for the *extreme violence and weight*.

Unable to stand or walk, he started crawling back to the British lines, still with his rifle and fixed bayonet. Eventually, regretfully – just like Private Ball in *In Parenthesis* – he discarded his rifle, with 'the fair flaw in the grain, / above the lower sling-swivel'. He was found by a friendly corporal who hoisted him onto his back. Not long after, in the half-dark, the pair came across their battalion second-in-command, a major. The corporal explained he was looking for stretcher-bearers for Private Jones. Jones himself never forgot the

major's reply: 'You will no matter *who* he is, drop the bugger *here*
. . . Stretcher-bearers will find him within a short time. Don't you
know there's a sod of a war on.' This was a story which Jones enjoyed
telling, particularly the last part – which, he said, had amused him
at the time because 'it was pretty obvious that a war was indeed
on'. One would like to think that he told it to Sassoon and that the
two had a good chuckle.

Neither, one assumes, alluded to Sassoon's dismissive description
of the arrival of Jones's battalion in *Memoirs of an Infantry Officer*,
although it perhaps hovered on the edge of their minds:

> they were unseasoned New Army troops . . . a jostling company of
> exclamatory Welshmen . . . a panicky rabble. They were mostly under-
> sized men, and as I watched them arriving at the first stage of their
> battle experience I had a sense of their victimisation . . . Two days later
> [actually five] the Welsh Division, of which they were a unit, was
> involved in massacre and confusion.

One other interesting coincidence they probably worked out was
that Graves too had been at Mametz Wood at almost exactly the same
time. In fact, on 20 July, five days after Jones's evacuation to England,
Graves too had been wounded, only half a mile from the wood. So all
three had been in the same firing line within a fortnight in July 1916,
and all three had survived: Sassoon with 'a splitting headache', Jones
with a Blighty, and Graves with a wound so severe that he had been
given up for dead and his mother sent the standard letter of condo-
lence. They survived but the lunch in 1964 makes clear that some forms
of damage can never be entirely repaired. Sassoon spoke for all the
survivors when he told Jones that 'however much he tried he could
never get that 1st War business out of his system'.

Sassoon and Jones both gave debriefings of the meeting to friends.
Jones's was lengthy and generous. The meeting had plainly meant a
lot to him despite the limits Sassoon had set on the conversation.
Writing to René Hague two days later, he emphasised how 'extremely
nice, gentle and pleasant' Sassoon had been, that 'he *couldn't* have been
more friendly and agreeable'. Sassoon had even proposed that he come
and stay at Heytesbury with a view to visiting Katharine Asquith at

Mells. This was kind even if both of them probably realised it would never happen. As it didn't.

Sassoon's brief post-mortem was anything but friendly and agreeable, or kind. Jones, he told Dame Felicitas a few weeks later was

> a pathetic, helpless seeming little man – ultra-sensitive. I talked to him alone for one and a half hours, and worked hard. He was a private in the 15th R.W.F. and wounded at Mametz Wood. His Battalion relieved ours after my day out bombing the Prussian Guard – Have you tried reading him? Father Sebastian specialised in *The Anathemata* – quite beyond me. *In Parenthesis* is an important war record – but doesn't reach me like *Undertones of War*.

Why this mean-spiritedness when beforehand he had called Jones 'undoubtedly a man of genius', and the meeting itself had apparently gone well? The likely answer is that at the time Sassoon really had enjoyed meeting Jones, and his friendly behaviour had been perfectly genuine. But, looking back, he had once again felt threatened as a poet. When he met Laurence Cotterell, whose pieces he had praised in *Poems from the Desert* (1944), he tersely reminded the young man not to forget that he, Sassoon, was *the* war poet. In putting down Jones so dismissively to Dame Felicitas, he was reaffirming his own pre-eminence as well as showing off to a relatively new but ardent admirer of his work. He was more generous later in the year, commenting on J H Johnston's *English Poetry of the First World War*: 'His theory about our inability to write war epics strikes me as professorial poppycock. The wonder was that we managed to record anything at all. But I am glad he has done well for David Jones.'

Sassoon's anxieties about his poetry persisted till the end. An honorary doctorate from Oxford in 1965 did little to diminish his acute disappointment at not receiving the Order of Merit when T S Eliot's death the same year created a vacancy. Even on his own death-bed, from inoperable cancer, in late August 1967, he was still desperately looking for poetic reassurance. 'My poems; they were all right, weren't they?' he asked Rupert Hart-Davis, his literary executor. To which Hart-Davis replied: 'Yes, Sieg, *more* than all right.' 'Every one a bull's-eye?' Sassoon pressed. 'No, Sieg,' Hart-Davis felt obliged to reply, 'not *every* one.' At which Sassoon regained his sense of humour and laughed. He died at home on the evening of 1 September. The day before his death he told his son George as though preparing to go over the top one last time: 'This is the final test of my endurance and I intend to put up a good show.'

Jones survived Sassoon by seven years. He died in the Calvary Nursing Home in Harrow on 29 October 1974. He had left his dug-out four years earlier, following a mild stroke and a broken hip. A growing band of supporters continued to promote his work. The year of his death saw *Agenda* devote a special issue to him, and Faber & Faber bring out a new volume, *The Sleeping Lord and Other Fragments*. That year he was made a Companion of Honour. At Calvary Nursing Home he still held court to visitors. The Canadian poet and Old Norse translator George Johnston described seeing Jones only a month before his death and, after a slow start, the two had an animated conversation about 'Olaf Tryggvason's conversion of the Northlands', feudalism, Aegir, and Geoffrey of Monmouth. 'What wonderful talk it was', Johnston reported; 'the pace seemed to be the pace of the ages.' In his person and in his work, David Jones clearly had, as he wrote of Christopher Smart, 'a strange and endearing genius'.

Epilogue

One more recent strange meeting stays in my mind. It brought the war poets before us not as they were in their own time and persons but in the way we have chosen to see them at the start of the twenty-first century. This was an exhibition, *Anthem for Doomed Youth: Twelve Soldier Poets of the First World War*, held at the Imperial War Museum from October 2002 till April 2003. All the poets were present except for Vera Brittain, Roland Leighton and Robert Nichols.

Rupert Brooke naturally came first. There were the famous Sherril Schell photographs from 1913 together with Brooke's typically charming disclaimer to Cathleen Nesbitt: 'I think they are really too revolting but I am sure that they are the kind of thing ladies would like to see on the front of a book of poems – God forbid I should write poems to match that face.' Many of his poems did match the face, including the five war sonnets. He could also be witty and sceptical, as the fair copy of his best Pacific poem 'Tiare Tahiti' showed. Other relics of his life-changing trip to the Pacific in 1913–14 included photographs of his Tahitian lover Taatamata. These raised the question of whether Taatamata really had a child by Brooke, as he hoped. If so, was that child Arlice Rapoto, who was still alive in the 1980s? It was possible, but when I contacted the daughter of James Norman Hall, who had known both Taatamata and Arlice, she was definite that Arlice's father had been a French naval officer.

Brooke's contemporaries speculated endlessly about what might have happened to him, had he survived the war. Virginia Woolf thought he would have gone into Parliament. Robert Graves imagined him editing the classics. He continued to fascinate them. When the last of the Bloomsberries, Frances Partridge, asked David Garnett in 1964 if he had really liked Brooke, Garnett replied: 'If the impossible were to happen and he were to ring up and ask me to go and see him now, I should be off like a shot.'

Charles Sorley's showcases were dominated by a pitted and corroded wooden signpost. This was the signpost that, at Marlborough College, he passed on his endless cross-country runs up on the Downs. He referred to it in 'Two Sonnets'. The sonnets reversed at the mid-point like an hourglass: octave, sestet, sestet, octave. In the octave of the first sonnet, death's 'straight and steadfast signpost' on the troop-filled roads in France reminded Sorley of school:

> I think it like that signpost in my land,
> Hoary and tall, which pointed me to go
> Upward, into the hills, on the right hand,
> Where the mists swim and the winds shriek and blow,
> A homeless land and friendless, but a land
> I did not know and that I wished to know.

'Two Sonnets', the disconcertingly jaunty 'All the hills and vales along' and the final, grim sonnet 'When you see millions of the mouthless dead' later became obligatory choices for any anthology of poetry from the Great War. His 28 April 1915 letter in which he attacked Brooke for his 'sentimental attitude' was much quoted after the revival of interest in the war poets in the 1960s:

He is far too obsessed with his own sacrifice, regarding the going to war of himself (and others) as a highly intense, remarkable and sacrificial exploit, whereas it is merely the conduct demanded of him (and others) by the turn of circumstances, where non-compliance with this demand would have made life intolerable. It was not that 'they' gave up anything of that list he gives in one sonnet: but that the essence of these things had been endangered by circumstances over which he had no control, and he must fight to recapture them. He has clothed his attitude in fine words: but he has taken the sentimental attitude.

Sorley was twenty when he died at the battle of Loos on 13 October 1915.

The most distinctive item in Siegfried Sassoon's showcases was not his 7.62 mm. Browning pistol but his trench boots. They were knee-length, brown and well-worn. The label read 'Maxwell, Dover Street', London. Officers with a private income like Sassoon could afford boots that fitted well and kept out the water and mud. Privates like Davies in Sassoon's poem 'In the Pink' and Rosenberg had to make do with army issue boots which often blistered and butchered their feet.

The 1997 film of Pat Barker's celebrated *Regeneration* trilogy showed Sassoon tending his men's feet in an almost Christ-like manner. Sassoon himself brought Jesus into his trench poems in a very different spirit. At the end of 'Stand-to: Good Friday Morning', an exhausted soldier tries to make a deal with Christ:

> O Jesus, send me a wound to-day,
> And I'll believe in Your bread and wine,
> And get my bloody old sins washed white!

It was the bitter truth-telling of poems like 'Stand-to', 'Base Details', '"They"' and 'Does it Matter?' that hit early readers like an electric charge.

Wartime photographs of Sassoon showed a face and mind haunted by horrors. But that was not how everyone saw him at the time. Glyn Philpot's aestheticised study, on display in the exhibition, was painted in the summer of 1917 at the height of Sassoon's protest, showing the poet in three-quarter profile with rouged lips and open-necked grey shirt. When Sassoon told Philpot the painting made him look 'rather Byronic', Philpot replied: 'You are rather, aren't you?' Sassoon's self-portrait in his prose memoirs and diaries was much more self-effacing and much less sensual. He concentrated on his protracted adolescence before the war and on the galvanising effect of the war itself. The published diaries took the story as far as 1925 but then appropriately stopped. Until the publication of several excellent recent biographies, most readers remained largely unaware of the complications of Sassoon's long post-war life: the decline in his poetry, his tormented affair with Stephen Tennant, his unhappy marriage to Hester, his late conversion to Catholicism. For all that, Anthony Powell's comment about meeting the old poet in 1964 remained true: 'for Captain Sassoon, though no longer himself involved in it, the first war was still in progress.'

Fittingly, Wilfred Owen followed Sassoon in the exhibition. Thirty years after Owen was killed, Sassoon wrote in his diary: 'His death made a gap in my life which has been there ever since', and the story of their friendship at Craiglockhart in the autumn of 1917 and its literary consequences was to become one of the Great War's central narratives. Owen's showcases contained his signed copy of Sassoon's *The Old Huntsman and Other Poems*, a copy of Brooke's *1914 and other Poems* (with a newspaper photograph of Brooke's grave), *More Songs by the Fighting Men* and Keats's *Endymion*. There were also his silver cigarette case and twin hairbrushes. The manuscript of 'Anthem for Doomed Youth', with Sassoon's pencilled annotations and dated 'Craiglockhart, September 1917', brought back the poetry.

By the 1970s and 1980s Owen was established as the defining poetic voice of the Great War in the English-speaking world, but that rise only happened slowly over decades. It began with Sassoon's and Edith Sitwell's publication of *The Poems of Wilfred Owen* in 1920 and gathered momentum with Blunden's 1931 edition, which contained a short memoir, and with the interest of the 1930s poets – Spender called Owen 'the most useful influence in modern verse'. But it was not until the inclusion of 'Anthem for Doomed Youth', 'Strange Meeting' and other Owen poems in Benjamin Britten's *War Requiem* (1961), closely followed by C Day Lewis's edition of his *Collected Poems* (1963), that his work gained wide acceptance, and he became, in Dominic Hibberd's phrase, 'the national poet of pity in the early 1960s'.

There were dissenters. Yeats excluded Owen from his *Oxford Book of Modern Verse* in 1936 on the grounds that he was 'all blood, dirt & sucked sugar stick'. Craig Raine described Owen's work in a 1973 review as 'perhaps the most overrated poetry in the twentieth century'. Larkin, after reviewing Jon Stallworthy's biography of Owen the following year, told Robert Conquest that he thought the poems remained good but that Owen himself seemed 'rather a prick. A brave prick, of course.' Modernist critics generally looked down on Owen, as they did on most of the war poets except for Isaac Rosenberg and David Jones. Owen's poems survived, however, because, as Ian Hamilton put it, 'he was able to tell us what war felt like and would feel like'.

Next to the manuscript of 'Anthem', a screen endlessly replayed jerky footage of patients at various war hospitals. On sports day at Alder Hey Hospital, Liverpool, there was a wheelchair race and shots of men on crutches trying to eat apples which bobbed on strings. During a sequence on War Neuroses, Private Meek, aged twenty-three, sat in a wheelchair, biting his thumb. He suffered from mutism. Private Press was nineteen. He had amnesia, word-blindness, but dived under the bed on hearing the word 'bombs'.

Robert Graves still had nightmares about the war in his eighties. The last of the major war poets, he died at ninety in 1985 (the same week as Philip Larkin and Geoffrey Grigson). Graves's long, prolific and maverick career reached its zenith in the 1950s and 1960s. His poetry was revered. His history of the muse, *The White Goddess*, was obligatory reading, as were his lively, highly eccentric Clark lectures on poetry. (Ted Hughes told Graves in a 1967 letter that *The White Goddess* had been 'the chief book' of his 'poetic consciousness'.) Throughout his life Graves turned out prose to free himself to write poetry. Ironically some of that prose – especially *Good-bye to All That* and the two Claudius novels – wore better than the poems it was written to support. One showcase displayed a copy of his first collection *Over the Brazier*, published by Harold Monro's Poetry Bookshop in 1916, price 8*d*. This was the collection which Sassoon thought Graves ought not to publish.

Anthologies, as much as individual collections, played a crucial role in promoting the war poets. Between them, Marsh's third volume of *Georgian Poetry* and E B Osborn's *The Muse in Arms*, both published in 1917, established Sassoon, Graves, Nichols, Sorley, Gurney and Rosenberg as significant or at least audible voices. Nearly fifty years later, I M Parsons's *Men Who March Away* (1965) began a steady succession of anthologies of Great War poetry which, despite some subsequent wrangling and special pleading, largely fixed the main poets and the main poems. Parsons set the tone by defending the war poets from accusations that they were 'narrowly personal and subjective'. 'They were concerned with something much larger,' he argued, 'something which has been the subject of poetry since time immemorial' – Owen called it 'The eternal reciprocity of tears'. In 1993, Martin Stephen's anthology *Poems of the First World War* offered an important modification to what had hardened into an orthodoxy. Stephen pointed out that Owen, Sassoon and the other war poets were poets first and soldiers second. Their poems did not represent the ordinary feelings of most who served in the war. Stephen's corrective was to place the by now celebrated poems among a wide range of more populist material, including soldier songs and verses from army newspapers.

Sassoon and Blunden helped to create Owen's posthumous reputation by editing collections of his work. Blunden helped Gurney in the same way, editing a first selection of his poems in 1954. Most of Blunden's own war poetry was written after the war. 'The Zonnebeke Road', displayed in manuscript in the exhibition, was included in the poetry supplement to his war memoir *Undertones of War* (1928): 'Agony stares from each gray face. / And yet the day is come; stand down! stand down! / Your hands unclasp from rifles while you can . . .' The war pressed fiercely if less explicitly on his other 1920s poems. In 'The Midnight Skaters' from 1925, the 'him' looking up through the ice in the third stanza was death:

> Then on, blood shouts, on, on,
>   Twirl, wheel and whip above him,
> Dance on this ball-floor thin and wan,
>   Use him as though you love him;
> Court him, elude him, reel and pass,
> And let him hate you through the glass.

The war taught Blunden that everyone was skating on thin ice, was dancing in the dark. Larkin dismissed him in 1966 as 'a faint amount of good once'. A judicious *Selected Poems* in 1982 and a sympathetic biography in 1990 did not markedly change that view.

Edward Thomas's reputation on the other hand rose steadily after his death on Easter Monday morning, 1917. Few wanted his poems during his lifetime; yet by the 1950s his 'Adlestrop' had become an anthology piece:

Yes, I remember Adlestrop –
The name, because one afternoon
Of heat the express-train drew up there
Unwontedly. It was late June.

Later, more ominous poems like 'Old Man', 'The Other', 'Fifty
Faggots', 'Rain', 'Lights Out' and the incantatory 'Out in the Dark'
took precedence, and Thomas began to be claimed by some as a vital
link in an ongoing English tradition and by others as a proto-Imagist.
He himself was always wryly unhopeful about his poetry. In March
1915, he told Walter de la Mare: 'I wrote (if anything) with a feeling
that I did use the Morse code. This is a fact. I only hope someone
besides myself will catch the accent.' His patriotism was much more
personal than Brooke's. When Eleanor Farjeon asked him what he
was fighting for, he 'picked up a pinch of earth' and said 'Literally, for
this'.

Eleanor Farjeon was unrequitedly in love with Thomas and wrote
one of the best books about him, *Edward Thomas: The Last Four Years*
(1958). This complemented his wife Helen's two volumes of memoir,
As It Was (1926) and *World Without End* (1931). Helen had much to put
up with. When in 1908, Thomas told her of his growing fondness for
a seventeen-year-old schoolgirl, Helen went straight to the point: 'Is
it to be the friendship of a middle-aged man, a man of letters etc.,
etc., and of a simple schoolgirl, the sort of idyllic affair that your
biographers will dote on. . . . Or is she meant to slip unconsciously
into something more . . . in fact a love affair, or what?' It was Farjeon,
not Helen, who understood that the imaginary book title *Armed Men
in Tears* in a letter of Thomas's from France in early 1917 meant he
and his company were en route for Armentières.

Thomas always used a clay pipe. He had just filled one on the
morning of 9 April 1917 when he was killed by the blast from a shell.
His pocket watch still recorded the exact moment when his heart
stopped: 7.36.12 a.m. Both pipe and watch were on show here.

Walking on, I found that the exhibition presented Ivor Gurney the
composer as much as Gurney the poet. Manuscript music as well as
manuscript poems were on display. A choice of his piano pieces played
softly in the background. Remarkably, he managed to compose even

while in the trenches; a reel of barbed wire underlined the point. Alive, Gurney never belonged. After his death in the Dartford Asylum in 1937, he remained equally hard to place. Piers Gray grouped Gurney together with Thomas and J R Ackerley in a fine book appropriately called *Marginal Men* (1991). Part of the difficulty with Gurney was establishing reliable texts and dates for his poems, particularly those written in the asylum: Blunden, P J Kavanagh, and R K R Thornton and George Walter successively wrestled with the problem. Others, like John Lucas, tried to rescue Gurney from the stigma of being a Georgian poet. This paralleled similar attempts to realign Thomas, Owen, Graves, Rosenberg and Sorley, as though a different critical branding would change the poetic product. The poets themselves thought differently. Graves and Rosenberg were eager to appear in Marsh's anthologies. Thomas was disappointed not to be chosen for *Georgian Poetry 1913–1915*, and de la Mare offered to make way for him in *Georgian Poetry 1916–1917*. Owen was delighted to be 'held peer by the Georgians'.

David Jones was a different matter entirely. *In Parenthesis*, his great prose-poem about the war, did not appear until 1937. Unlike the other poets, his work was long and complex and derived from an epic-heroic tradition and from the liturgy. Jones himself was anything but precious about *In Parenthesis*. 'Sometimes when I read it,' he told one friend, 'it seems to have a shape, at other times it sounds awful balls and full of bad jokes and strained meaning.' Some of the jokes were literary. The opening lines, for example, had the sixteenth-century poet Thomas Wyatt falling in on parade:

> '49 Wyatt, 01549 Wyatt.
> Coming sergeant.
> Pick 'em up, pick 'em up – I'll stalk within yer chamber.

Jones enjoyed puns: Corporal Quilter was described as having 'his private thoughts also'.

Few felt neutral about *In Parenthesis*. Larkin called it 'Richard Aldington rewritten by Ezra Pound'. Paul Fussell thought it an 'honourable miscarriage'. Bernard Bergonzi urged that 'like any major work it needs to be lived with before all its meanings become fully

alive'. The popularity of Great War poetry anthologies did not help
Jones. Lyric poems anthologised easily; epics did not. None of the
seven parts of In Parenthesis was sufficiently short or self-contained to
stand alone although Jon Silkin included a lengthy excerpt from Part
7 in his Penguin Book of First World War Poetry (1979).

As opposed to his poems, Jones's trench drawings, dashed off at
the time, were small-scale. His sketches registered the more mundane
aspects of army life: a soldier carrying a section of duckboard, a thin
platoon commander with hand outstretched, rats as big as cats. Jones
experienced more of the trenches than any of the poets except Blunden,
spending twenty-two months in and around the firing line to Blunden's
twenty-four. He used to talk of 'the excellent anonymity of the army',
and was another who never quite left the war behind. One photograph here showed a baby-faced Jones in greatcoat and regimental
cap – Dai Great-Coat was the name he gave one of his alter egos in
In Parenthesis. In the photo Jones was looking away from the camera
with a distracted stare, like someone who already inhabited a world
of his own.

Last came Rosenberg, the other working-class poet-painter. A photograph of the Slade School of Art picnic in 1912 highlighted how
much he too felt marginalised, showing him kneeling at the far left
of the group, arms crossed, slightly but noticeably separate from the
other students. Later photographs, after he enlisted, showed him thin,
exhausted, inward. However, a steel-helmeted self-portrait in black
chalk and gouache displayed wariness rather than weariness. The war
poems were equally devoid of self-pity.

While Jones felt anonymous in the army, Rosenberg felt that his
Jewishness made him conspicuous. He channelled his fury and disgust
into his play Moses. 'Moses symbolises the fierce desire for virility, and
original action in contrast to slavery of the most abject kind,' he told
a friend. Graves later admiringly described Rosenberg as – in poetic
terms – 'a born revolutionary'. He found his true poetic vein with
'Break of Day in the Trenches', and that poem, with 'Louse Hunting',
'Returning, We Hear the Larks' and 'Dead Man's Dump' eventually
became automatic choices for the war poetry anthologies. (Silkin –
an extreme example – gave Rosenberg seventeen poems and extracts.)
He owed his poetic survival primarily to Gordon Bottomley, who

edited *Poems by Isaac Rosenberg* (1922), and to Sassoon, who wrote a short foreword to *The Collected Works of Isaac Rosenberg* (1937). Sassoon described Rosenberg's work as 'Scriptural and sculptural' and detected 'a fruitful fusion between English and Hebrew culture'. He particularly admired 'Break of Day' for its depiction of 'Sensuous front-line existence . . . hateful and repellent, unforgettable and inescapable'.

I left the exhibition, with its maze of loaded showcases, my mind bombarded with objects and images: Brooke's cap, Sorley's signpost, Sassoon's trench boots, Owen's hairbrushes, Blunden's heavily taped cricket bat, Thomas's clay pipes. The exhibition had been a temporary shrine, a site of saints' relics, a place of pilgrimage. But outside in the daylight I thought of other ways of remembering those poets. They showed us war as adventure, as horror, as suffering, as squalor. Their poems did not prevent future wars but they changed for ever the way in which war could be thought about and written about. They asked fundamental questions to which we still have not found the answers:

> Was it for this the clay grew tall?
> – O what made fatuous sunbeams toil
> To break earth's sleep at all?

They showed human nature tested up to and beyond breaking point. They showed us courage, anger, humour, compassion. Their picture of war is the one we carry with us. They remain our contemporaries. They remind us what we are capable of.

Notes on Sources

For the most part, I only refer here to material I have actually quoted from in the main text. Where the full source is clear, I have not repeated the information. With quotations from poems, I have provided a general reference such as 'All extracts from Owen's poems are from *The Poems of Wilfred Owen*', unless the title is supplied in the main text, in which case I have also given it here. For quotations from letters, I have given where possible the date and volume title.

Epigraphs

Epigraphs are from Frederic Manning's *Her Privates We*, Philip Larkin's 'MCMXIV', *Whitsun Weddings* (1964) and Pat Barker's response to winning the 1995 Booker Prize for *The Ghost Road* (1995). Manning's laconic masterpiece about the First World War was first published in a limited edition in 1929 as *The Middle Parts of Fortune*, then republished the following year as *Her Privates We*. The Serpent's Tail edition (1999) with an introduction by William Boyd restores the original text but keeps the more familiar second title. Pat Barker's *Regeneration* trilogy (1991–5) and Sebastian Faulks's *Birdsong* (1993) did much to requicken interest in the Great War.

Prologue

The account of American troops reading Wilfred Owen, Siegfried Sassoon and Rupert Brooke in preparation for Afghanistan comes from Ben MacIntyre's article 'Dead Poets' Society Eases the Tensions of War', *The Times*, 1 November 2001. 'If in some smothering dreams' is from 'Dulce et Decorum Est', *The Poems of Wilfred Owen*, ed. Jon Stallworthy (1990) – henceforth *The Poems of Wilfred Owen*.

1. Breakfast at Eddie's

Siegfried Sassoon's *The Weald of Youth* (1942) is necessarily the primary source. This is the only first-hand account of the meeting between Sassoon and Brooke, and, unless otherwise stated, all Sassoon's comments and observations derive from here. His version might have been less fulsome, had he not felt obliged to show it to Eddie Marsh before publication.

Of the biographies of Brooke, two stand out: Christopher Hassall's more adulatory *Rupert Brooke: A Biography* (1964) – henceforth *Rupert Brooke: A Biography* – and Nigel Jones's more sceptical *Rupert Brooke: Life, Death & Myth* (1999) – henceforth *Rupert Brooke: Life, Death & Myth*.

Extracts from Brooke's poems are taken from *The Collected Poems* (1987) with a perceptive introduction by Gavin Ewart. Extracts from Brooke's letters are taken from *The Letters of Rupert Brooke*, ed. Geoffrey Keynes (1968) – henceforth *The Letters of Rupert Brooke* – except for Brooke's account of seducing Denham Russell-Smith, which is taken from his letter to James Strachey (10 July 1912) in *Friends & Apostles: The Correspondence of Rupert Brooke and James Strachey 1905–1914*, ed. Keith Hale (1998), which quotes the letter in full.

Details of Brooke's appearance, attributes and effect on others are drawn from a range of sources: Christopher Hassall, *Edward Marsh: A Biography* (1959) – henceforth *Edward Marsh: A Biography*; Joy Grant, *Harold Monro and the Poetry Bookshop* (1967); Edward Thomas, 'Rupert Brooke', *English Review*, 8 June 1915, from *A Language not to be Betrayed: Selected Prose of Edward Thomas*, ed. Edna Longley (1981) – henceforth *A Language not to be Betrayed*; *The Diaries of Lady Cynthia Asquith 1915–18* (1968) – henceforth *Lady Cynthia Asquith*; Gwen Raverat, *Period Piece* (1952); Paul Delany, *The Neo-Pagans: Friendship and Love in the Rupert Brooke Circle* (1987); *Song of Love: The Letters of Rupert Brooke and Noel Olivier 1909–1915*, ed. Pippa Harris (1991); and Henry James, Preface to *Letters from America by Rupert Brooke* (1916).

Brooke has inspired two recent novels: Stephanie Johnson's *The Heart's Wild Surf* (1996) and Jill Dawson's *The Great Lover* (2009).

There are now three excellent recent biographies of Sassoon: Jean Moorcroft Wilson, *Siegfried Sassoon: The Making of a War Poet, A Biography 1886–1918* (1999), and *Siegfried Sassoon: The Journey from the Trenches, A Biography 1918–1967* (2003) – henceforth *The Making of a War Poet* and *The Journey from the Trenches*; John Stuart Roberts, *Siegfried Sassoon* (1999) – henceforth *Siegfried Sassoon* (Roberts); and Max Egremont, *Siegfried Sassoon: A Biography* (2005) – henceforth *Siegfried Sassoon* (Egremont).

Sassoon's poems and lines come from *Collected Poems 1908–1956* (1961) – hereafter *Collected Poems* – except for *The Daffodil Murderer* to be found in an appendix to Michael Thorpe's *Siegfried Sassoon: A Critical Study* (1966). The sequence of lines beginning 'Passion with poisonous blossoms in her hair' is quoted from *Weald of Youth*, as is Marsh's 'you have a lovely instrument to play upon'. Sassoon's comment to Edward Carpenter that *The Intermediate Sex* had 'opened up the new life to me' is quoted in *The Making of a War Poet* as is Edmund Gosse's remark about Sassoon's 'richness of fancy and command of melodious verse'.

Christopher Hassall describes a Marsh remark as like a 'witty aside written in faded pencil' in his *Edward Marsh: A Biography*, also the source for Marsh's comment about 'the *feu sacré*' and Winston Churchill's 'You are a good little boy'. D H Lawrence's description of Marsh as 'a bit of a policeman in poetry' and 'a bit of a jig-saw puzzle', together with his grateful 'I call that manna', are from letters to Marsh (18 November 1913, 17 December 1913, 12 July 1913), *The Letters of D H Lawrence: Volume II, 1913–1916*, ed. George Zytaruk and James T. Boulton (1981). James Lees-Milne's diary entry for 22 April 1954 reports on Marsh's acts of devotion to young men, *A Mingled Measure: Diaries, 1953–1972* (1994). The quotation from Lawrence's 'The Snapdragon' comes from *Georgian Poetry 1911–1912* (1912).

The description of W H Davies and his habits blends details from *Weald of Youth*, Osbert Sitwell's *Noble Essences or Courteous Revelations* (1950) – henceforth *Noble Essences*, David Garnett's *Great Friends*:

Portraits of Seventeen Writers (1979) – henceforth *Great Friends* – and Grant's *Harold Monro and the Poetry Bookshop*.

Ezra Pound's connections with Marsh and *Georgian Poetry* are outlined in *Edward Marsh: A Biography*; these suggest that Pound was considerably keener on being included in the early *Georgian Poetry* anthologies than is usually assumed.

2. Fighting the Keeper

Edward Thomas's two reviews of Brooke's *1914 & other Poems* (1915) appeared in the *English Review* (8 June 1915), collected in *A Language not to be Betrayed*, and in the *Daily Chronicle* (18 June 1915).

All quotations from Brooke's poems are taken from *1914 & other Poems*. The extracts from his letters come from *The Letters of Rupert Brooke* except for his description of his five war sonnets as 'in the rough' (*Rupert Brooke: A Biography*) and 'I *might* turn out to be eminent' (*Rupert Brooke: Life, Death & Myth*). The *Daily News* and the *Star* tributes to Brooke are quoted in *Rupert Brooke: A Biography* and the *Morning Post* tribute in Michael Hastings, *The Handsomest Young Man in England: Rupert Brooke* (1967). *Edward Marsh: A Biography* describes the uncomfortable breakfast in March 1913 at which Thomas was 'unforthcoming and constricted, perhaps dyspeptic'.

Thomas's reviews of Thomas Hardy's *Time's Laughingstocks and Other Poems* (1909), Brooke's *Poems* (1911) and Robert Frost's *North of Boston* (1914) are all in *A Language not to be Betrayed*.

Helen Thomas in *As It Was* and *World Without End* (combined as *Under Storm's Wing*, 1988 – henceforth *Under Storm's Wing*) and Eleanor Farjeon in *Edward Thomas: The Last Four Years* (1958) – henceforth *The Last Four Years* – give the best accounts of Thomas's complicated and hypersensitive character. R George Thomas's *Edward Thomas: A Portrait* (1987) – henceforth *Edward Thomas: A Portrait*, William Cooke's *Edward Thomas: A Critical Biography, 1878–1917* (1970) – henceforth *Edward Thomas: A Critical Biography* and Jan Marsh's *Edward Thomas: A Poet for his Country* (1978) are all informative and perceptive.

Extracts from Thomas's letters, unless otherwise stated, are from *Edward Thomas: Selected Letters*, ed. R George Thomas (1995) – henceforth *Edward Thomas: Selected Letters*. Thomas's comment that faircopying *The South Country* was like 'returning to one's vomit' comes from a letter to Gordon Bottomley (1 October 1908) in *Letters from Edward Thomas to Gordon Bottomley*, ed. R George Thomas (1968). *The Life of the Duke of Marlborough* (1915) being 'the worst job I ever undertook' and the remark about 'sucking James Milne's –' come from letters to Gordon Bottomley (6 and 16 June 1915), held in the Edward Thomas Collection, Cardiff University Library – henceforth the Edward Thomas Collection. So too does Thomas's description of enlisting ('Seven of us were examined together') in a letter to Frost (15 July 1915). Thomas's letter to Marsh about Brooke (5 June 1915) is in the Berg Collection of New York Public Library – henceforth the Berg Collection. 'I run away from home' is quoted in Arthur Ransome's *The Autobiography of Arthur Ransome* (1976).

All extracts of Thomas's poems are from *The Collected Poems of Edward Thomas*, ed. R George Thomas (1978) – henceforth *The Collected Poems of Edward Thomas* – checked against *Edward Thomas: The Annotated Collected Poems*, ed. Edna Longley (2008). However, my discussion of 'Sedge-Warblers' and the claim that Thomas made a series of small changes to the beginning of the poem to avoid punning on the name of the recently deceased Brooke follows the suggested order of manuscripts in *The Collected Poems of Edward Thomas* rather than Longley's arrangement. Would Thomas really have cared about a Brooke/brook pun in a late May 1915 poem? After all, in July, he sent a version of 'Sedge-Warblers' containing the word 'brook' to Gordon Bottomley's *An Annual of New Poetry*, called a poem 'The Brook' and used the word in 'For These'. This is true, but by July Thomas had definitely decided to enlist if the army would have him. Any anxieties about Brooke/brook puns evaporated with this decision.

A steadily expanding critical industry is growing up around Thomas's poetry but Andrew Motion's *The Poetry of Edward Thomas* (1980) and Jeremy Hooker's 'Edward Thomas: The Sad Passion' and 'Edward Thomas' in *Poetry of Place: Essays and Reviews 1970–1981* (1982) remain essential reading.

Robert Frost's dicta that poetry should use 'a language absolutely unliterary' and caught 'fresh from talk' are from letters to John Bartlett (8 December 1913, 22 February 1914) from *Selected Letters of Robert Frost*, ed. Lawrance Thompson (1964). Frost's advice that Thomas should rewrite paragraphs from *In Pursuit of Spring* 'in verse form in exactly the same cadence' is quoted in *Edward Thomas: A Critical Biography*.

3. Rupert Brooke Must Have Been Rather Like You

Extracts from Vera's diaries come from *Chronicle of Youth: Vera Brittain's War Diary 1913–1917*, ed. Alan Bishop (1981) and extracts from her and Roland's letters from *Letters from a Lost Generation: First World War Letters of Vera Brittain and Four Friends*, ed. Alan Bishop and Mark Bostridge (1998). Paul Berry's and Mark Bostridge's *Vera Brittain: A Life* (1995) – henceforth *Vera Brittain* – was an invaluable secondary resource.

Vera's teasing put-down 'I shall look out for every atom of conceit' is from her *Testament of Youth: An Autobiographical Study of the Years 1900–1925* (1933) – henceforth *Testament of Youth*. So too are Roland Leighton's '*Je suis fiancé*', the extract from his poem 'Violets from Plug Street Wood', his final poem 'Hédauville', and the quotations and the details surrounding his death. The extracts from Vera's 'August 1914' and 'Perhaps –' are from *Because You Died: Poetry and Prose of the First World War and After* by Vera Brittain, edited and introduced by Mark Bostridge (Virago, 2008). Brooke's third sonnet 'The Dead' and the extracts from 'Heaven' and 'The Chilterns' are from *1914 & other Poems*.

A further blow for Vera in the aftermath of Roland's death was the publication of his 'Violets from Plug Street Wood', engineered by Mrs Leighton, Roland's mother. Clement Shorter at the *Sphere* published the poem with a note which, as Vera recorded in her diary, made it sound as though 'the poem had been written to his Mother'. This marked the start of Mrs Leighton's campaign for the repossession of her dead son, further pursued in *Boy of my Heart*, her memoir of Roland published in June the same year.

4. A Big Blot Has Hid Each Yesterday

Extracts from Sassoon's diary are from *Siegfried Sassoon: Diaries 1915–1918*, ed. Rupert Hart-Davis (1983) – henceforth *Diaries 1915–1918*. Sassoon's observations that Graves 'fairly got on people's nerves' and was 'a positive expert at putting people's backs up' are from *Memoirs of an Infantry Officer* (1930). Sassoon's letter to Edmund Gosse (22 February 1916), describing 'Robert G. [as] quite a dear' is in the Berg Collection as are the letters to Marsh (10 February 1916, 8 April 1915) containing the remarks 'I put "angry guns that boom and flash" in my poem' and 'one of the mugs'. His description of Graves's early war poems as 'violent

French lyrics about lice and corruption' is in a letter to Nellie Gosse (6 January 1916) in the Brotherton Library, University of Leeds.

All quotations from Sassoon's poems are from *Siegfried Sassoon: The War Poems*, arranged by Rupert Hart-Davis (1983) – henceforth *The War Poems* – except the extracts from 'Daybreak in a Garden', 'Before Day', 'Wonderment' and 'Storm and Sunlight', which are from *Collected Poems 1908–1956*. David Thomas's identification of Sassoon with the central character in *Hyacinth* and Sassoon's heartfelt exclamation to Marsh on 16 March 1915 ('O Eddie, you *must* get my poems printed soon') are quoted in *Siegfried Sassoon* (Egremont).

All extracts from Robert Graves's letters are from *In Broken Images: Selected Letters of Robert Graves 1914–1946*, ed. Paul O'Prey (1982) – henceforth *In Broken Images*. I have used Richard Perceval Graves's 1995 reissue of the original 1929 Jonathan Cape text of *Good-bye to All That: An Autobiography* – henceforth *Good-bye to All That*.

The extracts 'the slimy body of a dead corpse', 'military text-book or a rubbish novel', 'he would soon change his style' and 'Plato, the Greek poets, Shakespeare' are from *Good-bye to All That*. In his auto-biography Graves says that before their first meeting Sassoon had been reading the *Essays of Lionel Johnson*, but since *Post Liminium* (1911) seems to be Johnson's only collection of essays, I have assumed this was the one he meant.

Graves has been well served by his biographers: Martin Seymour-Smith, *Robert Graves: His Life and Work* (1983); Richard Perceval Graves, *Robert Graves: The Assault Heroic 1895–1926* (1986), *Robert Graves: The Years with Laura 1926–40* (1990) – henceforth *The Years with Laura* – and *Robert Graves and the White Goddess 1940–1985* (1995) – and Miranda Seymour's *Robert Graves: Life on the Edge* (1995) – henceforth *Robert Graves: Life on the Edge*. All extracts from Graves's poetry are from *Robert Graves: The Complete Poems in One Volume*, ed. Beryl Graves and Dunstan Ward (2000) – henceforth *The Complete Poems in One Volume*. 'A certain cure for lust of blood' comes from Graves's 'A Dead Boche'.

Anyone researching Charles Sorley owes a huge debt to Jean Moorcroft Wilson. Besides writing the only life of Sorley, *Charles Hamilton Sorley: A Biography* (1985), she has edited both his poems and letters: *The Collected Poems of Charles Hamilton Sorley* (1985) and *The Collected Letters of Charles Hamilton Sorley* (1990). Sorley's accusation that Brooke adopted 'the sentimental attitude' is in a letter (28 April

1915) in *The Collected Letters of Charles Hamilton Sorley*. The version of
the octave of the second of 'Two Sonnets' is from a letter of Graves's
to Marsh (24 February 1916) in *In Broken Images*. Graves has silently
improved Sorley's 'a-one in death' to 'at one in death'. The version of
Sorley's last poem 'When you see millions of the mouthless dead' is
from *The Collected Poems of Charles Hamilton Sorley*.

'Fatal Cleopatra' was Doctor Johnson's term for Shakespeare's
compulsive punning.

5. Gathering Swallows

This 'meeting' is indebted to *Edward Thomas: A Portrait* and to three
fine biographies of Owen: Jon Stallworthy's *Wilfred Owen* (1974),
Douglas Kerr's *Wilfred Owen's Voices* (1993) and Dominic Hibberd's
Wilfred Owen: A New Biography (2002) – henceforth *Wilfred Owen: A
New Biography*.

The opinions expressed in the 'imaginary conversations' between
Owen and Thomas are ones they really held and expressed. Most I have
taken from their letters: *Edward Thomas: Selected Letters* and *Wilfred
Owen: Collected Letters*, ed. Harold Owen and John Bell (1967) – henceforth *Wilfred Owen: Collected Letters*. Other sources are indicated below.

Thomas's 'the dullest flattest piece' is from *The Last Four Years*. His
'I wonder would you recognise me' is quoted from *Edward Thomas:
A Portrait*, as is 'There isn't a man I don't share'. Gordon Bottomley
in 'A Note on Edward Thomas', *Welsh Review*, September 1945, recalled
Thomas's 'husky mellow voice'. Walter de la Mare in his foreword to
Thomas's *Collected Poems* (1922) described his face as 'long and rather
narrow', his expression as 'rather distant and detached' and his hands as
'powerful and bony'. 'I could not keep out any longer' – quoted in John
Moore, *The Life and Letters of Edward Thomas* (1939) – was what Thomas
told his early countryman mentor and friend, 'Dad' Uzzell, the day after
passing his army medical in July 1915. Thomas's nickname 'The Iambic'
is from Keith Clark, *The Muse Colony: Rupert Brooke, Edward Thomas, Robert
Frost and Friends, Dymock 1914* (1992). Thomas's description of the beringed
Edmund John is from a letter to J W Haines (14 January 1916), held in
the Edward Thomas Collection. The anecdote about the young Thomas
at the *Daily Chronicle* is in H W Nevinson's *Changes and Chances* (1923).

Thomas's reference to Keats and soldiers and his opinions about

Keats's poetry are taken from his then forthcoming *Keats* (1916) in which he quotes the lines from *Endymion*, beginning 'Not hiding up an Apollonian curve', saying they show 'not a picture, but a painter at work'. Thomas's comments in the same book about the verbal music of 'To Autumn' anticipate the practical criticism of I A Richards and F R Leavis. His remark about often finding it hard to get in track with other people's poems was made in a letter to the poet John Freeman (April 1916), held in the Edward Thomas Collection. His own poem 'Rain' is in *The Collected Poems of Edward Thomas*.

Thomas clearly warmed to the painter Paul Nash – not least because he was good at finding birds' nests. Nash later said of Thomas: '[He] . . . always seems to have been oppressed by some load of sadness and pessimism. I believe I saw one of the happiest bits of his life while we were in the Artists [Artists' Rifles] – he was always humorous, interesting and entirely lovable', quoted in *Edward Thomas: A Critical Biography 1878–1917*. Thomas's diary entry for 8 April 1917 is taken from Appendix C in *The Collected Poems of Edward Thomas*.

Extracts from Owen's poems are from *The Poems of Wilfred Owen*. According to Harold Owen's *Journey from Obscurity*, III (1965) – henceforth *Journey from Obscurity* – it was during Harold's visit to Hare Hall Camp that Wilfred wondered what Keats and Shelley had to teach him under modern warfare conditions. There is no evidence that Owen read Thomas's reviews of Brooke's *1914 & other Poems* but he was in London in June 1915 and could well have done.

Aldous Huxley's witty coinage 'vindictive hagiography' was made of Middleton Murry's book on D H Lawrence, *Son of Woman* (1931), in a letter to G Wilson Knight (15 September 1931); *Letters of Aldous Huxley*, ed. Grover Smith (1969) – henceforth *Letters of Aldous Huxley*.

In *Wilfred Owen: A New Biography*, Dominic Hibberd plausibly suggests Saturday 19 February 1916 for Harold Owen's visit to his brother Wilfred in Hare Hall Camp. The time frame is tight. Owen was hoping for news of Harold on Wednesday 16 February and expecting the measles quarantine on his hut to be lifted. The following Wednesday (23 February) he went to London for his lecture course. Harold took ship on 28 February. The weekend of 19–20 February appears the only candidate and, since Owen seems to have secured a late pass, Saturday the most likely day.

When I had the idea of devising these imaginary conversations, I had not read Andrew Motion's intriguing 'Two Roads: The Life of Edward Thomas' in *Interrupted Lives*, ed. Andrew Motion (2004) – hereafter 'Two Roads'. Motion briefly imagines a rather different kind of meeting between the two poets at Hare Hall Camp.

6. A Good Man, Sir, but He's a Musician

Marion Scott's, Herbert Howells's and Charles Stanford's descriptions of the young Ivor Gurney are all quoted in Michael Hurd, *The Ordeal of Ivor Gurney* (1978) – henceforth *The Ordeal of Ivor Gurney*. This remains an indispensable source for information about Gurney's life.

Extracts from Gurney's letters come from R K R Thornton's *Ivor Gurney: Collected Letters* (1991) – henceforth *Ivor Gurney: Collected Letters*. Extracts from Gurney's poems or whole poems also come from this source, unless otherwise indicated. Extracts from 'Ballad of the Three Spectres' are from *Ivor Gurney: Severn & Somme* and *War's Embers*, ed. R K R Thornton (1997). Thornton's editions of these and Gurney's later collections are the most authoritative available. P J Kavanagh's *The Collected Poems of Ivor Gurney* (1982) – henceforth *The Collected Poems of Ivor Gurney* – contains an illuminating introduction. Also excellent is Piers Gray's too little known *Marginal Men* (1991) – henceforth *Marginal Men* – a group study of Gurney, Thomas and J R Ackerley. Gurney is the subject of plays by Gray and Jon Silkin: *The Ivor Gurney Show* (1995) and *Ivor Gurney* (1985) – and of a novel, *In Zodiac Light* by Robert Edric (2009).

John Lucas's *Ivor Gurney* (2001) provides another insightful introduction to the poetry. Lucas argues strongly that Gurney early on saw through Brooke and that his 7 and 14 February 1917 letters express his settled opinion of Brooke: 'He didn't really *believe* him.' Lucas makes a good case but, I think, underestimates the continuing fluctuation in Gurney's feelings about Brooke. Gurney advocates like to present him as un-'Georgian' (hence anti-Brooke as the quintessential Georgian). Like debates about who was and was not a modernist, this involves a degree of intellectual snobbery. One consequence is to under-read or ignore Brooke's witty 'Pacific' poems like 'Tiare Tahiti' and 'Heaven' and merely trot out his five war sonnets as stalking horses in a pre-arranged critical tournament.

It is hard not to imagine that Marion Scott was in love with Gurney.

He, though always grateful for her support and good offices, never gave any indication of returning her feelings. He treated her like a substitute older sister or 'friend aunt'. Gurney's sexual orientation remains mysterious. Graves, noting a single 'conventional love-lyric' in *Severn & Somme* ('To an Unknown Lady'), would probably have thought him 'so', i.e. homosexual. The homo-erotic strain in 'To His Love' from *War's Embers* might have confirmed his suspicions. On the other hand, Gurney seems to have been keen on the teenage Winnie Chapman and in late 1917 to have fallen for Annie Drummond, a VAD nurse at Edinburgh War Hospital, Bangour. Perhaps, as with many self-involved people, sexual feelings did not play a large part in his make-up.

Fond as Gurney was of F W Harvey, he was constantly competing with him poetically. On 18 January 1917 he asked Marion Scott (*Ivor Gurney: Collected Letters*): 'Would you mind telling me candidly sincerely as possible, what you think of my things were they collected in a book and compared to F.W.H.'s?' (Harvey's *A Gloucestershire Lad* had been published to popular acclaim in 1916.) Gurney thought that, apart from Harvey's 'In Flanders' and perhaps 'If We Return', his own poems were 'better on the whole and more poetical'.

7. Dottyville

The novelistic opening section here is intended as a nod to Pat Barker's fine fictional re-creation of this momentous meeting in *Regeneration*.

Owen's letters, Sassoon's account in *Siegfried's Journey 1916–1920* (1945) – henceforth *Siegfried's Journey* – and his *Diaries 1915–1918* are the main sources. Other secondary sources proved helpful: particularly *Wilfred Owen: A New Biography* and *The Making of a War Poet*. In the former, Hibberd demonstrates incontestably that the meeting took place on 18 August 1917, also that in *Siegfried's Journey* Sassoon conflates into a single evening his and Owen's final two evenings together in Edinburgh.

All extracts from Owen's letters and poems are taken from *Wilfred Owen: Collected Letters* and *The Poems of Wilfred Owen*. Unless otherwise noted, Sassoon's comments on Owen come from *Siegfried's Journey*. Quotations describing Sassoon's reactions on returning to France in late January 1917 are taken from *Diaries 1915–1918*, and extracts from his poems from *The War Poems*.

According to Peter Parker's *The Old Lie: The Great War and the Public School Ethos* (1987), Sassoon later described Owen as speaking with a 'grammar school accent'. However, it seems possible that the chameleon Owen, wanting to fit in and identify with his regiment, had acquired something of a Mancunian accent. He was certainly able to mimic one in 'The Chances' (probably drafted at Craiglockhart), with its distinctive northern 'Uz' for 'Us'.

Sassoon did send Owen's 'Song of Songs' to Ottoline Morrell after Owen had published the poem with Sassoon's 'Dreamers' in *The Hydra*. His comment, quoted in *Wilfred Owen: A New Biography*, is interesting: 'The man who wrote this brings me quantities & I have to say kind things. He will improve, I think.' Hibberd thinks this reflects Sassoon's 'real opinion of [Owen's] verse so far'. Perhaps it does. Equally, to his admirer Ottoline Morrell, he could simply have been casting himself as the 'old literary hand' discussing a young acolyte. This is no more creditable, of course.

The version of Owen's 'The Dead-Beat' given here is the first draft from *Wilfred Owen: Collected Letters*. Following Sassoon's suggestions, he substantially revised it. In *Siegfried's Journey* Sassoon quotes Owen's 'She dreams of golden gardens and sweet glooms' from 'The Kind Ghosts' as the sort of 'over-luscious' line he helped Owen to prune at Craiglockhart. Sassoon's memory may have slightly misled him, since an 8 August 1918 letter of Owen's to his mother seems to refer to both this poem and Sassoon's criticism as recent. Nevertheless Sassoon's objection to the line stands and characterises the constructive criticism he offered Owen.

Jon Stallworthy, Dominic Hibberd and Douglas Kerr all illuminatingly discuss the evolution of 'Anthem for Doomed Youth'. I have largely followed Stallworthy's account. Hibberd raises the intriguing possibility that the 'accepted final version' of the sonnet may not have been Owen's own final version though, sensibly, he does not argue that the latter is superior. Hibberd is tetchy about Jon Stallworthy's discussion, but himself misattributes Owen's use of 'wailful' to Keats's 'Ode to a Nightingale' rather than 'To Autumn'.

When Owen was in France in early 1916, he let his mother know his destinations in advance. Like Roland and Vera, the two had a code: the word 'Mistletoe' meant the opening letters of succeeding lines formed a word. Owen's 10 January 1916 letter alerted her that he was bound for Serre – where he was holed up in the dug-out for fifty hours, the experience later described in 'The Sentry'. As pointed out in *Wilfred Owen: A New Biography*, Owen, like Sassoon and Graves, routinely called the Germans 'the Bo(s)che' or 'the Hun'. These were not terms restricted to jingoistic warmongers. *Wilfred Owen: A New Biography* gives a particularly sensible account of the cowardice accusation against Owen.

When Sassoon was wounded in April 1917, the bullet – according to *Siegfried Sassoon* (Egremont) – 'narrowly missed the jugular vein and the spine'. The same source provides the extracts from Sassoon's note to his commanding officer, accompanying his public anti-war statement. The Under-Secretary for War's comment to the House of Commons about the 'extremely gallant officer' comes from *Wilfred Owen: A New Biography*.

What might Sassoon's and Owen's possible mutual confessions have amounted to? Both Hibberd and Stallworthy think Owen had already had some homosexual experience but inevitably the evidence is sketchy. Another problem in talking about Owen's sexuality is his avowed affection for children: understandably, no one wants to go there.

Gurney's reaction to Sassoon's poetry ('the Sassoons not as good') comes from *Ivor Gurney: Collected Letters*. Graves's comments to Owen on 'Disabled' are in a 17 October 1917 letter, Appendix C of *Wilfred Owen: Collected Letters*.

8. Cool Madness

Extracts from Isaac Rosenberg's letters and poems come from *The Collected Works of Isaac Rosenberg*, ed. Ian Parsons (1979) – henceforth *The Collected Works of Isaac Rosenberg* – except for the version of 'Ah, Koelue! . . .', which is taken from *Georgian Poetry 1916–1917*. Similarly, unless otherwise stated, all details and extracts about Robert Nichols's life are taken from Anne and William Charlton's sympathetic biography *Putting Poetry First: A Life of Robert Nichols 1893–1944* (2003) – henceforth *Putting Poetry First*. Extracts from Nichols's poetry come from his second collection *Ardours and Endurances* (1917), unless otherwise indicated. The details of Nichols's meeting and subsequent friendship with Philip Heseltine ('Peter Warlock') come from Nichols's contribution to Cecil Gray, *Peter Warlock: A Memoir of Philip Heseltine* (1934).

The Times for Monday 13 October 1913 reported Lloyd George's Land Reform speech at Bedford which contained the reference to pheasants and mangolds (mangel-wurzels).

Nichols describes the trenches as 'an ignominious rabbit-warren to the eye and sewage-farm to the nose' in the introduction to his *Anthology of War Poetry 1914–1918* (1943) – henceforth *Anthology of War Poetry 1914–1918*. The details of Nichols's various army medical boards come from the Army Records at the National Archives, Kew. Graves's account of Nichols's syphilis is in a 25 January 1917 letter to Sassoon in *In Broken Images*. Graves mentions that Nichols was having salvarsan injections. Salvarsan, an arsenical compound nicknamed 606, was discovered by Paul Ehrlich in 1910; it was more effective than previous methods of treating syphilis, though apparently not a complete cure. In a letter c. 1943, see chapter 14, Graves gives a highly spiced résumé of Nichols's life. Graves of course was a great embellisher, but so was Nichols.

Nichols's postscript to Henry Head ('Is "Assault" poetry? . . . It's something I'm sure') is in a 21 November 1916 letter supplied by Anne and William Charlton, now with other Nichols manuscript material in the British Library.

Masefield's comment that Nichols, Graves and Sassoon were 'singing together like the morning stars' is quoted by Graves in a letter to Sassoon (3 July 1917) in *In Broken Images*. Extracts of reviews of *Georgian Poetry 1916–1917* are from *Georgian Poetry 1911–1922*, ed. Timothy Rogers (1977) – henceforth *Georgian Poetry 1911–1922*.

The version of 'Break of Day in the Trenches' that Rosenberg sent Marsh almost certainly differed slightly from his final version which I give here. Bottomley's remark about Rosenberg swamping them all except Lascelles Abercrombie is quoted in Jean Moorcroft Wilson, *Isaac Rosenberg: Poet and Painter* (1975). This and Joseph Cohen's *Journey to the Trenches: The Life of Isaac Rosenberg 1890–1918* (1975) offer full accounts of Rosenberg's too short life. Edmund Gosse's comment 'Who is Rosenberg?' is quoted in *Edward Marsh: A Biography*.

9. At Mrs Colefax's

This meeting gathers material from a wide range of sources. Sassoon's comments are either from *Diaries 1915–1918* or *Siegfried's Journey*. Extracts from his poems are from *The War Poems*. All Nichols's comments, etc., preceding the two readings, unless otherwise stated, come from *Robert Ross: Friend of Friends*, ed. Margery Ross (1952).

Gosse's review of *Ardours and Endurances* is in *Georgian Poetry 1911–1922*. *The Times Literary Supplement* guaranteed Nichols literary immortality on 12 July 1917, and the *Morning Post* on 21 June 1917 called him 'the most remarkable of the new soldier poets'. Details about sales and printings of *Ardours and Endurances* come from the Chatto & Windus ledger No. 8, 543, University of Reading. The description of Ross's flat in Half Moon Street is from Dominic Hibberd, *Wilfred Owen: The Last Year* (1992) – henceforth *The Last Year*.

Cynthia Asquith gives accounts both of poetry readings and of Nichols's and Sassoon's appearance and delivery styles in *Lady Cynthia Asquith*. It was she who called Sibyl Colefax a 'duchess-snob'. Vita Sackville-West's verdict on Nichols is quoted in Victoria Glendenning's *Vita: The Life of V. Sackville-West* (1983).

The Making of a War Poet and *Siegfried Sassoon* (Egremont) both state that Sassoon read 'The Hero', 'The Rear-Guard' and '"They"'. There is, however, a tiny mystery. 'The Hero' and '"They"' are in *The Old Huntsman and Other Poems*, but 'The Rear-Guard' had been written more recently. So, did Sassoon have a copy of the poem with him (unlikely) or know the poem by heart (not impossible, but it is twenty-five lines long, and he was nervous)? A possible solution is that someone had a copy of E B Osborn's anthology *The Muse in Arms* (1917) which contains 'The Rear-Guard' and that Sassoon read from that.

The idea that Sassoon was taking a swipe at Nichols in 'Glory of Women' assumes the poem was written in the wake of the Colefax evening and also as a result of Sassoon's visit to his mother in late November 1917. Exact dating of Sassoon's poems from this period is tricky, but Rupert Hart-Davis in the introduction to *The War Poems* comments that 'There is ample evidence to show that usually a finished poem which the poet thought good enough was almost immediately sent to a periodical and published there within a few days'. That would support a post-Colefax composition. However, if 'Glory of Women' was written before the Colefax evening, Sassoon's ironic use of the word 'ardours' still stands.

Lyndall Gordon in *Eliot's Early Years* (1978) says the second Colefax reading was for the Red Cross. Edmund Gosse had been, perhaps still was, chairman of the Red Cross Committee. Cynthia Asquith describes Yeats's performance at the April 1916 reading for the Star and Garter Fund and the second Colefax reading as 'smaller, more *intime*, and above all *shorter*'.

Gosse's jibe about 'Mrs Colebox and Madame Fan-the-Devil' is in a letter to Ross (18 November 1917) in British Library Manuscripts Room, Add. 81715. Virginia Woolf's comment on Mrs Colefax ('a bunch of red cherries on a hard black straw hat') is from *Moments of Being: Unpublished Biographical Writings of Virginia Woolf*, ed. Jeanne Schulkind (1976). Ezra Pound's description of Gosse's *Life of Swinburne* as 'the attempt of a silly and pompous old man' is quoted in Ann Thwaite's indispensable *Edmund Gosse: A Literary Landscape* (1984). This is also the source of Gosse's remark to John Drinkwater about the Sitwells' 'beautiful manners'. Gosse's engagement diary is lodged in Special Collections at Leeds University Library.

Graves's 'The Picture Book' and 'The Dead Fox Hunter' are in *The Complete Poems in One Volume*. T S Eliot's comments prior to the second Colefax reading are from *The Letters of T. S. Eliot, Volume 1: 1898–1922*, revised edition, ed. Valerie Eliot and Hugh Haughton (2009).

My account of the second Colefax reading blends details from the following sources: *Letters of Aldous Huxley*; Osbert Sitwell's *Laughter in the Next Room* (1949) and *Noble Essences*; Sibyl Colefax's Commonplace Books in the Colefax Archive at the Bodleian Library, Oxford; *Lady Cynthia Asquith* and Arnold Bennett's 'War Journal' in the Arnold Bennett Archive at the Potteries Museum and Art Gallery, Hanley, Stoke-on-Trent. I've tried to deduce a possible running order for the reading from the available evidence.

According to Osbert Sitwell, the Gosse poem read by Nichols concluded with the line: 'The centaur crashes through the under-growth.' Perhaps it did, though, if so, I have failed to find the poem. Equally, Sitwell could well have made up the line as a parody of Gosse's pseudo-classical manner or, just conceivably, he might have been half remembering the line from Eliot's 'Mr Apollinax': 'I heard the beat of centaur's hoofs over the hard turf'. 'Mr Apollinax', a zany exercise in social caricature, would have been a suavely subversive poem for Eliot to have read on such an occasion. Unfortunately, there is no other evidence that he did. 'The Hippopotamus' which he certainly did read and which Cynthia Asquith called 'quite a funny poem' and Bennett 'the highlight of the whole occasion' is in *Collected Poems 1909– 1962* (1963).

Philip Heseltine's letter (20 July 1917) reassuring Nichols that he left 'the Lawrences and Hodgsons and Abercrombies and de la Mares' far behind is in the British Library, Add. 57795. Graves's championing of 'we three inevitables' is in a letter to Sassoon (*c.* November 1917) from *In Broken Images*.

10. The Physic Garden

Most authorities give Saturday 17 August 1918 as the date of the final meeting between Owen and Sassoon. However, Hibberd in *Wilfred Owen: A New Biography* makes the strongest possible case for Thursday 15 August, and I have followed his dating.

Extracts from Owen's letters are from *Wilfred Owen: Collected Letters*, and most quotations from his poems are from *The Poems of Wilfred Owen*. However, the lines 'Beauty is yours . . .', later recycled in 'Strange Meeting' and first published in *The Athenaeum*, 13 August 1920, are quoted in *The Last Year*, which also gives the full text of Owen's proposed Preface ('This book is not about heroes') with corrections, excisions and parentheses.

Extracts from Sassoon's poems are from *The War Poems* and comments on his daily life from *Diaries 1915–1918* unless otherwise stated. Sassoon's note to Owen ('Why *shouldn't* you enjoy your leave?') is in the Oxford English Faculty Sassoon Archive, 3:452. Sassoon's (second) 'Testament' ('For the last time I say') is quoted in *The Last Year* and his letter to E M Forster ('I fear they'll do me in this time') in *Siegfried Sassoon* (Egremont). His account of being shot on 13 July 1918 is taken from *Sherston's Progress* (1936), the third volume of his lightly fictionalised *The Complete Memoirs of George Sherston* (1937). Sassoon's comment on T S Eliot's 'intellectualities in verse' is from *Siegfried Sassoon: Diaries 1920–1922*, ed. Rupert Hart-Davis (1981) – henceforth *Diaries 1920–1922*.

Graves's poetic tip to Owen ('Best thing, I find') is from his 22 December 1917 letter in Appendix C of *Wilfred Owen: Collected Letters*. Miranda Seymour in *Robert Graves: Life on the Edge* queries Graves's story about Nancy and the marital vows, pointing out he was nowhere near Nancy on the morning of the wedding and that on the way to the church Nancy said to her father: 'Father, this is fun.'

Robbie Ross's persecution by Noel Pemberton Billing and homophobia in wartime England are brilliantly teased out in Philip Hoare's *Wilde's Last Stand: Decadence, Conspiracy & the First World War* (1997).

Wilfred Owen: A New Biography gives the fullest account of Harold and Wilfred Owen's last meeting and their discussion of homosexuality. Harold himself left two accounts, one in a 1950 letter to Edmund Blunden, the other a late addition to his memoir *Journey from Obscurity* in the mid-1960s. Since both accounts were set down so many years after the event, their reliability is certainly questionable. But some such exchange clearly took place. According to Harold, he included the memoir version to scotch rumours of his brother's homosexuality. However, his portrayal of Owen here and throughout the memoir so crackles with resentment that one wonders whether his less conscious intention may really have been to 'out' his indulged and preferred older brother.

Charles Scott Moncrieff's lines to Owen ('Nor blame head heart') are quoted in *The Last Year*. Graves later claimed that Scott Moncrieff did seduce Owen, but he is not a reliable witness.

Philip Larkin's lines are from 'Annus Mirabilis' in *High Windows* (1974). Stephen Maguire's 'Tory mild' quip in the *New Age* is quoted in *Siegfried Sassoon* (Egremont). The suggestion that Thomas would have cautiously admired *The Waste Land* is made in 'Two Roads'. James Fenton's essay 'Wilfred Owen's Juvenilia', from his *The Strength of Poetry* (2001), persuasively explores the 'complicated set of forces' which released Owen from his early poetry and also raises some reservations about his poetic future.

11. Good-bye to All That

The main sources on Edmund Blunden are his own *Undertones of War* (1928; reissued 1982) – hereafter *Undertones of War*, Barry Webb's *Edmund Blunden: A Biography* (1990) – henceforth *Edmund Blunden: A Biography* – and Blunden's review copy of *Good-bye to All That*. The original of the latter is in the Berg Collection, and all Blunden's and Sassoon's annotations quoted here are taken from that source –

although many also appear in Richard Perceval Graves's edition of *Good-bye to All That*.

Extracts from Blunden's poems are taken from *Edmund Blunden: Selected Poems*, ed. Robyn Marsack (1982) – henceforth *Edmund Blunden: Selected Poems*, except for 'The Pike', 'The Estrangement' and 'Third Ypres: A Reminiscence' which are from *Edmund Blunden: Overtones of War, Poems of the First World War*, ed. Martin Taylor (1996).

The main source for Graves is *Good-bye to All That* itself. Extracts from his letters are from *In Broken Images* and extracts from poems from *The Complete Poems In One Volume*. Graves's recipe for his autobiography is given in 'Postscript to "Good-bye to All That"' in *But It Still Goes On: An Accumulation* (1930).

Virginia Woolf's description of Blunden ('a London house sparrow') is from *Diary of Virginia Woolf*, vol. 2, ed. Anne Olivier Bell (1981). Blunden's comment that *Good-bye to All That* was a 'bombastic and profit-seeking display' is quoted in *Siegfried Sassoon* (Egremont). His 1921 complaint about Graves's critique of his poems is quoted in *Edmund Blunden: A Biography*.

Sassoon's 2 June 1922 diary entry about his 'war-harnessed' relationship with Graves is in *Diaries 1920–1922* as are his reflections on his 'kinship of mind' with Blunden (also 2 June) and Mary Blunden's 'considerable adroitness' (16 June).

Laura Riding's term the 'three-life' is quoted in *The Years with Laura* as is Geoffrey Phibbs's declaration that he was '*not* going to continue to live with or near Laura'. In some versions of Riding's jump, she is said to have leapt out of a fourth-floor window, but *Robert Graves: Life on the Edge* makes an overwhelming case for the window being on the third floor. Presumably the title of *Good-bye to All That* was meant in part as a covert tribute to Riding's line as she jumped: 'Goodbye, chaps.'

T E Lawrence's description of the Riding-dominated Graves as 'bewitched and bitched' is quoted in *Robert Graves: Life on the Edge*. Nichols's account of how Sassoon turned *Good-bye to All That* into 'a roaring farce' is in a letter to Henry and Ruth Head (26 October 1930), supplied by Anne and William Charlton from manuscripts now lodged in the British Library.

Blunden's account of friends literally being blown to bits occurs in *Undertones of War* as does his depiction of pastoral France. Sassoon's idyllic 'The Flower Show Match' and hunting reminiscences, and their overshadowing by death in the trenches, are in *Memoirs of a Fox-hunting Man* (1928).

In Broken Images contains both sides of the acrimonious Graves–Sassoon correspondence, following the publication of *Good-bye to All That*. Stephen Tennant's perceptive reading of Graves's feelings comes from his journal (27 February 1930), quoted in *Siegfried Sassoon* (Egremont).

Blunden's account of Duleepsinghji appears in 'Lord's, June 27th, 1930' in *Edmund Blunden: A Selection of his Poetry and Prose*, ed. Kenneth Hopkins (1930). His analogy between poetry writing and finding a landmine is from 'Edmund Blunden' in *The Poet Speaks*, ed. Peter Orr (1966), as is his remark about how he always remained haunted by the war.

12. Strange Hells

The primary sources for this chapter are: Helen Thomas's account in *Under Storm's Wing* of visiting Gurney at Stone House, *The Ordeal of Ivor Gurney* and the Gurney Archive at Gloucestershire Archives – henceforth the Gurney Archive. Francine Payne's *Stone House: The City of London Asylum* (nd) was also helpful with some background information.

All extracts from Gurney's letters, unless otherwise stated, come from *Ivor Gurney: Collected Letters*. Extracts from Gurney's poems come from *Ivor Gurney: 80 Poems or So*, George Walter and R K R Thornton (1997) or from *Best Poems and The Book of Five Makings*, ed. R K R Thornton and George Walter (1995) – except for the extract from 'Ballad of the Three Spectres' from *Severn & Somme* and the lines from 'Strange Hells' in *Collected Poems of Ivor Gurney*.

Marion Scott's reminiscence of Gurney singing 'Twa Corbies' 'with gruesome intensity' is in the Gurney Archive, Box 5. Gray tells the story of Gurney, the policeman and the gun in *Marginal Men*. Ronald Gurney's reaction is quoted in *The Ordeal of Ivor Gurney*, as is Gurney's poignant 'It is too late'. Arthur Townsend's description of Stone House as 'an eminently suitable place' is in a letter to Marion Scott (1 December 1922), Gurney Archive, Box 4. Gurney's 10 November 1932 letter to Marion Scott reproduced here in full (square brackets with question marks mine) is in the Gurney Archive, Box 10, as is his undated letter (perhaps never sent) to Marion Scott, thanking her for sending his poems to Helen Thomas. Two other letters from Box 10 refer to Edward Thomas: one, undated, contains the cryptic 'ET is not (it is Hell)'; the other, dated September from sometime in the mid-1930s, includes the ominous 'Perhaps autumn has come – but it may need Edward Thomas poems to carry it through'.

Robert Bridges, sent Gurney's *Severn and Somme* by Charles Stanford, thought him indebted to the Gerard Manley Hopkins poems in his 1916 anthology *The Spirit of Man*, which Gurney had certainly read. This makes sense: syntactical contractions are a trademark Hopkins feature. However, Pamela Blevins in *The Ivor Gurney Society Journal*, vol. 6, 2000 offers a different (though not mutually exclusive) explanation. Arguing that Gurney suffered from bi-polar disorder (manic depression), she sees such compressions as a product of his condition, 'fingerprints of his mental illness'.

There is now a considerable literature on what was really wrong with Gurney. Apart from Michael Hurd in *The Ordeal of Ivor Gurney*, Pamela Blevins's 'New Perspectives on Ivor Gurney's Mental Illness' and Anthony Boden's 'Ivor Gurney: Schizophrenic?' in *The Ivor Gurney Society Journal*, vol. 6, 2000 are worth consulting. Malarial therapy, i.e. deliberately inoculating patients with a mild form of malaria, was apparently a common treatment for syphilis from *c*.1917 up to the 1950s.

Edward Thomas's 'Lights Out' is from *Poems* (1917) by Edward Thomas ('Edward Eastaway'), as this is the version Gurney would probably have known. The only difference from the standard version is in the punctuation. Edward Thomas's walking maps are held in the Edward Thomas Collection. The handwriting at the top of Ordnance Survey sheet 81, saying 'Shows my home St Mary's', must, I think, be Gurney's.

13. Hope Divine

Reports of the PPU meeting in Bristol appeared in the 14 January 1937 editions of the *Bristol Evening Post*, *Western Daily Press* and *Bristol Evening World* (Colindale Newspaper Library).

Brittain's reaction to Sassoon is quoted in *Vera Brittain*, as is her letter about treating her war experience as autobiography rather than fiction. Her question 'Why should these young men . . . ?' is from *Testament of Experience: An Autobiographical Story of the Years 1925–1950* (1957) – henceforth *Testament of Experience*. 'What a head-cracking week' is from *Chronicle of Friendship: Vera Brittain's Diary of the Thirties*, ed. Alan Bishop (1986) – henceforth *Chronicle of Friendship*. Colonel Charles Hudson's account of her brother Edward's potential disgrace and death is told in *Vera Brittain*. There seems no question as to its reliability. *Chronicle of Friendship* provides the description of Brittain's father's dead face. Brittain's comment on 'the ideal life' is quoted in *Vera Brittain*, as is her claim 'I am wholly a heterosexual person'. 'As I came out of the home' is from *Chronicle of Friendship*; her reflection that the League of Nations was 'merely a camouflage' is quoted in the *Bristol Evening Post* on 14 January 1937. Brittain describes Winifred's funeral service and her own 1936 visit to Germany in *Chronicle of Friendship*. Her account of 'Dick' Sheppard near Dorchester is in *Testament of Experience*.

All extracts from Sassoon's poems are from *Collected Poems*, except his elegy for 'Dick' Sheppard which is quoted in *The Journey from the Trenches*. The phrases 'poetry that springs direct from the heart' and 'pretentious verbiage' appear in 'Aunt Eudora and the Poets', *The Spectator*, 31 January 1936. The photograph of Sassoon as Elizabethan bard is reproduced in both *The Journey from the Trenches* and *Siegfried Sassoon* (Egremont). His initial responses to Hester are quoted in *Siegfried Sassoon* (Egremont).

14. No Fire Brigade Was Needed for the Thames

Putting Poetry First is the source for: Nichols's performance and speech in Nashville, Nancy Cunard's 'Lord had I but known', the *Morning Post*'s praise, and Nichols's memories of Boar's Hill.

Extracts from Nichols's poems come from 'Winter Overnight', *Aurelia and Other Poems* (1920); *Fisbo* (1934); 'Epic Wind', *Anthology of War Poetry* and 'From "Swansong"' and 'Don Juan's Address to the Sunset', *Such was My Singing* (1942).

Quotations from Nichols's plays are from *Guilty Souls: A Drama in Four Acts* (1922) and *Wings Over Europe: A Dramatic Extravaganza on a Pressing Theme* (1932). Nichols reviewed *Good-bye to All That* in *The*

Listener (4 December 1929). His description of *Morning Heroes* is in a letter to Henry and Ruth Head (26 October 1930) supplied by Anne and William Charlton, now with other Nichols manuscript material in the British Library.

Gosse's letter of reprimand to Nichols (17 July 1919) is in Nichols's papers at Trinity College, Oxford. Norah Nichols's 'On Being the Wife of a Poet' is in *The Star* (27 August 1928). Huxley's comments on *Wings Over Europe* appeared in 'Notes on the Way', *Time and Tide* (14 May 1932). The *Observer* review is quoted from *Putting Poetry First*. Similarly, the review of *Fisbo* in the *Manchester Guardian* is quoted in *Putting Poetry First*. Marsh's reactions to *Fisbo* and to Nichols's death are from *Edward Marsh: A Biography*. The *New Statesman* and *Adelphi* reviews of *Such Was My Singing* appeared on 25 July 1942 and April–June 1943 respectively. Desmond MacCarthy's review of *Anthology of War Poetry 1914–1918* appeared in *The Sunday Times*, 8 August 1943. Kenneth Tynan reviewed *Kosumo* in the *Observer*, 13 October 1955, Milton Shulman in the *Evening Standard*, 9 November 1955. The extract from the *Financial Times* review is quoted from *No Turn Unstoned: The Worst Ever Theatrical Reviews*, compiled by Diana Rigg (1982).

Blunden's reminiscences of Nichols on Boar's Hill are quoted in *Edmund Blunden: A Biography*. Blunden's comment that Nichols was 'almost worshipped by R.G.' is in the Berg Collection copy of *Good-bye to All That*. His poem 'In Memory of Robert Nichols' is in *Poems of Many Years* (1957).

Extracts from Graves's letters are from *In Broken Images*. 'Another poet on Boar's Hill' is from *Good-bye to All That*. 'Recalling War' can be found in *The Complete Poems in One Volume*. Nichols reproduces line three of the third stanza of Graves's 'Recalling War' as 'Such tasteless honey oozing from the heart' rather than the more familiar 'tasty honey'. This was correct at the time. When I queried the point with Graves's editor Dunstan Ward, he very helpfully commented: 'Graves has "tasteless" in the first two printings of "Recalling War", *Collected Poems* (1938) and *No More Ghosts* (1940). He changed it to "tasty" in *Collected Poems 1914–1947* (1948), and it remained as "tasty" through five subsequent printings up to *Collected Poems* (1961), after which he removed the poem, most regrettably, from the canon.' Laura Riding's reproving letter to Nichols is quoted in *Putting Poetry First*.

Sassoon's description of Nichols's wedding is from *Diaries 1920–1922*. Osbert Sitwell's 'Alive – Alive Oh!' can most readily be found in his *Collected Stories* (1974).

15. Sacred Intimacies

The phrase 'most sacred intimacies' is from Sassoon's indignant letter to *The Times* (1 October 1957), complaining about the *Sunday Express* reporter's intrusion on his privacy.

David Jones's account of their meeting is in a letter to Harman Grisewood (17 July 1964) in *Dai Greatcoat: A Self-Portrait of David Jones in his Letters*, ed. René Hague (1980) – henceforth *Dai Greatcoat*. Keith Alldritt's biography *David Jones: Writer and Artist* (2003) was also useful. Sassoon's version of the meeting is in a letter to Dame Felicitas Corrigan (5 August 1964), quoted in full in *Siegfried Sassoon* (Roberts).

Jones's description of Sassoon's 'timeless craggy Jewish face' is from '9 September 1972' in William Blissett's *The Long Conversation: A Memoir of David Jones* (1981) – henceforth *The Long Conversation* – as is the '1969' recollection of Jones's 'what for his friends is a cold'. Jones's comments on 'Liberal' Catholics are from a letter to Harman Grisewood (6 July 1964) in *Dai Greatcoat*. His comments about 're-calling' in *Anathemata* are from 'Autobiographical Talk', his 1954 radio talk, in *David Jones: Epoch and Artist*, ed. Harman Grisewood (1959) – henceforth *Epoch and Artist*; his comment that the poem's 'a bit of a bugger on the surface' is from a letter to H S ('Jim') Ede (17 December 1952) in *Dai Greatcoat*. The extract from *In Parenthesis* (1937) is from Part 7, 'The Five Unmistakable Marks'. Jones's depiction of the poet as a rememberer is from 'Past and Present' in *Epoch and Artist*. His account of being wounded is from two letters to René Hague (1 January 1973 and 27 September 1974) in *Dai Greatcoat* and from Part 7 of *In Parenthesis*. George Johnston's account of Jones's talk is in a letter to Blissett (1 October 1974) in *The Long Conversation*. Jones's description of Christopher Smart as 'a strange and endearing genius' is from 'Christopher Smart', *The Tablet*, January 1939, collected in *Epoch and Artist*.

Sassoon's description of Jones as 'undoubtedly a man of genius' is in a letter to Alan Lascelles (1 July 1964), quoted in *The Journey from the Trenches*. Sassoon's view of Philip Larkin's *The Less Deceived* is quoted in *Siegfried Sassoon* (Egremont). The extracts from 'Cleaning the Candelabrum' and 'The Trial' are from *Collected Poems 1908–1956*. His view of *In Parenthesis* as 'an important war record' is from his letter to Dame Felicitas Corrigan (5 August 1964) in *Siegfried Sassoon* (Roberts). His reiteration that *Good-bye to All That* was 'full of inaccuracies' comes from '9 September' in *The Long Conversation* as does 'details of trench life . . .' ('3 June 1971').

Sassoon's phrase 'day out bombing the Prussian Guard' is from his letter to Dame Felicitas Corrigan (5 August 1964) quoted in *Siegfried Sassoon* (Roberts). Sassoon's other recollections of 5 July 1916 and the 'New Army troops' are from *Memoirs of an Infantry Officer*. His comments on Jones and J H Johnston's *English Poetry of the First World War* are in a letter to Mr Bell (19 August 1964), item 58, Owen Archive 6, English Faculty Library, Oxford. Sassoon's and Hart-Davis's last conversation about his poetry and Sassoon's words to George ('This is the final test') are quoted in *The Journey from the Trenches*.

Anthony Powell's account of visiting Sassoon is in *The Strangers All Are Gone* (1982). 'Separate Ways', Larkin's review of *Sequences*, is in *Further Requirements: Interviews, Broadcasts, Statements and Book Reviews 1952–1985*, ed. Anthony Thwaite (2001). Graves's comment that *In Parenthesis* is 'a war-book by Joyce out of Eliot' is quoted in *Robert Graves: Life on the Edge*.

Epilogue

The main source is *Anthem for Doomed Youth: Twelve Soldier Poets of the First World War*, http://www.iwm.org.uk from which all quotations are taken unless otherwise indicated. I went round the exhibition twice in April 2003.

David Garnett's 'If the impossible were to happen' is noted by Frances Partridge in her diary (21 May 1964), *Other People: Diaries 1963–1966* (1998). Sorley's lines are from 'Two Sonnets', *The Collected Poems of Charles Hamilton Sorley*; his 28 April 1915 letter is in *The Collected Letters of Charles Hamilton Sorley*. Sassoon's 'Stand-to: Good Friday Morning' can be found in *The War Poems*. The Sassoon–Philpot exchange is quoted in *Siegfried Sassoon* (Egremont). Anthony Powell's comment on Sassoon ('for Captain Sassoon') is from *The Strangers All Are Gone*. Sassoon's diary entry (10 February 1948) that Owen's death 'made a gap in my life' is quoted in *Siegfried Sassoon* (Egremont).

Spender's comment that Owen's was 'the most useful influence in modern verse' is quoted in *Wilfred Owen: A New Biography* where Hibberd calls Owen 'the national poet of pity in the early 1960s'. Yeats's famous complaint that Owen was 'all blood, dirt & sucked sugar stick' is from a letter to Dorothy Wellesley (21 December 1936) in *Letters on Poetry from W B Yeats to Dorothy Wellesley* (1940). Craig Raine dubs Owen's 'perhaps the most overrated poetry in the twentieth century' in 'Wilfred Owen', collected in *Haydn and the Valve Trumpet* (1990). Larkin called Owen 'rather a prick' to Robert Conquest in a 9 January 1975 letter in *Selected Letters of Philip Larkin 1940–1985*, ed. Anthony Thwaite (1992) – henceforth *Selected Letters of Philip Larkin*. Ian Hamilton's comment on Owen is from *Against Oblivion: Some Lives of the Twentieth-Century Poets* (2002).

Ted Hughes told Graves *The White Goddess* was 'the chief book' of his 'poetic consciousness' in a letter (20 July 1967), *Letters of Ted Hughes*, ed. Christopher Reid (2007). Extracts from Blunden's poetry can be found in *Edmund Blunden: Selected Poems*. Larkin's brisk dismissal of Blunden is in a letter to Robert Conquest (5 March 1966) in *Selected Letters of Philip Larkin*. Thomas's 'Adlestrop' and other poems can be found in both *The Collected Poems of Edward Thomas* and Edna Longley's *Edward Thomas: The Annotated Collected Poems*. His comment about using 'the Morse code' is quoted in the Preface to *Edward Thomas: Selected Letters*. Eleanor Farjeon recalled Thomas picking up 'a pinch of earth' in *The Last Four Years*. Helen Thomas asked her husband about his relationship with Hope Webb in a 19 January 1908 letter, quoted in *Edward Thomas: A Portrait*.

Jones's comment on *In Parenthesis* ('Sometimes when I read it') is in a 2 December 1935 letter to René Hague, *Dai Great-Coat*. Larkin called *In Parenthesis* 'Richard Aldington rewritten by Ezra Pound' in a 26 April 1980 letter to Kingsley Amis, *Selected Letters of Philip Larkin*. Paul Fussell called it an 'honourable miscarriage' in *The Great War and Modern Memory* (1975), and Bernard Bergonzi a 'major work' in an excellent chapter on Jones in *Heroes' Twilight* (1980). Rosenberg's comment that 'Moses symbolises the fierce desire for virility' was made in a June 1916 letter to R C Trevelyan, *The Collected Works of Isaac Rosenberg*. The introduction to the same work contains Graves's comment that, poetically, Rosenberg was 'a born revolutionary'.

General

There is now a huge literature about the war poets (individually and collectively) and about the Great War and its different contexts. My notes list the most crucial sources. (I apologise for any omissions.) My more general debt to this literature is too overwhelming to try to list. However, here are three books not mentioned above which in their very different ways I have found particularly useful, moving and inspiring: Geoff Dyer's *The Missing of the Somme* (1994); Niall Ferguson's *The Pity of War* (1998); and Ben Shepherd's *A War of Nerves: Soldiers and Psychiatrists 1914–1994* (2000).

Acknowledgements

For permission to reproduce material, published and unpublished, I should gratefully like to acknowledge the following: Michael Asquith (Lady Cynthia Asquith, diary extracts); Margi Blunden and Michael Sissons (Edmund Blunden, poetry and prose extracts); Dr Isaac Gewirtz, Berg Collection, New York Public Library (Edmund Blunden and Siegfried Sassoon extracts in Blunden's copy of *Good-bye to All That*); Mark Bostridge and Timothy Brittain-Catlin, Literary Executors for the Estate of Vera Brittain 1970 (for permission to reproduce extracts from Vera Brittain's poetry, letters, diaries and prose); the Estate of T S Eliot and Faber and Faber (T S Eliot, poetry extract and letter extracts); Michael Schmidt and Carcanet Press (Robert Graves, poetry, letter and prose extracts); Michael Schmidt and Carcanet Press, the Ivor Gurney estate and Gloucestershire Archives (Ivor Gurney, poetry and letter extracts); Georges Borchardt Inc (Aldous Huxley, letter extract); Nicholas Elkin (David Jones, poetry, prose and letter extracts); the Estate of Philip Larkin and Faber and Faber (Philip Larkin, poetry, prose and letter extracts); Pollinger Limited (D H Lawrence, poetry and letter extracts); David Leighton (Roland Leighton, poetry and letter extracts); Anne Charlton (Robert Nichols poetry, diary, prose and letter extracts); Jon Stallworthy (Wilfred Owen, poetry extracts); Oxford University Press (Wilfred Owen, letter extracts); Bruce Hunter of David Higham (Anthony Powell, extracts from *The Strangers All Are Gone*); Bernard Wynick and Chatto & Windus (Isaac Rosenberg, poetry and letter extracts); Rogers, Coleridge & White (Francis Partridge, diary extract); Barbara Levy Associates and Faber and Faber (Siegfried Sassoon, poetry, diaries, letters, prose and letter extracts); Susan Usher of English Faculty Library Oxford (Siegfried Sassoon note, letter extract and inscription in flyleaf to Wilfred Owen's copy of *The Old Huntsman and Other Poems*); Mrs R Vellender, Oxford University Press and Cardiff University Library (Edward Thomas, poetry, prose and letter extracts). For permission to reproduce illustrations, as listed, I should like to thank the institutions and individuals named in the List of Illustrations at the beginning of the book. Every effort has been made to contact publishers and copyright holders; I sincerely apologise for any omissions and would be glad to rectify these.

For research and study leave from teaching, I should like to thank Victoria University of Wellington, New Zealand.

For help with my research, general encouragement and inspiration, I should like to thank the staff at the British Library and the Gloucestershire Archives, and the following, with apologies to anyone whom I have inadvertently left out: Laurie Atkinson, Zoe Bennett (Cambridge Theological Federation and Anglia Ruskin University), Mark Bostridge (for advice on Vera Brittain), Duncan Campbell (China Centre, the Australian National University), Justin Cargill (Victoria University of Wellington Library), Rachel Cohen (whose book *A Chance Meeting: Intertwined Lives of American Writers and Artists*, 2005, came along at the right moment), Stephen Crook (Berg Collection, New York Public Library), Max Egremont (for advice on Sassoon's various poetry readings), Alex Frame, Isaac Gewirtz (Curator, Berg Collection, New York Public Library), Clare Hopkins (Trinity College Library, Oxford), Douglas Kerr (for advice on Owen's poetry), Kate and P J Kavanagh (for advice on Ivor Gurney's poetry and help with my not very fruitful attempts to discover more about Irene Rutherford McLeod), Peter Keelan (Head of Special Collections and Archives, Cardiff University Library), Ray Oblitas (for reminiscences of Edmund Blunden in Hong Kong), the late Lieutenant-Colonel D J Patrickson, Jayne Ringrose (Honorary Archivist, Pembroke College, Cambridge), Jean Rose (Random House Group Archive & Library), John Shapcott (Arnold Bennett Society), Chris Sheppard (Head of Special Collections, Leeds University Library), my colleague and friend Jane Stafford, Jon Stallworthy (Wolfson College, Oxford), Ann Thwaite (for advice on Edmund Gosse), Susan Usher (English Faculty Library, Oxford) and Dunstan Ward (for advice on the dating of Robert Graves's war poems).

More particularly I should like to thank my literary agent Deborah Rogers for her help, friendship and enthusiasm; my editor Jenny Uglow for her continuing patience, support and perceptive reading, Parisa Ebrahimi for her assistance with many details, and Vicki Robinson for the index; David Kynaston for forty years of friendship and for unflagging encouragement and expert advice at every stage of this book; and my wife Belinda whose love and good humour kept me going.

Index